The Rise of the State
Profitable Investing
and Geopolitics
in the 21st Century

Yiannis G. Mostrous,
Elliott H. Gue,
David F. Dittman

D1449267

Vice President, Publisher: Tim Moore
Associate Publisher and Director of Marketing: Amy Neidlinger
Executive Editor: Jim Boyd
Editorial Assistant: Pamela Boland
Development Editor: Russ Hall
Operations Manager: Gina Kanouse
Senior Marketing Manager: Julie Phifer
Publicity Manager: Laura Czaja
Assistant Marketing Manager: Megan Colvin
Cover Designer: Chuti Prasertsith
Managing Editor: Kristy Hart
Project Editor: Betsy Harris
Copy Editor: Geneil Breeze
Proofreader: Apostrophe Editing Services
Indexer: WordWise Publishing Services
Compositor: Nonie Ratcliff
Manufacturing Buyer: Dan Uhrig

This book is sold with the understanding that neither the author nor the publisher is engaged in rendering legal, accounting, or other professional services or advice by publishing this book. Each individual situation is unique. Thus, if legal or financial advice or other expert assistance is required in a specific situation, the services of a competent professional should be sought to ensure that the situation has been evaluated carefully and appropriately. The authors and the publisher disclaim any liability, loss, or risk resulting directly or indirectly, from the use or application of any of the contents of this book.

FT Press offers excellent discounts on this book when ordered in quantity for bulk purchases or special sales. For more information, please contact U.S. Corporate and Government Sales, 1-800-382-3419, corpsales@pearsontechgroup.com. For sales outside the U.S., please contact International Sales at international@pearson.com.

Company and product names mentioned herein are the trademarks or registered trademarks of their respective owners.

Printed in the United States of America
First Printing August 2010

ISBN-10: 0-13-715387-2
ISBN-13: 978-0-13-715387-9

Pearson Education LTD.
Pearson Education Australia PTY, Limited.
Pearson Education Singapore, Pte. Ltd.
Pearson Education North Asia, Ltd.
Pearson Education Canada, Ltd.
Pearson Educatión de Mexico, S.A. de C.V.
Pearson Education—Japan
Pearson Education Malaysia, Pte. Ltd.

Library of Congress Cataloging-in-Publication Data
Mostrous, Yiannis G.
 The rise of the state : profitable investing and geopolitics in the 21st century / Yiannis G. Mostrous, David F. Dittman, Elliott H. Gue.
  p. cm.
 ISBN 978-0-13-715387-9 (hardback : alk. paper) 1. Investments—Developing countries.
2. Natural resources—Developing countries. 3. Capital movements—Developing countries.
4. Developing countries--Politics and government. 5. International relations. I. Dittman, David F., 1971- II. Gue, Elliott H. III.
Title.
HG5993.M68 2010
332.67'3091724—dc22
                    2010017279

"Events can move from the impossible to the inevitable without ever stopping at the probable."

Alexis de Tocqueville

To our parents.

Contents

Past and Prologue 1

Chapter 1   Tectonic Shifts .9
Peace and Prosperity. 10
State Capitalism. 12
The Great Game 14
Polycentricism 19
Dividing the World 23

Chapter 2   The Wealth of Sovereigns 27
Welcome to America. 30
The Next New Order 38

Chapter 3   The Road to Pan-Asia 47
Arabian Knights. 49
Vanguard of the Middle Kingdom 55
East Is East 61

Chapter 4   Rumble in the Jungle 67
China on the Lead. 72
Of Tigers and Bears. 77

Chapter 5   A New Oil Age .83
Oil for Transportation 86
The American Roadmap. 88
The New Oil Age. 91
The Supply Constraint 94
The Death of Cantarell 98
Fallen Giants 102

Chapter 6   To the Ends of the Earth 111
Brazil: King of the Deep. 115
The Deepwater Gulf. 118

West Africa 119
Going Unconventional 121
Russia, Iraq, and Iran 126
Beyond the Producers. 130
Shifting East 132

Chapter 7 Natural Gas: The 21st-Century Fuel 135
Electricity and Industrial 136
The Gas Choice. 140
Liquid Energy 150
Unconventional Boom 154
The Conventional Choice 158

Chapter 8 Coal: The World's Workhorse 163
Steam and Met 164
Environmental Issues 169
Supplying the Demand. 174

Chapter 9 The Other Energy 181
Nuclear and Hydroelectric 183
Wind and Solar 191

Chapter 10 Water Is Money .199
A Closer Look at Asia 201
The Water Investment Theme
Is Under Way. 203
Demand Reduction. 207
Improve Efficiencies. 212
Fishing Profits 214

Chapter 11 Back to the Future 221
China Shortens the Distance 222
Faster, Longer, Heavier 228
A Race Against Time. 231
Beyond Rail. 235

Chapter 12   Age, Youth, and Upward Mobility 239
             China Changes Its Course 242
             Pharma's Opportunity 243
             Big Pharma Still Strong 246
             Medical Products and Services 249
             The Time for Education 252
             The Chinese Opportunity 256
             Other Asian Educators 258

Chapter 13   The Asian Frontiers: Mongolia,
             Cambodia, Vietnam 261
             Mongolia 263
             Thirty Years After 269
             Vietnam's Doi Moi 275

             Index 281

Acknowledgments

The Rise of the State would have been difficult to complete without the contributions of Jason R. Koepke and Benjamin Shepherd. The former's extremely refined and elevated levels of intellectual curiosity and the latter's solid research skills were materially important.

Thanks are also due to Angelos A. Kovaios for the extensive discussions on geopolitical developments. Thank you to Gregg S. Early for being a big advocate and supporter for the need to always press on to conclusions. Thank you to Roger S. Conrad for helping us navigate the difficult waters of the financial advisory newsletter business in the past ten years, thus allowing us to also gain extensive knowledge in explaining our investment ideas to people.

Thank you also to Jim Boyd, our executive editor at FT Press, for supporting us during a very difficult 2008 and allowing sufficient time for the work to be completed.

Finally, a special thank you to our families for putting up with the distractions of writing.

About the Authors

Yiannis G. Mostrous is Editor of the *Silk Road Investor* (www. SilkRoadInvestor.com), a financial advisory dedicated to emerging markets, a field that he has been covering since 2001. He is also an Associate Editor of *Personal Finance*, a widely circulated financial newsletter. He has been a guest on radio shows around the country and Canada. He is a coauthor of *The Silk Road to Riches: How You Can Profit by Investing in Asia's Newfound Prosperity*. He holds an MBA degree from Marymount University.

Elliott H. Gue is Editor of *The Energy Strategist*, the premier financial advisory dedicated to energy markets, a field he has been covering since 2002. He is also editor of *Personal Finance* (www. pfnewsletter.com). He is a regular guest on "Clean Skies TV" (www. CleanSkies.com) and on radio shows in North America. He is a coauthor of *The Silk Road to Riches: How You Can Profit by Investing in Asia's Newfound Prosperity*. He holds a Masters of Finance degree from the University of London.

David F. Dittman is Editor of the *Maple Leaf Memo*, a weekly newsletter dedicated to the analysis of the Canadian economy and financial markets. He is also an Associate Editor of *Canadian Edge* (www.CanadianEdge.com), a financial advisory that identifies investment opportunities in Canada. He holds a *juris doctor* from the Villanova University School of Law.

Past and Prologue

At a party during a trip to China in the 1930s Nikos Kazantzakis, one of the foremost writers and thinkers to emerge from Greece in the 20th century, became involved in a deep conversation with a mandarin. Kazantzakis noted that both the communists and the Japanese were advancing toward Beijing from different directions. Was the man scared? Kazantzakis asked. The mandarin, at one time China's ambassador to France, smiled. "Communism is ephemeral, Japan is ephemeral, but China is eternal," he said.

China is not new to the power game. For 500 years Imperial China was the world's preeminent force. At the height of its influence, between 1440 and 1433 AD, China's navy was the most formidable in the world in terms of sheer size as well as reach. Chinese Admiral Cheng Ho commanded ships that weighed 1,500 tons, with firepower and cargo capacity incomprehensible to his European counterparts.

Control of the seas and the extensive trade relationships it facilitated were the foundation of China's economic and political superiority. Because of a strategic decision to shift resources to strengthening its defenses against potential land invaders, by 1436 the mighty Chinese navy had been disassembled. The end of its power was not far off.

More than 500 years on and China is leading emerging economies in a rebalancing of the world's economic and geopolitical order. The increase in global trade, coupled with pragmatic leadership, set the stage for the awakening of what was a slumbering dragon. Furthermore, other countries that have also benefited from free trade and that also enjoy continentlike characteristics complement the rise of

China's star, Brazil, India, and Russia—the remaining three elements of the BRIC mosaic—are each in its own right important elements in the world's transformation.

Only in the aftermath of the crisis that nearly ruined the financial system in 2008-09 did the majority of people start understanding the growing importance of these emerging nations to global economic well-being. For the first time in financial history, major emerging economies were able not only to avoid total destruction when the developed economies were in dire straits, but also the leaders among them have actually delivered solid growth amid what was otherwise the worst economic downturn in seven decades. The relative resilience of these economies, primarily China and India, has helped the global economy absorb what would otherwise have been fatal blows.

The multiyear process that resulted in these economies playing a prominent role in stabilizing the global system, unfolded while the West was engorging itself on cheap credit and unsustainable consumption. During these fat years of self-congratulation, relatively little attention was paid by the West to the serious structural reform that Asian countries, in particular, in the wake of the regional crisis of 1997-98, had undertaken. The reality is that strong economic growth in the emerging world allowed the majority of the Anglo-Saxon economies to follow spendthrift fiscal and easy monetary policies, prolong the economic cycle on the upside, shorten it on the downside, and only delay an inevitable reckoning.

Responding to what now looms as the first in a series of upsets that will result in its eventual decline as the global hegemonic power, U.S. leaders—financial and political—managed, sadly, to discredit John Maynard Keynes in the eyes of the majority of Westerners. This result, however, springs from the vanity and hunger for power that led those who would relegate Keynesianism to history's dust heap to disregard Lord Keynes' advice in 1946 that the "classical medicine"—letting a recession run its natural course—must also be allowed to work and that government intervention would be ineffective in the long term otherwise. Our sophisticated society ignored substance in favor of superficiality and so the financial system continues to wither. Western countries, typified by the largest, the United States, lived beyond their means for too long, all the while developing a sense of invulnerability to the economic cycle and contempt for other growth models. It was not just the greed of "evil bankers" that brought the Western financial system to its knees. The greed of the public, the most dangerous of all avarice, also played a great role.

The failure of the state to effectively monitor markets beforehand led directly to inevitable, extraordinary intervention after the fact of the near-collapse of the financial system—the de jure and de facto control of the economy by the state. What we have, too, is the looming danger of moral hazard, a culture in other words of nonpayment, where everyone has recourse to a central authority. Because neither side of the great American political divide properly understands even what are considered well-known theories on the role of government in the economy, and the people who elect them aren't seriously concerned because they've effectively voted themselves rich, the door is now open, at least partially, to the destruction of the free market-based model of growth. This is the breach the West has opened.

But the crisis of 2008 also revealed that there are different ways to foster economic development, and that these varying structures can also lead to positive outcomes. Beginning in the mid-2000s serious economic researchers warned that "the cross-country evidence on the growth benefits of capital-account openness is inconclusive and lacks robustness." As the global recession that closed the decade revealed, relying less, not more, on foreign capital for growth has been a better recipe for success than the majority of economic experts and other Western commentators would have had us believe. The financial crisis demonstrated that countries that followed gradual approaches toward more open capital accounts had one less thing to worry about once the situation deteriorated rapidly in late 2008. Others, those in a hurry to follow the Holy Grail of Western financial success had significantly more exposure to cover.

Until recently a substantial part of Western elites propped up the idea that emerging economies would support the spending habits of their Western customers in perpetuity by financing their consumption via the endless purchase of bonds. These export-based economies in need of destination markets for their products had no alternative. This assumption is as false today as it was in the waning days of the 20th century when it was first advanced. What most expert commentators failed to notice was that while these economies did lend money to their Western customers, they were at the same time strengthening their own financial infrastructure.

The primary manifestation of this maturation is the rapid expansion of existing and proliferation of new sovereign wealth funds (SWF). The strong growth of these investment vehicles has set in motion a process through which emerging economies will evolve from creditors into owners. The rise of SWFs is a direct consequence of globalization. Oil-related SWFs have been around since the early 1950s; the expansion of global trade and the gradual opening of international markets have endowed nonresource-rich, export-based economies to support the creation of similar state-owned asset managers. Without free trade, SWFs would have remained what they have always been, namely a loose pool of money trying to find ways to diversify away from oil.

Asian nations have been at the forefront of this SWF process. The structural economic boom in the emerging economies has allowed new players such as China to enter the investment arena with money that's basically controlled by the state but is allocated primarily with investment returns in mind. Nevertheless, only the most naïve observer would suggest that investment decisions made by SWFs are entirely devoid of geopolitical considerations; the long-term economic development of one particular nation-state is inevitably a matter of strategic importance to its neighbors, and vice versa. Sovereign influence is a fact of international capital flows and always has been. That SWFs overtly owned by the states that sponsor them has nevertheless aroused a great deal of suspicion among the US- and EU-based commentariat.

Despite the short-term distractions caused by ambitious politicians, SWFs are here to stay. And the most significant investment development for the next decade will be SWFs soliciting funds from individual investors in their respective countries on a widespread basis. Singapore's Temasek Holdings, in the summer of 2009, was the first SWF to raise funds from institutional investors, making the next leap all the more possible to imagine. That SWFs will eventually tap their own citizens is not so far-fetched; in fact, the domestic base is theoretically preferable to foreign institutions because the latter are prone to withdraw funds for reasons other than investment performance.

Right now we can only contemplate the impact allowing, for example, Chinese to invest in China Investment Corporation (CIC), the country's primary SWF, would have on the global financial system. Apart from the pure amount of funds that would be at its disposal, this would represent yet another step toward a global system in which government plays not simply a supportive, nurturing role but a robust, active role in economic and financial decisions. Governments in the major emerging economies are already deeply entrenched in the financial game. Governments in the Western economies are, alarmingly, increasing their presence in it. Greater interconnectedness between the public and private sector is the inevitable outcome.

The rise of the state, the way it is viewed here, is about two things. First, geopolitical developments will have increasingly greater influence on the way investment funds are allocated as the coming decade unfolds. Second, government will have greater involvement in people's financial affairs—this is the great legacy the financial crisis of 2008 will leave with us.

The recent course of action undertaken by the US government provides a good example of what you should expect from duly constituted authorities around the world in the future. The US government now controls outright or has significant financial interests in some of the biggest, most important industries in the economy. It essentially owns nearly 50 percent of the domestic mortgage market. It owns an iconic automobile manufacturer. It controls large stakes in the major financial institutions that have only gotten bigger since they were deemed "too big to fail." Only hope informs the view that governmental involvement will be relatively short-lived or easily rolled back and that things will return to "normal" sooner rather than later. The financial problems the US federal and state governments face are of unprecedented proportion. The makeup of American society is also changing. The Baby Boomers—around 70 million people born between 1946 and 1960—are entering their 50s and 60s, and their financial needs are changing rapidly. Saving is now more important than spending. The idea of a safety net is a lot more personal, which makes people more amendable to the idea of greater government involvement in their financial affairs. American individual investors have stepped up their purchases of US government bonds, another indication of alignment of interests with the state and their search for income.

History clearly demonstrates that governments are reluctant to give up control of the economy. Successful challenges to authority in matters of commerce usually come from the people, during times of strong growth, as entrepreneurs struggle against burdens placed on them by the state. If, therefore, we've entered a period of structural stagnation and deregulation is viewed suspiciously by the majority of the people, it's impossible to imagine government ceding control soon.

We are in the early stages of an economic and social transformation the end of which could see governments in control over—though not owners of—the means of production. This is not a new idea. The Austrian economist Joseph A. Schumpeter discussed this outcome, in the context of a market-based economy, in his book *Capitalism, Socialism and Democracy* in the early 1940s. The liberal democracies of the West have now reached the point where implementation of a mild version of the ideas Schumpeter expressed can't be dismissed out of hand. Such a shift will be gradual and relatively seamless, through a democratic process, thus engendering relatively little opposition.

This is a book about ideas, the main one of which is that sustainable economic growth increases geopolitical power, which in turn allows for greater assertion in the pursuit of economic greatness. Consequently the investments made by the new powers, domestically and internationally, are more aggressive as well as different in nature than before.

As the book was written with the long-term investor in mind, we have identified the investment themes we believe will emerge as our forecast for the next decade. The majority of these themes share the characteristic that governmental involvement is present usually as a facilitator, but often as a partner to the private sector. Our energy theme is a good example, as governments are now more involved in every phase of the production chain, while also supporting new energy alternatives through elaborate subsidized schemes.

We also name many companies as potential investment candidates, but these recommendations are simply points of departure for more rigorous analysis the realities of time and space don't allow here.

At the same time, noninvestors will also benefit from understanding the themes we address. The political and economic rise of new powers will affect everyone. The ability to separate reality from fiction is, after all, the most useful characteristic of a citizen of a democracy.

We hope you find *The Rise of the State* a useful tool as you make your way through what is a fast-changing world, where the blurring of private and public will only increase.

Yiannis G. Mostrous

McLean, Virginia

March 2010

1

Tectonic Shifts

Governments have always interfered in the investment process. Our contention is that the state's role in finance and the economy will only increase in scope and scale in the decade ahead, for two reasons.

Developed-world economies are in a precarious condition in the aftermath of the great economic collapse of 2008–09. This instability and the extreme measures required to counteract it have exacerbated stresses long-term commitments to citizens have placed on government balance sheets. A paradigm of entitlement has gripped these societies and will prove a difficult burden to shed. At the same time, rising powers feature governments that have traditionally been much more involved in financial and economic matters—practitioners of what many observers have defined as state capitalism.

Here we describe, in broad strokes, the world as it was under US dominance and how it will evolve going forward. Understanding this evolution is most important for the long-term investor. One must look no further than Central Asia to see how economic and political games today's great powers are playing in the region affect the rest of the world. Polycentricism is fast becoming the new norm among states.

Our assessment of how the world will be divided going forward is an effort to prepare the reader for the deep transformation that's already underway. We make no claim that the new financial and geopolitical order we envisage will be a better one. For Westerners, however, the new normal may not be as agreeable as the state of affairs. The example of political and economic order represented by China is a direct challenge to two centuries of accepted wisdom.

Economic and geopolitical scales are tilting eastward. Investors—and citizens—who understand and adapt will find this new world a profitable and exciting one.

In the 1980s, UK Prime Minister Margaret Thatcher was instrumental in blocking the Kuwait Investment Authority (KIA) from controlling more than 25 percent of British Petroleum. The Iron Lady objected on the grounds that she didn't want to see a national treasure owned by a foreign government. The KIA, which was owned by the Kuwaiti government, had to reduce its share of the company to less than 15 percent.

Apart from leading a revival of England's collapsed economy and injecting a dynamism that it until recently possessed, Lady Thatcher was a big proponent of capitalism. She acknowledged, however, that governments had occasionally to interfere, for a variety of potential reasons, in otherwise free markets.

History is full of examples of states intervening in the financial arena for political and economic reasons. The most characteristic examples involve the use of investments or other financial engagements as a geopolitical negotiating technique,[1] as was the case with the English East India Company and the Dutch East India Company. Both companies were founded in the early 1600s to exploit business opportunities in Asia, with initial focus on India and the Indian Ocean, respectively. Both were also involved in politics and acted as agents of the imperialistic aspirations of their countries.

Even the US, which has long projected the image of a free-enterprise haven, maintained high-tariff policies until World War II. "Freedom to trade" rather than "free trade" remains the maxim of its leaders. As recently as 2008, Germany adopted a bill that blocks non-European investors from owning more than 25 percent of a German company.

Peace and Prosperity

As World War II came to an end, the US had clearly evolved into a power financially and militarily able to lead a new era. Its isolationist pretentions were quickly put aside as the new global power was getting ready to take central stage.

President Truman, in an April 1946 speech to a joint session of Congress, observed, "The free people of the world look to us for support in maintaining their freedoms. If we falter in our leadership, we may endanger the peace of the world—and we shall surely endanger the welfare of our own nation." America's "sphere of interest" was now global.[2]

Although the US has been quick to use force in furtherance of its strategic goals, it's also responsible for important institutions with global reach. The most significant in the geopolitical arena are the North Atlantic Treaty Organization (NATO) and the United Nations (UN).

NATO may initially have been designed as its first secretary-general, Lord Ismay, allegedly said, "to keep the Russians out, the Americans in and the Germans down." In practice, it did shelter Western Europe from communism, and the threat of US power guaranteed stability—a prerequisite for economic growth.

The UN's role has been the subject of much criticism. But the UN, overall, has been a positive force in the world—even for the small countries that constantly note their underrepresentation in key decision-making circles. At the end of the day, as Paul Kennedy has observed, "We have a central, self-selected world security body that can be summoned day and night in the event of a new emergency and threat to international order. It is as strong or weak as its permanent members wish it to be. At least, the Great Powers remain inside the tent. At best, they can do great things."[3]

Mainly because of the leadership and restraint it exercised in its post-World War role as one side of a bipolar global power structure, the US has been able to exercise its military and economic power on a global scale essentially unopposed for more than 60 years. The phenomenon of economic globalization, as Baldev Raj Nayar has noted

> ...is not something that has occurred as simply the outcome of some autonomous economic process, but is fundamentally rooted in the geopolitical fact of the global reach of American military power. It is precisely the globe girdling American military presence that has provided the political framework—because of the accompanying security and stability that it assures—within which the Western regime of "embedded

liberalism" has functioned and the massive flows of post-war foreign direct investment have taken place.[4]

America's dominance was also helped by the failure of its two most important adversaries to keep up with a changing world. The Soviet Union eventually collapsed under the weight of its own mis- guided policies and disastrous economic planning. China suffered more than 30 years of "warlord-ism," genocide at the hands of the Japanese, financially disastrous policies, and oppression under Chi- ang Kai Shek. It didn't fare better under Mao Zedong, whose "Great Leap Forward" led to the starvation deaths of about 40 million Chi- nese. The Middle Kingdom's economy, by 1962, was decimated.

State Capitalism

As time passed US economic success, the consequences of which were greater power-projection capabilities and domination of the world's geopolitical scene, made a great impression on the rest of the world. Russia and China set out to emulate this Western model— once given the chance. China, under the guidance of Deng Xiaoping in the late 1970s, was finally able to reverse Mao's disastrous policies and establish a trajectory of economic growth the spectacular likes of which very few people around the world would dare even contem- plate at the time. To its credit American leadership at the time, from 1977 and up to the presidency of George H. W. Bush, understood the implications of Deng's market-oriented reforms and, by building upon former President Richard M. Nixon's initiatives, laid a founda- tion that would allow American companies and investors to capitalize on opportunities in China for years to come.

Ironically, it was Mao's political instinct—a great asset during the early days of his leadership—that led him to bring Deng to Beijing in 1952. Deng was promoted rapidly to secretary general of the party. In terms of importance, he ranked behind Liu Shaoqi, then Chairman of the Standing Committee of the National People's Congress, and Zhou Enlai, the first Premier of the People's Republic of China. According to Mao's contemporaneous view, "Deng is a rare and talented man; he finds solutions. He deals with difficult problems responsibly."[5] These qualities the future leader of China would put to good use for years to come.

In the late 1980s, when the communist states in Eastern Europe were falling apart and the Chinese leadership was wracked with anxiety, Deng famously observed, "Don't be impatient; it is no good to be impatient. We should be calm, calm, again calm, and quietly immerse ourselves in practical work to accomplish something—something for China."[6] Deng's resolve to "do something for China" was a stark contrast at the time with the chaos surrounding the recently dissolved Soviet Union. The disastrous years of the Yeltsin administration, the main achievement of which was the humiliation of Russia on a global scale, pushed economic and institutional reform back by a decade. With the ascent of Vladimir Putin in 1999, Russia regrouped and began to make good use of its strategic natural resources. Proceeds from these strategic assets—contrary to past practice—have been used to secure Russia's future and to modernize its economy. The economic and geopolitical rise of the so-called BRIC countries (Brazil, Russia, India, China) demonstrates that economic growth comes wrapped in many political covers—liberal democracy is not a prerequisite for successful economic expansion. The one-size-fits-all policies advocated by Western operatives and financial zealots in the 1990s proved to be nothing more than nonsense, and actually almost destroyed countries as old and large as Russia.

The financial crisis of 2007-09 demonstrates the failure of the governments in the Anglo-Saxon sphere of economic influence to properly police the system. This failure may not destroy the capitalist model, but has altered it decisively. The failure of state agencies to perform their duties—provide a level playing field, intervene where there's foul play—was deconstructed, vividly, during Congressional hearings about the Bernard Madoff scandal.[7] When the state did intervene in the financial markets, during the years leading up to the crisis's peak in 2008, it did so in a way that invited high levels of moral hazard. The Federal Reserve's moves during the mini-crash of 1987 and the rescue of Long-Term Capital Management (LTCM) set a tone that permitted the 2007-09 bailouts that define the current era of American finance. The 1987 incident, had it been allowed to run its natural course, would not have undermined the US economy overall or the average American's economic security. But, stepping in as it did, the Fed demonstrated a reluctance to allow market forces to correct excesses. Traditionally, such excesses end with the punishment of unscrupulous, arrogant participants. As one observer noted at the time, high finance rewards success, but in the twilight years of the 20th century, it strangely protected failure as well.[8]

It was worrisome then and it's worrisome now that authorities in capitalist economies would step in to ensure endlessly rising markets. Implicit in their actions is the message that nothing can go wrong. This implied guarantee eventually almost caused the Western financial system's demise in 2008–09. This crisis revealed that for the first time in 65 years America doesn't hold all the cards in the global economic and political game.

The Great Game

For centuries Central Asia has been a key piece on the geopolitical chessboard. Its relevance peaked in the 19th century, when Great Britain and Russia vied for control of the region. Russia's desire for expansion and England's fear that the Russians were after India and access to the Indian Ocean created an explosive situation that brought the two great imperial powers to the brink of war numerous times. This competition came to be called "The Great Game."

The US, China, and Russia are the main actors in a 21st century version of The Great Game. Complicating the updated version are the natural resources that Central Asian countries have in abundance.

In 1997 Deputy Secretary of State Strobe Talbot, describing America's long-term view of the region, noted

> If economic and political reform in the countries of the Caucasus and Central Asia does not succeed—if internal and cross-border conflicts simmer and flare—the region could become a breeding ground of terrorism, a hotbed of religious and political extremism, and a battleground for outright war.
>
> It would matter profoundly to the United States if that were to happen in an area that sits on as much as 200 billion barrels of oil. That is yet another reason why conflict-resolution must be Job One for US policy in the region: It is both the prerequisite for and an accompaniment to energy development.[9]

Central Asia is home to the second-most important regional alliance in the world. The Shanghai Cooperation Organization's

(SCO) global influence is exceeded only by NATO's. The SCO, which was established June 15, 2001, includes China, Russia, Uzbekistan, Kazakhstan, Kyrgyzstan, and Tajikistan. Its secretariat is located in northeast Beijing. The SCO was formed to resolve issues between China and the states of Central Asia. It gradually expanded its reach into counterterrorism, defense, energy, and economic cooperation. The US tried to get observer status at the SCO in 2005 but was turned down. India, Iran, Mongolia, and Pakistan currently enjoy observer status.

The West has routinely dismissed the SCO as nothing more than a talk shop. But geopolitical events, particularly the US-led war in Afghanistan, have proved this assessment wrong. If countries that now hold observer status eventually attain full membership the alliance will represent more or less half of the world's population and four nuclear powers. Critically, the SCO has brought China and Russia closer together, aligning their interests, to a point, with regard to issues arising in Central Asia and beyond. The two countries have jointly voiced their opinions about global and regional issues, using the SCO as a platform. The SCO's advocates' major geopolitical argument is made in favor of "multilateral diplomacy." The organization's communiqués regularly include language that gently cautions the US about its global plans.

In late summer 2008, the heads of the SCO's member states gathered in Dushanbe, Tajikistan's capital, to discuss issues of international and regional importance.

The introduction to the official statement released following the meeting characterizes the thinking among policymakers around the world:

In the 21st century interdependence of states has grown sharply, security and development are becoming inseparable. None of the modern international problems can be settled by force; the role of force factor in global and regional politics is diminishing objectively.

Reliance on a solution based solely on the use of force faces no prospects, it hinders comprehensive settlement of local conflicts; effective resolution of existing problems can be possible only with due regard for the interests of all parties, through their involvement in a process of negotiations, not through isolation. Attempts to strengthen one's own security to the prejudice of security of others do not assist the maintenance of global security and stability.

Search for effective response to common challenges and threats that are global in nature must be conducted in strict accordance with the UN Charter and generally accepted norms of the international law, by uniting the efforts of all states, overcoming the bloc mentality, bloc politics and unipolarity, using the means of multilateral diplomacy.

The member states of the SCO believe that in modern circumstances the international security must be built on the principles of mutual trust, mutual benefit, equality and cooperation. The creation of a global antimissile defense system does not assist the maintenance of strategic balance, international efforts on weapons control and nuclear nonproliferation, strengthening of trust among states and regional stability.[10]

Central Asia is now vital to the maintenance of geopolitical stability. The rise of radical Islam and its military manifestation, jihadism, in the area is a critical danger. The US, China, Russia, and India share a common interest in drastically containing this phenomenon, the only geopolitical interest these four states share in common. US Special Representative for Afghanistan and Pakistan Richard Holbrooke said during a trip to Central Asia in February 2010:

I think the real threat in this region is less from the Taliban but from al Qaeda, which trains international terrorists...this is an issue of common concern to the United States and to all the countries of this region. And by all the countries I definitely include Pakistan and China and India.

The war in Afghanistan makes many countries in the region important in terms of establishing supply routes for Western armies. Part of Russia's air space has been opened to Western military traffic as well, an indication that the Russian government continues to support US efforts. Russia has a keen interest in seeing militant Islam defeated or drastically contained. For this reason Russia has provided an air corridor for American and European supply lifts to Afghanistan, which remain open and was actually expanded more during the conflict with Georgia in August 2008, when Russia was being heavily criticized by America's mass media establishment. Although Russia and the US compete in the area, both their efforts to gain influence in Central Asia and the Caspian and a slice of the region's hydrocarbons have as a prerequisite minimizing the influence and actions of the jihadists.

Most important, a global consensus views instability in the region as extremely dangerous to the global situation. Afghanistan's neighbor Pakistan could also suffer greater destruction at the hands of radical Islamists, who could potentially gain access to the country's nuclear arsenal.[11] According to Seymour M. Hersh of *The New Yorker*, this scenario is at the top of Washington, DC, policymakers' discussions, as Pakistan's military and secret services are believed to have relationships with Islamic fundamentalists.[12]

Russia's problem with violent Islam is centered on what's called the *Caucasus Emirate*, which was founded in 2007. This is the latest manifestation of a jihadist movement that's plagued the northern Caucasus since the mid-1990s. Russia has long-term relationships with these newly independent countries. Their proximity to its borders means Russia can't afford to be a bystander to the changing military and strategic balance of power in its backyard, particularly as Russia has traditionally considered the region a strategic buffer against outside threats.

China is also tied to Central Asia. It shares common borders totaling more than 3,000 kilometers (1,864 miles) with Kazakhstan, Kyrgyzstan, and Tajikistan. Its long-term strategic plan for the region includes three priorities: Keep Central Asia stable; use the region as another way to diversify its energy resources; and contain separatist movements in its oil-rich Xinjiang province. China also views the region as a potential destination for its exports; already many Chinese products are found in Central Asian countries, and they're gradually displacing Russian-made goods.

The first strategic interest is rooted in China's history and the centuries-old internal debate over Chinese strategic security between proponents of maritime power and land power. Land-power advocates often prevail in these debates, a fact reflected by Central Asia's significant presence in China's strategic thinking.

The second interest concerns efforts by China to reduce its dependence on oil imports from the Middle East. Roughly 80 percent of Chinese oil imports pass through the 600-mile Strait of Malacca, which divides Singapore from the Indonesian island of Sumatra; Chinese officials see this as a weakness because the route can be easily closed down during conflicts, particularly where the conflict would involve China and the US. Pipelines from Central Asia are considered more reliable and are therefore highly desirable.

In 2005 the 1,000 kilometer oil pipeline connecting Atasu in Kazakhstan to Alashankou in western China started pumping oil. The pipeline, which boasts capacity of 20 million tons, was an important milestone in China's investment in the region, not only because it allowed China to further diversify its energy deliveries. China also financed most of the USD800 million construction cost for the project completed in ten months, record time for such an undertaking. In December 2009 China signed a deal with Turkmenistan to build a 1,800 kilometer pipeline to deliver gas from Turkmenistan to China. The pipeline, which will also pass through Uzbekistan and Kazakhstan, will deliver up to 40 billion cubic meters of natural gas a year to China by the time it reaches full capacity in 2013 and should serve the Middle Kingdom for the next 30 years.

The third long-term strategic interest—keeping the region stable—has to do with what the Chinese view as an unstable situation in the Xinjiang Uighur Autonomous Region (XUAR). The more than seven million ethnic Turkic Uighurs living in the region, who are largely Muslim, identify more closely with their Central Asian neighbors than with ethnic Chinese. Because many Uighurs desire greater autonomy—and it's believed that foreign-based, radical Islamic organizations are instigating a separatist movement—Chinese leaders view them as a potentially destabilizing force.

China's fast and decisive moves to secure natural gas and oil from Central Asian countries coupled with Russia's equally swift moves to guarantee Central Asian gas will keep flowing through Russian pipelines have made similar efforts supported by the US and other Western interests seem less viable. The best example is the highly advertised Nabucco gas pipeline, a 3,300 kilometer pipeline that's supposed to bring natural gas from the Caspian Sea to Eastern and

Central Europe, bypassing Russian territory. Initial talks about the project took place in February 2002; the timetable calls for transporting gas by 2014. According to market studies the pipeline has been designed to transport a maximum of 31 billion cubic meters per year. Estimated investment costs, including financing costs, for a complete new pipeline system amount to approximately EUR7.9 billion (USD11 billion). Set aside the high cost and the engineering challenges the Nabucco project entails, because of the projects detailed above involving Central Asian countries and China and Russia, there's simply not enough natural gas to fill this pipeline and make it even remotely economical. Azerbaijan, which would supposedly supply most of the volume, doesn't have enough gas.

Further complicating matters, Russia has already signed a deal with Italian, Bulgarian, Greek, and Serbian energy companies to push its South Stream pipeline forward and double its capacity. The South Stream will take gas from Russia to South and Central Europe from an entry point on the Bulgarian coast. This is one of two additional pipelines planned by Russia to deliver gas to Europe, both of which avoid Ukraine's pipeline network and the problems associated with it. Another very important project is the Nord Stream pipeline, which would deliver gas from Russia directly to Germany through the Baltic Sea.

If the Nabucco project fails to live up to expectations, the US will eventually abandon its heavy involvement in Central Asia, although it will continue to cooperate on issues that are vital to its operations in Afghanistan and the Middle East.

Polycentricism

Sustainable economic growth increases individuals' and governments' confidence. Ideas once expressed only amid casual conversation are now incorporated in official statements.

Over the past five years government officials around the world have repeatedly expressed a particular way of thinking about energy security. The world tends to view energy security issues through the lenses of developed economies. These economies were able, through government actions, to establish an energy status quo that, though it's been stable, was based on the premise that developed-economy leaders could dictate the politics of the international energy trade. At the same time, smaller nations, because they lacked the financial and economic muscle, weren't invited to participate in the decision-making process. They had to go with the flow.

Today China and India are at the forefront of a global effort to change this arrangement. Chinese and Indian political elites now exercise their right to strike energy deals according to their own interests and needs rather than the geopolitical considerations of others. Although this doesn't mean the sensitivities of their partners are discarded, the fact remains that it's incomprehensible to Indians, for instance, why their relationship with Iran is used by the US as a pressure point, particularly as more than 12 percent of India's oil imports come from Iran. To Indians the issue for the US is purely geopolitical—namely, the nuclear threat that Iran may in the future pose to Western interests. India has co-existed with an extremely unstable and economically deficient neighbor with a nuclear arsenal for a long time. This country, Pakistan, has offered its expertise on nuclear weapons, under the guidance of the notorious A. Q. Khan, to an assortment of rogue states, while all the time being an ally of the US in its "global war on terror."[13] Indian officials, as well as many Indian businesses, have often yielded to US pressures on these issues, against their will, because the US is a necessary ally and economic partner. But US actions are increasingly viewed in India the same way Western commentators view "resource nationalism." In other words, states that control natural resources are applying pressure to consumers via threats to cut supplies.

The US usually uses access to its markets as well as access to nuclear and other technologies as negotiating levers, what government officials and elites describe as "strategic interests." India will soon have enough standing to defy similar US requests that it considers contrary to Indian interests, particularly if Indians don't perceive their actions as threatening regional and global security and stability.

China and Russia are the main proponents of the concept of polycentricism. Their call is to return to the more stable situation that prevailed in the immediate aftermath of World War II, during which the US wasn't venturing around the world à la Gulliver, trying to "take care of business." The emerging Asian powers envisage a more subtle, diplomatic approach as the best road forward. Political scientist G. John Ikenberry expressed a similar idea in 2001. He noted that

> The institutional model of order building is based on a potential bargain between unequal states after a war...what makes the institutional deal attractive is that the leading state agrees to restrain its own potential for domination and abandonment in exchange for greater compliance by subordinate states. Both sides are better off with a constitutional order than in an order based on the constant threat of the indiscriminate and arbitrary exercise of power.[14]

The Chinese, for obvious reasons, have been very vocal in assuring the world that its rise will be peaceful. Its official policy position, expressed in a white paper on defense, indicates that China

> [W]ill encourage the advancement of security dialogues and cooperation with other countries, oppose the enlargement of military alliances, and acts of aggression and expansion. China will never seek hegemony or engage in military expansion now or in the future, no matter how developed it becomes.[15]

The US has been heavily involved in Asia since the mid 1800s, when marines landed in Guangzhou to protect American citizens from Chinese mobs. It became the dominate force in the region after its conquest of The Philippines in 1899. Forty-five years later the US ended World War II in Asia by guaranteeing that Japan had no choice but to surrender and making it essentially a vassal state. The US turned the island into a stationary carrier from which the rest of Asia could easily be accessed. As Professor Yoshihide Soeya of Keio University has said, there are three traumas from which the Japanese people are still reeling: defeat in the war, occupation by Americans, and the solidification of their country's subordination to the US.[16]

Nevertheless, the US, acting as the guarantor of regional stability, served Asia well. Its presence worked for the region overall, as long as communism was seen as a threat and the Japanese atrocities of old, mainly in China and Korea, were still fresh in people's minds. Neither of these conditions is present now. China's economic ascent is seen as a positive for the region, and the majority of Asian governments are more than willing to cooperate with China; a developing Chinese economy is good for their own economies. China is, after all, a neighbor state that will be there forever. Good relations are the right way to go.

The US has responded negatively to geopolitical change and the idea of polycentricism. America's ideas about its own exceptional status and the universality of its values are expressed prominently in dealings with other states. Although these ideas and the policies crafted to further them aren't new, the way they've been carried out over the past 10 to 15 years, combined with the economic rise of China, has created notable discomfort for governments around the world. Many countries are starting to identify with John Adams' words about the British and their handling of peace negotiations: "The pride and vanity of that nation is a disease; it is a delirium; it has been flattered and inflamed so long by themselves and others that it perverts everything."[17]

George H. W. Bush, whose gentlemanly approach to diplomacy advanced US interests around the world without eliciting serious opposition, noted in 1975 while in China as the head of the United States Liaison Office (USLO), that

> The American people do not have any concept of how others around the world view America, we think we are good, honorable, decent, freedom-loving. Others are firmly convinced that...we are embarking on policies that are anathema to them.[18]

Although this is the nature of international politics—not everyone looks at an issue the same way or has the same interests—it is still the case in America that people are genuinely puzzled when they find out that others don't necessarily see eye to eye with the US on a lot of issues. But geopolitical and economic developments are gradually laying this mind-set to rest. Probably—eventually—the US will once again adhere to the principles of its founders, who erected their constitutional regime on the sound proposition that power must be checked and balanced.[19]

Dividing the World

In March 1991, Richard Nixon went to Georgia, a trip that, because of his status as a former president, indicated US support for the former satellite's independence from the Soviet Union.

According to Dmitri K. Simes, an aide to Nixon who attended the meeting, the 37th president was alarmed when Zviad Gamsakhurdia, then president of Georgia, told him that not only was the Soviet Union dissolving, but also Russia itself was weak. The time might be right, he advised, to deliver a final blow. "Mr. President," Nixon replied, "there are two kinds of people in Washington you are going to encounter— those who will tell you what you want to hear and those who will tell you what you need to hear. And what you need to hear is that no matter what your friends and admirers in the United States may tell you, America is not going to go to war with Russia because of Georgia."[20] Nixon's words were prophetic. During the Russia-Georgia conflict 17 years later, Russia stopped short of taking over Tbilisi of its own accord, not because of the presence of the US army, which was not there. Russian President Dmitry Medvedev said in an interview a month later, "The last time I talked with President Bush on the phone it was during the active phase of military operations, and I told him that 'in this situation you would have done the same thing, only perhaps more severely.' He did not argue with me."[21]

The biggest contributions powerful states have made to global social progress have come during periods of cooperation that followed profound disruptions to established order. The need to restore stability has driven successful settlements such as those that followed the Napoleonic Wars in 1815 and World War II in 1945. Other arrangements, however, were doomed from the outset. The settlement of World War I, for example, led directly to a sequel only 20 years later. Although no shots were fired during the most recent disruption to established order, recent events have shaken public confidence in the prevailing global economic and financial architecture. What transpired during 2007 to 2009 will have long-term consequences similar to those that sprang from wars in the 19th and 20th centuries. Among them, the world will once again be informally divided into spheres of influence, determined primarily by geography.

The US, weakened in absolute terms by the financial and economic crises, is also in economic decline relative to China, Russia, and India. This is not to suggest the US won't be an important actor in the world's stage; this is not a zero-sum game. But an overstretched America is silently trimming its financial and military commitments abroad. As economic conditions in China, Russia, and India improve, their people will grow more eager to see their countries taken more seriously on the global stage. The first step toward making these aspirations reality is to enhance military strength; all three will beef up their armed forces to keep neighbors at bay and minimize potential interference in economic development and the well-being of their respective populations. This page is taken directly from the script followed by the US and other powers before it. This plot line has endured the test of time, and its logic is easily understood.

China will become the undisputed power in Asia. The US will maintain a presence, but only as a symbolic suggestion of balance. The Middle East will remain under the influence of the US, though Iran won't be materially destabilized because China has significant investments there, and it's also of interest to Russia and India. Central Asia will be the domain of Russia and China. South America will remain under US domination. Africa will stay open to all—the logic of economic cooperation will eventually supersede short-term political differences among the biggest players. Jihadism, a potential security threat in North Africa, is something all parties will have to deal with. The US will continue to try and influence Eastern European states, but the EU seems strong enough to remain the main relevant economic and political force in the Continent.

Finding this new equilibrium requires all interested parties to make concessions. The US, for example, must cease NATO expansion, and China, Russia, and India have to support US policy in the Middle East. But these are relatively minor points in the big picture. The exercise of restraint is already emerging as the defining characteristic of responsible global actors in the 21st century.

Emotional responses to this nascent order threaten what would be a mutually beneficial division of global influence. Suspicion aroused for domestic political purposes, direct confrontation, and unilateralism will undermine—perhaps undo—the profound economic progress the world has experienced over the last three decades.

"For the future, like the past," historian William H. McNeill observed in the early 1980s, "depends upon humanity's demonstrated ability to make and remake natural and social environments within limits set mainly by our capacity to agree on goals of collective action."[22]

Endnotes

[1] *Geopolitics* is the analysis of the geographic influences on power relationships in international relations. The word "geopolitics" was originally coined by the Swedish political scientist Rudolf Kjellén about the turn of the 20th century. Its use spread throughout Europe in the period between World Wars I and II (1918–39) and came into worldwide use during the latter. In contemporary discourse, geopolitics has been widely employed as a loose synonym for international politics—*Encyclopedia Britannica* online edition. It is the latter definition that is being used throughout the book.

[2] Francis Pike, *Empires At War: A Short History of Modern Asia Since World War II* (London: I. B. Tauris, 2010), 109.

[3] Paul M. Kennedy, *The Parliament of Man: The Past, Present, and Future of the United Nations* (New York: Random House, 2006), Vintage Books Edition 2007, 286.

[4] Baldev Raj Nayar, *The Geopolitics of Globalization: The Consequences for Development* (New Delhi: Oxford University Press, 2005), Paperback edition 2007, 82.

[5] Pike, *Empires At War*, 584.

[6] David Shambaugh, *China's Communist Party: Atrophy and Adaptation* (Washington, DC: Woodrow Wilson Center Press, 2008), 46.

[7] Testimony of Harry Markopolos, CFA, CFE, before the US House of Representatives committee on financial services, February 4, 2009.

[8] Roger Lowenstein, *When Genius Failed: The Rise and Fall of Long-Term Capital Management* (New York: Random House, 2000), 219.

[9] Strobe Talbott, "US Policy Toward Central Asia and the Caucasus," speech delivered at the Central Asia Institute of The Paul H. Nitze School of Advanced International Studies of The Johns Hopkins University on July 21, 1997.

[10] Dushanbe Declaration of the Heads of the Member States of the Shanghai Cooperation Organisation, 28 August 2008, http://www.sectsco.org/EN/show.asp?id=90 (accessed January 2010).

[11] Gordon M. Hahn, "U.S.–Russian Relations and the War Against Jihadism," A Century Foundation Report 2009.

[12] Seymour M. Hersh, "Defending the Arsenal: In an unstable Pakistan, can nuclear warheads be kept safe?" *The New Yorker*, November 16, 2009.

[13]   For more on the issue see http://www.globalsecurity.org/wmd/world/pakistan/khan.htm.

[14]   G. John Ikenberry, *After Victory: Institutions, Strategic Restraint, and the Rebuilding of Order after Major Wars* (New Jersey: Princeton University Press, 2001), 258–59.

[15]   "China's National Defense in 2008" Information Office of the State Council of the People's Republic of China, Beijing, January 2009, 7.

[16]   Cited by Masahiko Ishizuka in "How Far will Abe Go in Defying Japan's 'Postwar Regime'?" Japanese Institute of Global Communications, June 4, 2007, http://www.glocom.org/opinions/essays/20070604_ishizuka_how/index.html (accessed January 2010).

[17]   Barbara W. Tuchman, *The March of Folly: From Troy to Vietnam* (New York: Ballantine Books, 1985), 229.

[18]   Jeffrey A. Engel, ed., *The China Diary of George H. W. Bush: The Making of a Global President* (New Jersey: Princeton University Press, 2008), 463.

[19]   Robert W. Tucker, and David C. Hendrickson, "The Sources of American Legitimacy," *Foreign Affairs*, 83:6 (November/December 2004), 28.

[20]   Dmitri K. Simes, "Westerners Resist Perception of Georgian Aggression," *The Washington Times*, September 17, 2008.

[21]   Meeting with Participants in the International Club Valdai, September 12, 2008. http://eng.kremlin.ru/speeches/2008/09/12/1644_type82912type82917type84779_206409.shtml.

[22]   William H. McNeill, *The Pursuit of Power: Technology, Armed Force, and Society since A. D. 1000* (Chicago: The University of Chicago Press, 1982), 387.

2

The Wealth of Sovereigns

Sovereign wealth funds have existed for more than half a century. The truth is government has and will always have a critical role in the economy. We are now in a period in which the state's prominence is on the rise.

The early response from US leadership to the proliferation of state-sponsored actors in the economy was more about establishing domestic political advantages than enlightening the public to the realities of globalization. Contrary to the worst fears catered to by officials, SWFs and their like have proven to be no more political than a typical pension or mutual fund.

But the Great Recession changed everything. SWFs played a key role in stabilizing the global financial system, providing significant capital to Western institutions at critical moments. Their legitimacy confirmed, SWFs have been among the most aggressive global investors in the early days of the recovery. The rise of SWFs is just one sign of the changing balance of power in the world economy.

The most remarkable aspect of sovereign wealth funds (SWF) and related vehicles is what their emergence says about the present and future of the global economy.

Special-purpose investment funds or businesses created and owned by the general government for macroeconomic purposes have existed for decades. The term "sovereign wealth fund" was coined by Andrew Rozanov in a May 2005 article in *Central Banking Journal* to describe, generally, government investment activities. The definition most useful for our purposes, which is to understand the rising role of the state and how this impacts decisions for individual investors, comes from Bryan J. Balin's paper *Sovereign Wealth Funds: A Critical Analysis*:

> Sovereign wealth funds are defined by the US Treasury Dept as "government vehicles funded from foreign exchange earnings but managed separately from foreign reserves." Along with financing, sovereign wealth funds also differ from other government vehicles in their objectives, terms, and holdings: while foreign reserves have historically invested in sovereign fixed income notes for the purpose of intervention on the foreign exchange market, SWFs typically take a longer-term approach, where international equities, commodities, and private fixed income securities are used to achieve the long-run strategic and financial goals of a sovereign.
>
> It should be strongly noted that sovereign wealth funds are **not** the only vector through which sovereign entities make foreign private investments. Another way through which countries invest in foreign entities is through purchases by state-owned enterprises.[1]

The history of such activities has been traced to 1953, when the Kuwait Investment Board was created to manage the excess oil revenue for what was then still an "independent sheikhdom under British protectorate." But rapid growth in their number and a shift in investing behavior brought SWFs and state-owned enterprises (SOE) to the attention of politicians and the public shortly before an otherwise normal downturn became the Great Recession with the near-collapse of the Western financial system. SWFs, several of which came to the aid of weakened US and European banks, have proven resilient in the aftermath of the 2007-09 turmoil. Once happy to quietly work the wings, SWFs have fixed themselves prominently on an otherwise evolving global financial and economic stage. The composition of the leadership will change, with less agile markets receding in importance. The influence of these types of vehicles, however, will only grow. They are important instruments that will help sponsoring countries diversify their economies, provide for future generations, stabilize government revenue in times of economic crisis, and also access particular knowledge that will help development in the present.

Controversy stoked for domestic political purposes in the US obscures the more nuanced case that on the whole state-sponsored entities present no inherent threat to public markets, and that their long-term focus, objectives, and behavior as investors in fact add to financial and economic stability. Whether convenient for the US and the West, SWFs are here to stay. Current estimates—because so few report portfolio information in the manner of Western institutional investors, these are ballpark figures—place their total assets under management somewhere between USD1.5 trillion and USD3 trillion.

During the proliferation phase of 2005–08, some market observers projected SWFs aggregate assets under management would reach USD12 trillion, USD15 trillion, even USD20 trillion by 2020. One study has identified more than 2,500 investments worth an aggregate USD3 trillion in the listed equity of private firms by state-owned investment companies, stabilization funds, commercial and development banks, pension funds, and state-owned enterprises. Including state purchases of government and corporate bonds, SWF holdings and foreign exchange reserves, the total value of state-owned financial assets may already exceed USD15 trillion.[2]

It wasn't until an SOE tried to buy strategic US assets that the new prominence of state actors in the global economy came to wide political and public attention in the US. Shortly thereafter the US financial system began to buckle under the weight of subprime-mortgage-backed securities, among other synthetic financial instruments; sovereign wealth funds were able to at least paper over balance-sheet holes in the short term via the infusion of more than USD31 billion into three US-based financial institutions.

Indeed, the economic crisis forced a reevaluation of deeply held convictions about the role of the state and state-sponsored entities in the economy. Among the many issues still under consideration by global policymakers are the roles of regulation and regulators in financial markets. In addition, governments and extra-governmental organizations have had to reconsider how foreign trade and capital flows impact at the local as well as the international level. Specifically regarding the West, the crisis has also forced a reassessment of economic orthodoxy that touts the self-regulating nature of free market economies and suffers lightly intrusions by the state into private economies. The top criticism of SWFs is that they lack transparency; however, the depth and breadth of the global recession can be blamed on a financial crisis arguably caused by opacity in the over-the-counter derivatives market, in the composition of synthetic mortgage-backed securities and with regard to banks and special investment vehicles.

Understanding the reasons for and the consequences of the increasing prominence of state actors in the global economy will help open-minded investors profit in the coming decade.

This trend emerged well before an ordinary recession became a global financial and economic crisis and has only strengthened with the extraordinary participation of Western governments in the rescue and support of their respective economies.

Treated with skepticism by Western elites in 2005-08, Middle East and East Asia-based SWFs and SOEs have become critical pillars of the global financial system in the aftermath of the Great Recession. Their rapid growth in the years preceding the crisis resulted from the accumulation of massive excess foreign reserves by sponsoring governments due to the rapid rise in the oil price and credit-fueled consumption in the West. Their contribution to mitigating the worst effects of the global economic downturn at home and abroad as well as the resumption of consumption trends that will help them grow mean the individual investor with a long-term view must understand their activities.

Welcome to America

In January 2006, a semi-retired lobbyist, Joseph A. Muldoon Jr., was retained by Fort Lauderdale, Florida-based port operator/stevedore Eller & Company as part of a last-ditch effort to derail the proposed acquisition of Peninsular & Oriental Steam Navigation Company, a British firm known widely as P&O, by Dubai Ports World. Eller & Company, through its subsidiary Continental Stevedoring & Terminals, was engaged in two joint ventures with P&O. It was concerned that DP World would impair contracts Continental had to conduct stevedoring operations at the Port of Miami; in addition to hiring Muldoon, Eller & Company also filed a lawsuit in a Florida circuit court.

In addition to the Port of Miami, P&O held the operating leases for ports in New York/New Jersey, Philadelphia, Tampa, Baltimore, and New Orleans. These leases, as well as stevedoring contracts at 16 more ports scattered up and down the Atlantic and Pacific coasts, would be assumed by DP World. DP World had begun the process of gaining the necessary approvals from the federal government for a foreign entity seeking to acquire US assets. It first contacted the Committee on Foreign Investment in the United States (CFIUS) in October 2005, before a deal with P&O had even been struck. The CFIUS screens potential acquisitions of US assets by foreign entities for national security threats. The panel is headed by a representative of the US Treasury Department and includes top officials from the Department of Defense, the Department of State, the Department of Commerce, and the Department of Homeland Security. More than 250 officials at the second and third tiers of the federal government reviewed the proposed DP World-P&O transaction on substantive grounds. There were no objections raised—neither from the Pentagon nor Homeland Security, in particular, which at that point had been under intense political pressure for perceived shortcomings in their respective performances.[3] In February 2006, DP World advised in its dealings with the review board by former President Bill Clinton, received the approval of the CFIUS for its takeover of P&O.

The Eller & Company subsidiary, Continental, simply did not want to become what it called an involuntary partner of DP World.[4] It asked a judge to block the takeover and for USD10 million in damages. It said it didn't believe the company, Florida, or the US government could ensure DP World's compliance with American security rules. Its lawyers alleged in a Florida circuit court filing that the sale to Dubai was prohibited under Continental's partnership agreement with P&O and "may endanger the national security of the United States." This was the flashpoint for a controversy that brought widespread attention to the proliferation of state-sponsored entities among participants in private markets around the world.

Joe Muldoon, his rural Maryland horse farm a short drive from Washington, DC, started making the rounds on Capitol Hill that month. He, along with his son Joseph A. Muldoon III, focused on members of the Senate Banking Committee from both sides of the aisle. He also targeted members of Congress who represented states and districts where ports included in the transaction were located. Senator Charles Schumer (D-NY) met both criteria. But it wasn't until Muldoon got in touch with an *Associated Press* reporter that the extent of direct state involvement in global markets became a topic for cable news discussion and major daily front-page headlines. The lead paragraph of a February 12, 2006, *AP* story set the tone for the hysterical debate that followed over the course of the ensuing three weeks:

> A company in the United Arab Emirates is poised to take over significant operations at six U.S. ports as part of a corporate sale, leaving a country with ties to the Sept. 11, 2001, hijackers with influence over a maritime industry considered vulnerable to terrorism.[5]

On February 13, 2006, Senator Schumer, encouraged by Representative Rahm Emanuel, then the Democratic Congressional Campaign Committee chairman who would lead his party in the November 2006 midterm elections as it reclaimed a majority in the House of Representatives, held a press conference during which he called on the US Department of Homeland Security to investigate the CFIUS decision. He added, "Foreign control of our ports, which are vital to homeland security, is a risky proposition. Riskier yet is that we are turning it over to a country that has been linked to terrorism previously." Representative Emanuel told Senator Schumer he thought he "had something here"; Senator Schumer said he knew he did.[6] One of the terrorists who flew a plane into the World Trade Center on September 11, 2001, Marwan al-Shehhi, was born in the United Arab Emirates; he and another hijacker carried UAE passports. Other hijackers traveled through the UAE on their way to the US. Congressman Peter King (R-NY) described the UAE as "the heartland of al-Qaida."[7] By comparison, 15 of the hijackers carried passports issued by Saudi Arabia, and more had direct contact with Great Britain, home of P&O's original owner, than with the UAE. The UAE had allowed the US Army and Navy access to its territory while conducting operations related to the war on terror, but it still bore a stigma. John Negroponte, the director of national intelligence, told the Senate Armed Services Committee that the CFIUS assessed the threat to US national security posed by DP World to be low. "In other words," he said, "we didn't see any red flags come up during the course of our inquiry."

But Dubai Ports World is a subsidiary of Dubai World,[8] an investment company that manages a portfolio of assets on behalf of the government of Dubai. Not only is DP World domiciled in the UAE, it is owned by Dubai, one of the seven city-states that comprise the Middle Eastern nation. This is the only aspect of the AP story that understated the facts. DP World was created in 2005 by the merger of state-owned Dubai Ports Authority and Dubai Ports International. Dubai World was established by decree of Sheikh Mohammed bin Rashid Al Maktoum, Vice President and Prime Minister of the United Arab Emirates and Ruler of Dubai to manage the emirate's investment portfolio. The Sheikh is the majority owner of Dubai World.

By mid-February a bipartisan coalition of senators, representatives, cable TV pundits, and bloggers had formed against the deal, though DP World was widely recognized as one of the top port operators in the world. It now runs 49 terminals in 31 countries on all five continents. By March the deal was dead; testifying before the Senate Commerce Committee DP World CEO Edward Bilkey confirmed that Dubai World, the holding company that owned DP World, owned a Dubai customs office that enforced the emirate's participation in an Arab League boycott of products made in Israel.[9] Support from Israel's largest shipping firm couldn't overcome this final transgression.[10] DP World divested the US assets acquired along with P&O in late 2006.[11]

At the time DP World made its offer to buy the company in October 2005, P&O had 27 container terminals and logistics operations in more than 100 ports, with a presence in 18 countries. The British government had earlier that year granted conditional approval to DP World's plan to invest GBP1.5 billion to develop a deepwater container port and a logistics business, the London Gateway, on the north bank of the River Thames at Thurrock, Essex. The port will be open to the largest container ships in the world and will be able to handle 3.5 million twenty-foot equivalent units (TEU) a year. The business, an important one during a time of rising global trade, is growing.

DP World oversaw the growth of the UAE ports of Rashid and Jebel Ali into the tenth-largest operation in the world and has successfully used this experience to expand abroad. It wanted P&O for strategic business purposes: access to its Asia routes. The US assets comprised 10 percent of P&O's revenue; the real prize was access to the emerging center of global growth, East Asia. It would have made no substantive changes to day-to-day operations at P&O's US locations. Though not yet conditioned to steer entirely clear of political trouble, management was mindful of the sensitive nature of its proposed deal; after all, it hired a former US president to lobby on its behalf, which raised some controversy when his wife, then-Senator Hilary Clinton, weighed in against the deal. According to its Web site, in 2008, DP World handled more than 46.8 million TEU across its portfolio from the Americas to Asia, an increase of 8 percent over 2007 levels. Its development pipeline spanning key growth markets in India, China, and the Middle East, TEU are forecast to reach 95 million over the next ten years. If Dubai or any malefactors associated with it wanted to harm the US through DP World, it would have plenty of launch points beyond North America from which to do so. DP World's intent with P&O was entirely economic. The deal made sense within a broader strategy to leverage expertise gained at home—essentially exporting its port-management services.

As instructive as the DP World pursuit of P&O is about state-controlled funds' goals, the DP World debacle may prove to have been a last desperate victory for the so-called Washington Consensus and the global infrastructure established to perpetuate it. The term "Washington Consensus" was first used in 1989 by John Williamson to describe a set of ten economic policy prescriptions that should comprise the standard reform package promoted for crisis-wracked developing countries by Washington, DC-based institutions such as the International Monetary Fund (IMF), the World Bank, and the US Treasury Department.[12] It evolved into a broader description that, among other things, implied a preference for private as opposed to public solutions to problems of economic growth. Williamson later expressed concern that "the term...has come to be used to describe an extreme and dogmatic commitment to the belief that markets can handle everything."[13]

Ironically, new questions about state-controlled entities and their ownership of US-based companies arose in 2007 and 2008 as the corrosive impact of subprime mortgages ate away at crisis-wracked US financial institutions' balance sheets. Between March 2007 and April 2008 investment vehicles backed by the governments of Abu Dhabi (like Dubai one of the United Arab Emirates), Singapore, Kuwait, Korea, and China invested a total of approximately USD31 billion in Citigroup, Merrill Lynch, and Morgan Stanley. Establishing relationships with what were then considered the world's leading banks was another way to diversify. These investments were about long-term considerations—for returns, opportunities for further investment, and for access to investment skill.[14]

Western leaders were forced to consider their opposition to foreign investors buying key US-based assets in light of the capital needs of a financial system critical, those leaders themselves argued, to stabilizing to domestic economy. In a July 30, 2007, post on the *Financial Times* Economists' Forum blog, Lawrence Summers, then the Charles W. Eliot University Professor at Harvard, now Chairman of the Council of Economic Advisors, expressed the root of American concern:

> The question is profound and goes to the nature of global capitalism. A signal event of the past quarter-century has been the sharp decline in the extent of direct state ownership of business as the private sector has taken ownership of what were once government-owned companies. Yet governments are now accumulating various kinds of stakes in what were once purely private companies through their cross-border investment activities.[15]

Attitudes evolved as the crisis worsened. Politicians who once clamored for investigations and restrictions now at least conceded SWFs' critical role in providing capital at an important moment. Pundits openly campaigned for SWF cash.[16] Western states were now concerned that structural problems at home and the need to prop up certain debt-ridden peers would force SWFs to reallocate capital inward rather than into the US and European economies.[17]

Senator Schumer, in opening remarks before a February 13, 2008, hearing of the Joint Economic Committee of the Senate Banking Committee on the question, "Do Sovereign Wealth Funds Make the US Economy Stronger or Pose National Security Risks," grudgingly noted this beneficial role. But his previously UAE-specific concern became a generalized suspicion of SWFs. He concluded his prepared statement by granting the importance of foreign investment but questioning state-controlled funds' transparency and whether their investments were in fact based on financial and economic considerations:

> We have seen plenty of private foreign investors put money into U.S. companies without much evidence that they are investing for non-economic purposes. But it would be perfectly rational to expect a foreign government-controlled fund to have non-economic motivations....
>
> In this regard, sovereign wealth funds are their own worst enemies. Most are not transparent or publicly accountable, and we know little about their governance structures or fiduciary controls. So the bottom line is that we don't know if their decisions are made exclusively on an economic basis.[18]

During his April 2008 keynote address to the Luxembourg Foreign Trade Conference, Bader M. Al Sa'ad, Managing Director of Kuwait Investment Authority, responded to what he considered the hypocrisy of Western officials. After he briefly described KIA's history, Al Sa'ad turned to present matters and the then-persistent calls for transparency for SWFs:

> Let me go to the main point: how was this crisis created? It is important to identify the root for the creation of funds which permitted entities to borrow 30 to 40 times their capital, without any discussions or calls for any regulation of these entities. Based on public information, these funds apparently grew geometrically without any governance or oversight.
>
> Sovereign Wealth Funds have acted responsibly and swiftly during these highly volatile times. They have taken on the responsibility of pumping more than 65 billion US dollars in some of the impacted financial institutions. At the end, these Sovereign Wealth Funds will be held responsible by their

stakeholders and their citizens, the ultimate owners of these funds.

If a set of principles or codes of conduct are established for Sovereign Wealth Funds, then recipient countries should also have the same set of principles for all pools of capital, including Hedge Funds, Private Equity Funds, Pension Funds, Savings Funds, and other non listed funds, in OECD and non OECD countries. There should be a common and level playing field for all.

"If it is not broken, don't fix it." There is no evidence, over the past many decades, of any wrong doing by any Sovereign Wealth Fund.[19]

SWFs' attempted rescue of beleaguered financial institutions proved frustrating for them, in terms of the early paper losses and the resulting domestic backlash—while much of the suspicion in Western recipient countries was washed away by a greater sense that they needed SWF cash, citizens of the investing countries wanted to know why these funds could not be put to better use at home, particularly as the global downturn gained steam and oil consumption and trade declined—as well as the reaction of an inhospitable West. SWFs then sought to lower their profiles at home and in the corridors of official power by investing through private equity funds. This strategic shift has been interpreted by critics as another indication of SWF secrecy.[20] It's actually a return to the methods they employed before the 2005-08 proliferation period, when what we now call sovereign wealth funds were known only to a few elite actors in the global financial system.

Only weeks before the Luxembourg Foreign Trade Conference, the IMF had announced, on March 21, 2008, the creation of an international working group of sovereign wealth funds to begin drafting proposals for best-practice guidelines.[21] Critically, it was agreed that IMF staff should work with SWFs to develop these practices. In addition, this group's work "would be coordinated with the work of the Organization for [Economic] Cooperation and Development (OECD) on practices for recipient countries as appropriate."

Considering their reputation for secrecy, there is surprisingly ample information available about sovereign wealth fund investment behavior. At the time of its debut, the Monitor-FEEM Sovereign Wealth Fund Database included data on 1,216 individual equity investments in private companies worth more than USD350 billion made by 35 SWFs between January 1986 and September 2008. This information is revealing; for example, a comparative study based on a database of 14,000 SWF and 11,700 mutual fund investments in equity did not suggest that their investment motives were radically different.[22] If drivers of SWF investment decisions tend to be mainly financial rather than political, they should enjoy a level playing with field with other global institutional investors, including hedge funds and similar unregistered vehicles.

The International Working Group of Sovereign Wealth Funds (IWG) eventually produced the Santiago Principles, a set of best practices for SWFs, in October 2008. SWFs now have an opportunity to "go a step further by making an active contribution to the development of the norms and principles that will provide long-term stability to global financial markets. They need to play a key role in the construction of an institutional framework that will provide overall guidance to market participants."[23]

Participating in a global response to the financial and economic crisis of 2007-09 is in the direct interest of SWFs. Opting out of global efforts to govern their behavior leaves them exposed to the risk that national legislation will overcome any supranational effort and that they'll face a patchwork of regulatory schemes around the world.

The Next New Order

SWFs attracted the attention of economists and fiscal and monetary bureaucrats for three reasons. There was a significant uptick in the number of funds after 2003. Funds—new and old—rapidly accumulated assets. Their sheer size and scope put several in company with some of the largest public-pension plans and central bank reserves in the world.

What politicians and the media initially emphasized is that SWFs are owned by the state. There are fascinating intellectual debates about the propriety of government involving itself in markets; there are vital practical debates about whether such entities will destabilize foreign markets and governments at the behest of their political bosses. But overwhelming evidence indicates that, since first appearing more than half a century ago, while making many equity investments abroad, including in iconic names such as Chrysler in 1973, SWFs have acted as responsible investors. The Abu Dhabi Investment Authority (ADIA), the world's largest SWF, recently recruited a key decision-maker from the Canadian Pension Plan Investment Board (CPPIB) to establish an in-house infrastructure investment operation. ADIA is perhaps the most secretive of SWFs; that it hired the person who started CPPIB's infrastructure practice, one of the institutional management world's first, is a sure sign ADIA is on the prowl for global assets and for knowledge to bring home for long-term domestic modernization. Equally important, this personnel move illustrates the similar nature of SWFs and traditional institutions such as pension funds. The record suggests that their long-term focus in fact improves market stability. And SWFs have largely accepted that, with regard to their cross-border investments in publicly traded companies, they must be seen as passive investors lest they be the subject of political controversies.

There's nothing particularly remarkable about SWF managers' sheer stock-picking ability. Available data reflect the fact that SWF returns don't stand out relative to the broader market; in fact, part of SWFs' collective notoriety can be traced to international—and domestic—reaction to significant losses related to high-profile investments in damaged Western financial institutions. Half of the investments included in the Monitor-FEEM database occur after June 2005, in line with the mid-decade surge in SWF activity. As such, performance numbers are skewed because to the historic correction that got underway in the fourth quarter 2007. As of December 31, 2008, almost one-third of the number and more than half of the dollar value of SWF investments were directed toward financial firms. Although the Gulf Cooperation Council (GCC) funds suffered losses on paper of between one-fifth and one-quarter of their value, as a group they performed better than funds based in the Asia-Pacific region as well as certain high-profile funds and endowments in North America and Europe. Older funds with large, diversified portfolios fared better than those that had pursued aggressive investment strategies and participated in significant leveraged transactions.

But our advice is not to chase stocks in which SWFs invest. Rather, the value of SWFs to the individual investor is primarily what their emergence says about the changing nature of the global economy. That's not to say, however, that SWFs don't emit important signals to investors. The Middle East and East Asia will be key centers of growth in the coming decade. Because in many cases SWF investments reflect, for example, the resource needs of the domestic economy, their choices broadly lead us to markets such as Australia and Canada because of their coal and precious metals reserves. A partnership with a leading technology manufacturer suggests the China Investment Corporation (CIC) would like to both expedite and profit from the spread of computers and the use of the Internet in its home country. On one hand changes in the global consumption profile still leave oil producers and the SWFs their governments sponsor in good position to realize steady foreign currency flows. Fossil fuels remain the key input for economic growth. The export-modeled powerhouses of Asia, on the other hand, will have a more difficult path to future funding as the US undergoes its now-mandatory deleveraging—although the Chinese, because of their sheer number, have the potential to replace some of the consumption slack left by the American consumer's behavior change, higher savings rate for the world's No. 1 consumer.

Criticism of sovereign wealth funds often centers on the concern that they'll pursue politicized investment objectives and that they're nontransparent, particularly those headquartered in Asia and the Persian Gulf. However, it's the larger threat, to an order that has only taken shape during the last three decades, driving the backlash in the US. The US is ostensibly committed to the principle that private actors allocate capital better than public actors. The rise of SOEs and SWFs by some accounts is a direct challenge to this orthodoxy. Politicians have invoked emotion to stir opposition, and their actions suggest that, no matter what principles and standards of practice, for investing SWFs as well as recipient countries, international institutions establish, governments will defend themselves as they see fit. This emotional approach provides a stark contrast with SWFs' behavior. The notable thing about SWFs during the financial crisis and the recession it exacerbated is not that they made particularly savvy investment deals; rather, they didn't panic. They proved to be steady, reliable sources of capital. Many withstood withering criticism for decisions made in 2007 and 2008, not only from recipient countries but also from domestic officials and citizens.

Some observers in the US, critical of the political response to the DP World-P&O deal and the suspicions expressed following the massive infusions of capital made by SWFs into crippled financial institutions, worried that these sources of capital would simply avoid the US in favor of more hospitable jurisdictions, places where their activities wouldn't be subject to the kind scrutiny hyperpartisan domestic political theatrics and a 24-hour news cycle hungry to be fed by same naturally subjects them to. Paradoxically, however, the record suggests SWFs avoid such considerations altogether. They are focused on long-term returns, wherever they can find them.

In testimony before the House Committee on Foreign Affairs on May 21, 2008, Dr. Gal Luft, Executive Director of the Institute for the Analysis of Global Security, noted:

> The rise of sovereign wealth funds (SWF) as new power brokers in the world economy should not be looked at as a singular phenomenon but rather as part of what can be defined a new economic world order. This new order has been enabled by several mega-trends which operate in a self-reinforcing manner, among them the meteoric rise of developing Asia, accelerated globalization, the rapid flow of information and the sharp increase in the price of oil....[24]

Sovereign wealth funds, on the whole, made it through the Great Recession and are now fixtures in the global financial system. The most substantial funds are stronger now than they were before the crisis began. SWF leaders—namely ADIA—won the 2006-2008 transparency struggle with Western financial elites. The Santiago Principles for the most part reflect their influence.

In a December 6, 2009, *The New York Times* article describing the impact of the rally that commenced almost exactly nine months earlier, sovereign wealth funds were described as "white knights" now collecting ample profits from their once-distressed investments.[25] Their second act has gotten off to a better start than the first. But there remain serious questions about how—and whether—governments should act in the economy, much less as shareholders, both in the near term and over the longer term. These questions are important with regard not only to China, Singapore, Russia, Abu Dhabi, and the other GCC states. They are also important in light of the extraordinary efforts by policymakers in the US and the United Kingdom to prop up their respective economies. How the US government handles its exit from financial institution- and the auto sector-ownership and the manner in which the Fed rolls back extraordinary liquidity measures will have at least as much impact on the global economy in the short term as any move CIC or the ADIA makes. These tasks are much more fraught with risk: The government has to keep these businesses alive while simultaneously overseeing their fundamental transformation. SWFs, by contrast, are simply seeking long-term returns.

Along with the proliferation of state-run companies and pools of capital in the middle part of the last decade came rising suspicion about the motives of such actors; were they investing based on pure financial and economic considerations, or were they advancing the interests of their sponsoring regimes? Recent events have exposed SWFs as generally responsible, long-term-oriented investors that provide liquidity and stability during times of duress. Broader motivations for investment decisions include diversifying economies; setting aside funds for future generations; establishing a fund to cover general government expenditure during times of low commodity prices; and investing in foreign companies to gain access to particular expertise that will enhance domestic development. At the end of the day decisions are made based on logical, rational considerations made by professionals.

The recent rise of SWFs and their relative health in the aftermath of one of the most severe market downturns in decades is strong evidence of a changing global financial and economic architecture. Their behavior is worthy of understanding by the individual investor because of what it says about changing consumption patterns around the world and where the growth is. Those who pay attention will profit.

Endnotes

1 Bryan J. Balin, "Sovereign Wealth Funds: A Critical Analysis," September 23, 2009, http://ssrn.com/abstract=1477725 (accessed December 21, 2009).

2 Bernardo Bortolotti, Veljko Fotak, and William L. Megginson, "Sovereign Wealth Fund Investment Patterns and Performance," April 6, 2009, http://admin.darden. virginia.edu/emupload/uploaded2009/swf-invest-patterns-perform-nov288.pdf (accessed July 12, 2009).

3 John Harwood and Gerald F. Seib, *Pennsylvania Avenue: Profiles in Backroom Power* (New York: Random House, 2008) pp. 5–8.

4 Peter Overby, "Lobbyist's Last-Minute Bid Set Off Ports Controversy," National Public Radio, March 23, 2006, http://www.npr.org/templates/story/story. php?storyId=5252263 (accessed September 9, 2009).

5 Ted Bridis, "Arab Firm May Run 6 U.S. Ports," Associated Press, February 12, 2006, http://seattletimes.nwsource.com/html/politics/2002800202_ports12.html (accessed September 9, 2009).

6 Harwood and Seib. *Pennsylvania Avenue*, p. 11.

7 Staff, Newsmax.com, "Peter King: Dubai Ports Company in 'Al Qaida Heartland,'" Newsmax, February 20, 2006, http://archive.newsmax.com/archives/ic/2006/2/20/120409.shtml (accessed September 9, 2009).

8 Dubai World achieved a new level of notoriety in November 2009 when it asked for a standstill on interest payments due on USD59 billion of liabilities. Abu Dhabi, the largest of the United Arab Emirates, provided USD10 billion to help Dubai avoid default. Dubai World is an SOE, not an SWF. Though both structures are extensions of the state, generally speaking SOEs involve operating companies, while SWFs focus on passive financial investments and generally eschew management responsibilities. Dubai World is remarkable among entities in the SWF/SOE class for the level of leverage it employed in its operations.

9 Carl Hulse, "New Concerns Are Raised in Congress on Ports Deal," *The New York Times*, March 1, 2006, http://query.nytimes.com/gst/fullpage.html?res=9C06E4D61631F932A35750C0A9609C8B63 (accessed September 9, 2009).

10 Israel's largest shipping firm, Zim Integrated Shipping Services, came out in support of the deal. "During our long association with DP World," wrote Idan Ofer to Senator Hilary Clinton (D-NY) in a letter dated February 22, 2006, "we have not experienced a single security issue in these ports or in any of the terminals operated by DP World. We are proud to be associated with DP World and look forward to working with them into the future." Ed Henry, Phil Hirschkorn, and Paula Newton, "Israeli Shipper Endorses DP World," CNN.com, March 2, 2006, http://www.cnn.com/2006/POLITICS/03/02/port.security/index.html (accessed September 9, 2009).

[11] DP World sold the US assets to AIG Global Investment Group, which was rebranded as Pinebridge Investments in 2009 to create distance from its embattled parent, US-government owned American International Group.

[12] John Williamson, "What Washington Means by Policy Reform," Peterson Institute for International Economics, November 2002, http://www.iie.com/publications/papers/paper.cfm?researchid=486 (accessed August 11, 2009).

[13] John Williamson, "What Should the World Think about the Washington Consensus?" Peterson Institute for International Economics, July 1999, http://www.iie.com/publications/papers/paper.cfm?ResearchID=351, (accessed August 11, 2009).

[14] Steven Davidoff, "What You Didn't Know about Sovereign Wealth Funds," *The New York Times*, January 29, 2008, http://dealbook.blogs.nytimes.com/2008/01/29/what-you-didnt-know-about-sovereign-wealth-funds-2/ (accessed January 29, 2008).

[15] Lawrence Summers, "Sovereign Funds Shake the Logic of Capitalism," *Financial Times*, July 23, 2007, http://blogs.ft.com/economistsforum/2007/07/sovereign-funds.html/ (accessed August 11, 2009).

[16] Ibrahim Warde, "Sovereign Wealth Funds to the Rescue: Are They Saviors, Predators or Dupes?" *Le Monde Diplomatique*, May 15, 2008, http://fletcher.tufts.edu/news/2008/02/Warde_May16.shtml (accessed August 2, 2009).

[17] Daniel Gross, "SWF Seeks Loving American Man," Slate.com, January 24, 2008, http://www.slate.com/id/2182746 (accessed August 11, 2009). Kristin Halvorsen, then the minister of finance of Norway, whose SWF controls an estimated USD322 billion, drily noted, "They don't like us but they want our money." Summers, at the same 2008 Davos Conference during which Halvorsen made her observation, conceded that "there's not much that SWFs have done to date that one can be critical of."

[18] Senator Charles E. Schumer, "Do Sovereign Wealth Funds Make the U.S. Economy Stronger or Pose National Security Risks?" Opening Statement, Joint Economic Committee Hearing, February 13, 2008, http://jec.senate.gov/archive/Hearings/02.13.08%20SWF/SWF%20hearing%20-%20CES%20statement%20press_Formatted.pdf (accessed September 17, 2009).

[19] Bader M. Al Sa'ad, Keynote Speech at the First Luxembourg Foreign Trade Conference, "Overview of the Kuwait Investment Authority and Issues Related to Sovereign Wealth Funds," April 9, 2008, http://www.kia.gov.kw/En/About_KIA/Overview_of_KIA/Documents/FINA_SPCH_LUXEMBORG_APR_9_092.pdf (accessed August 11, 2009).

[20] Service Employees International Union, "Sovereign Wealth Funds and Private Equity: Increased Access, Decreased Transparency," Service Employees International Union, April 2008, http://www.behindthebuyouts.org/storage/Sovereign%20Wealth%20Funds%20and%20Private%20Equity%20Final%20Report%20April%202008.pdf (accessed August 12, 2009).

[21] IMF Survey Online, "IMF Board Endorses Work Agenda on Sovereign Funds," International Monetary Fund, March 21, 2008, http://www.imf.org/external/pubs/ft/survey/so/2008/NEW032108A.htm (accessed August 12, 2009).

[22] Rolando Avendaño and Javier Santiso, "Are Sovereign Wealth Funds' Investments Politically Biased? A Comparison with Mutual Funds," Organization for Economic Cooperation and Development, December 2009, http://www.oecd.org/dataoecd/43/0/44301172.pdf (accessed January 11, 2010).

[23] Sven Behrendt, "When Money Talks: Arab Sovereign Wealth Funds in the Global Public Policy Discourse," Carnegie Endowment for International Peace, October 2008, http://www.carnegieendowment.org/files/arab_sovereign_wealth_funds.pdf (accessed June 25, 2009).

[24] Gal Luft, "Sovereign Wealth Funds, Oil and the New World Economic Order," Testimony, House Committee on Foreign Affairs, May 21, 2008, http://foreignaffairs.house.gov/110/luf052108.htm (accessed July 12, 2009).

[25] Eric Dash, "Big Paydays for Rescuers in the Crisis," *The New York Times*, December 6, 2009, http://www.nytimes.com/2009/12/07/business/global/07bank.html (accessed December 7, 2009).

3

The Road to Pan-Asia

During the last decade SWFs evolved into critical strategic tools in the Middle East and East Asia. The rising price of crude and insatiable Western demand for cheap imports lifted what had been low-key but significant global financial players into topics for front-page stories. Their rapid proliferation and their potential for long-term growth suggest that SWFs are here to stay.

SWF activity is directly linked to economic diversification in both emerging regions, and this role will only become more important during the next decade. What's of greatest long-term significance is the potential for Gulf Cooperation Council (GCC) and East Asian SWFs to lead the establishment of a third market to stand alongside the US and the EU. Understanding the behavior of SWFs will help the long-sighted investor profit in the coming decade.

Although several rank among the world's top institutional investors, as a group sovereign wealth funds (SWF) still represent a relatively small slice of total invested assets. Their recent proliferation is a function of the rapid accumulation of foreign reserves among emerging market countries, notably in petroleum-exporting countries in the Middle East, driven by the historic strength of oil prices in the mid-2000s,[1] and in East Asia, a response to reforms implemented after the 1997-98 regional crisis as well as to US demand for exports. According to International Monetary Fund (IMF) data, reserves increased from about USD1 trillion in 1990 to an estimated USD7 trillion by June 2008,[2] the result of insatiable demand stoked by easy credit in the US for oil and cheap manufactured products.

SWFs and their related cousin state-owned enterprises (SOE) are key instruments as East Asia and the Middle East mature into critical financial centers and the engines of growth for the global economy. Their activities—the types of investments they make and why—are broadly focused on generating long-term returns; research supports the conclusion that SWFs are no more political in their investment decisions than mutual funds. This does not mean, however, that their choices are not strategic. Only the most naïve observer would deny that positive long-term performance for the China Investment Corporation (CIC) and/or the Abu Dhabi Investment Authority (ADIA) will enhance China's and the United Arab Emirates' (UAE) economies, which, in turn, will boost their respective standing on the global stage. Insofar as SWFs represent a threat, the actual strategic exposure is the US consumer funding a massive accumulation of currency reserves by East Asian and Middle Eastern exporters. SWFs are an outgrowth of this phenomenon.

Early signs suggest officials in both subregions appreciate the long-term potential of a robust financial and development nexus between the Far and Middle East. Such a union could co-occupy the global economic leadership role with the United States. Discussions about potential investments between Chinese officials—representatives of both the government and the CIC—and the UAE intensified in early 2010, extending the cooperative relationship that led to a favorable outcome for the International Working Group of Sovereign Wealth Funds and its Generally Accepted Principles and Practices (GAPP).

SWFs sponsored by Asian exporters are sending out important signals about the direction of the global economy. Suspicion about state-owned companies gave way to obsequiousness as the last decade's pendulum swung from credit-driven excess to credit-driven privation and crippled banks sought new sources of capital. This— not their absolute or relative size (although their rate of growth is impressive and suggests they'll be moving up the financial chain)—is the overarching lesson about SWFs: Their "arrival" is still more evidence of a shift of global economic influence eastward. Understanding why and where their capital flows will help individual investors profit.

Arabian Knights

The first SWF has its roots in the Kuwait Investment Board, which was established in 1953 in the City of London "with the aim of investing surplus oil revenues to reduce the reliance of Kuwait on its finite oil resource."[3] Through the Kuwait Investment Office in London, the sheikdom, then a protectorate of the United Kingdom, diversified its economy through investments in financial assets in other countries.

This problem of a finite resource is a regional one, shared Kuwait and its fellow members of the GCC: the UAE, which includes Abu Dhabi, Dubai, Sharjah, Ajman, Umm al-Quwain, Ras al-Khaimah, and Fujairah; Bahrain; Saudi Arabia; Oman; and Qatar. The GCC states, seeking a way to produce income once petroleum resources are exhausted—to replace depleting assets with financial assets—now sponsor a total of 14 sovereign wealth funds, seven of which are tied to the UAE. These SWFs and similar state-sponsored vehicles invest domestically, but because these economies are so small relative to the world economy, it's inevitable that they would pursue investments beyond their borders.

SWFs hold, manage, or administer financial assets to achieve financial and economic objectives,[4] and employ a set of investment strategies, which include investing in foreign financial assets. They're commonly established out of balance of payments surpluses, official foreign currency operations, the proceeds of privatizations, fiscal surpluses, and/or receipts resulting from commodity exports. The capacity to operate over long-term investment horizons makes SWFs and their capital attractive to companies and recipient countries. SWFs are less risk-averse compared to agencies managing traditional foreign exchange reserves. Other types of assets held by governments include foreign currency reserve assets held by monetary authorities only for the traditional balance of payments or monetary policy purposes, government-employee pension funds, or assets managed for the benefit of individuals.

SWFs have various specific purposes, among them providing for future generations; providing an emergency fund in the event government revenues decline; and providing access to markets, technologies, resources, and knowledge to bring back home to help the domestic economy. The primary reasons most of the GCC SWFs exist are to reduce dependence on a depleting resource in the short term and, a related goal, to diversify to better position the domestic economy for long-term growth. Resource-dependent national and subnational governments all over the world have followed Kuwait's lead. In 1974 Singapore began the trend of noncommodity exporters establishing SWFs. Since 1953 more than 50 SWFs have been established, nearly two-thirds of them during the last decade as a response to booming oil prices and rising export demand from the US. Though Arab wealth has found its way West to American and other developed economies for decades, as the GCC states accumulated reserves there was a definite shift in the direction of greater risk-taking by their SWFs. SWFs, including the KIA, the ADIA, and the Qatar Investment Authority (QIA), also took more direct stakes in firms, bypassing the money managers previously used as conduits for their activity. The QIA emerged during the oil boom with a mandate to complement ambitious domestic socioeconomic development plans. The explicit purpose of the QIA is to support domestic economic development through investments made abroad.[5]

Like the KIA two decades earlier, the ADIA was created in 1976 to manage excess oil revenue and to reduce its sponsoring state's economy's dependence on petroleum. The ADIA, with assets under management estimated to be as much as USD875 billion, is recognized as the largest SWF in the world. That number would also place it among the top institutional money managers in the world. Abu Dhabi generates an annual surplus of USD50 billion with oil at USD100 per barrel; much of a given year's surplus is channeled to the ADIA.[6] Yet the ADIA was able to maintain a low public profile until the mid-2000s, despite the fact that it was active all over the globe almost from its founding. Part of the reason for its anonymity was the fact that it held small equity stakes that fell below levels that required public disclosure. Another is that it allocated as much as 80 percent of its assets to outside managers.[7]

In 2007 local and regional investment activity was passed to the Abu Dhabi Investment Council (ADIC) to be managed by the new entity Invest AD. Invest AD's mandate is to attract institutional investors to opportunities in the Middle East and North Africa. It is the primary tool in Abu Dhabi's ambitious Vision 2030 strategy. Vision 2030

> establishes a common framework for aligning all policies and plans that contribute to the ongoing development of the Emirate's economy. It seeks to create opportunities for the local and international private sector in the Emirate of Abu Dhabi, and new employment opportunities for UAE nationals, particularly in highly-skilled, export-oriented sectors.[8]

In late January 2010, Invest AD opened talks with state-backed and private investors in China about jointly investing in the Middle East and Africa. CEO Nazem Fawwaz Al Kudsi said Invest AD was seeking long-term partnerships in infrastructure projects and development of financial services. "Recognizing China's global importance, it is crucial for us to establish a proper partnership with China in the MENA region," Al Kudsi said, referring to the Middle East and the North African region where his firm is most active.[9]

Another offshoot, the USD22 billion Mubadala Development Company, was established in October 2002. It is organized as a public joint stock company (PJS) within the meaning of UAE law, owned entirely by the government. Mubadala manages "an extensive and economically diverse portfolio of commercial initiatives...either independently or in partnership with leading international organizations." It is "both a catalyst for, and a reflection of, the drive for economic diversification of the Emirate of Abu Dhabi. Its impact is evident domestically and internationally in sectors such as energy, aerospace, real estate, healthcare, technology, infrastructure, and services."[10] Following the example of Asian SWFs like Singapore's Temasek Holdings, which focuses on regional development, Mubadala has been extremely proactive in the Middle East. It provides an excellent example of the two-way nature of SWF investment: Mubadala's 5 percent stake in Ferrari brought with it the potential for increased tourism to Abu Dhabi in the form of the Ferrari theme park. Mubadala has also invested USD8 billion in a partnership with General Electric, which, in turn, will boost investment and increase technology transfers to the UAE.

The man who oversees day-to-day operations at the ADIA was not born in the UAE; he is Jean Paul Villain, No. 1 in Arabian Business's ranking of the most influential expatriates working in the

Middle East.[11] A Frenchman, Villain was a finance professor before joining Banque Paribas in 1971. He left in 1982 to become the ADIA's regional manager for Europe and came back in 1987 as the first CEO and chief investment officer of the newly created Paribas Asset Management.[12] The acquisition of top talent has been one of ADIA's most important initiatives over the last decade; in addition to Villain, the SWF, like many of its peers, has drawn from the deep pool of institutional investor-talent in the West. The ADIA recruited Chris Koski away from the Canadian Pension Plan Investment Board (CPPIB), an early mover among global-scale pension funds on the infrastructure theme, to head up the ADIA's own group to buy up roads, ports, and bridges. The ADIA's sole shareholder is the Abu Dhabi government, as is the case for Invest AD and Mubadala. The managing director of ADIA, Sheik Ahmed bin Zayed al-Nahyan, No. 27 on *Forbes'* list of the world's most powerful people,[13] died in a late March 2010 glider accident. His successor will be named by the chairman of the ADIA, Sheikh Khalifa bin Zayed al-Nahyan, Ahmed's oldest brother and the current president and emir of Abu Dhabi.[14]

The KIA was the first SWF, but the ADIA led the group into new types of assets. When it was founded in 1976, its portfolio included equities, fixed-income securities, and real estate. It added a commodities arm in 1986, and in 1989 it started investing in private equities. Though it began investing in emerging markets early in its history, in 2005 the ADIA created a division to focus exclusively on the group.[15] Some analysts have suggested as well that the ADIA was involved in hedge funds as early as the 1980s. During a January 2010 interview with Germany-based business daily *Handelsblatt*,[16] Sheik Ahmed said ADIA continuously looks for alternative investments, which he described as an important element of any diversified portfolio.

In a wide-ranging interview with *Business Week* published June 6, 2006,[17] Ahmed revealed the ADIA's asset allocation. Alternative investments such as private equity funds, hedge funds, emerging markets, and infrastructure account for 34 percent of assets. The ADIA now has approximately 60 percent of its money invested in index funds, an upward adjustment from 45 percent inspired by the underperformance of high-priced outside managers. Asset allocation ranges were as follows: developed-market stocks, 45 to 55 percent;

emerging-market stocks, 8 to 12 percent; small-cap stocks, 1 to 4 percent; government bonds, 12 to 18 percent; corporate and other bonds, 4 to 8 percent; alternative investments such as real estate (5 to 10 percent), private equity, (2 to 8 percent), and infrastructure (0 to 4 percent); and cash, 0 to 5 percent. Because of the dollar's depreciation leading up the period when the decision was made and the increase in value of assets in other regions, the ADIA was underweight US equities. Rather than buy USD1 billion pieces of several US financials, management opted to pay USD7.5 billion for a 4.9 percent stake in Citigroup. "We were underweight in US equities, large companies, and credit," said Jean-Paul Villain in his first public interview in his role as head of investment strategy at the ADIA. "Citigroup was reducing the risk of the portfolio."

Prioritizing diversification and focusing on long-term trends, in Ahmed's words, "come together to form our shared long-term view of the world." Portfolio composition is based on "allocations with fixed weights to more than two-dozen asset classes and subasset classes. We adjust this only when our view of the long-term outlook for the global economy changes in a fundamental way." For the first half-century of their existence, Arab SWFs invested around the world without destabilizing markets or engaging in overtly political tactics. In short, their activities were known only to the most inside of the global financial elite, the business partners who executed trades and moved assets on their behalf.

"One day someone woke up in the morning and considered this to be a threat, a danger," Bader Mohammed al-Saad, managing director of the KIA, noted in an interview with German-based *Spiegel Online*.[18] Following the uproar over the DP World-P&O transaction and the series of SWF investments in Western financial institutions, the ADIA realized it no longer served its long-term interest to remain in the wings of the global financial stage.

On March 20, 2008, the ADIA reached an agreement with the US Treasury Department on principles for SWF investment.[19] It was a recognition that US financial institutions' capital needs, at that time not likely to be satisfied through conventional channels though not yet dire enough for government involvement, outweighed domestic political concerns. It was also an opportunity for the ADIA, legitimized by the US Treasury Secretary, to assert its commitment to responsible investing on a highly public stage. Shortly after this agreement was announced, the IMF, with the cooperation of participating SWFs, created the International Working Group of Sovereign Wealth Funds (IWG).

In the months that followed, the ADIA's public profile continued to increase, as did its impact on the debate about SWF best practices. Within weeks the SWF updated its Web site with more detailed information about its history and portfolio composition. At the time it defined its investment strategy as follows, stating unequivocally that it is a passive investor:

> ADIA manages a substantial global diversified portfolio of holdings across sectors, geographies and asset classes including public listed equities, fixed income, real estate, and private equity. With a long tradition of prudent investing, ADIA's decisions are based solely on its economic objectives of delivering sustained long-term financial returns. ADIA does not seek active management of the companies it invests in.[20]

In October 2008, US Treasury Secretary Henry Paulson co-authored an "open editorial" with Hamad al Hurr al-Suwaidi, Under Secretary of Finance of Abu Dhabi, and Tharman Shanmugaratnam, Minister of Finance of Singapore, supporting the Santiago Principles, the set of guidelines set down by representatives of 26 SWFs that signed up to support the IMF's and the OECD's efforts to bend their activities to Western norms. Hamad al Hurr al-Suwaidi served as a co-chair of the International Working Group of Sovereign Wealth Funds (IWG). The Santiago Principles were lauded as "a milestone in building trust in open markets."[21] Even this defense of the Santiago Principles by those who laid its foundation reveals the largely symbolic nature of the effort—and the new influence these emerging-market leaders exert. The Santiago Principles call for but do not require reporting of activity in recipient countries. They acknowledge that SWFs have thus far acted on financial and economic rather than political grounds. Finally, critically, the principles reflect the most important interest of SWF sponsor states: that their reporting obligation is ultimately to their owners.

Vanguard of the Middle Kingdom

Among the many points of confusion about SWFs is exactly what the term means. Countless government agencies, think tanks, investment banks, and academic researchers have set forth definitions, and these efforts are important insofar as they determine, too, estimates of assets under control by state-owned vehicles. The critical considerations for individual investors, however, is not what an SWF is or how much money in aggregate it controls. The important considerations are the reasons for their existence and what their behavior says about investing in a global economy.

For example, most definitions of "sovereign wealth fund" imply that the source of capital for the entities described is excess foreign currency reserves, the amount above what a government needs to conduct normal balance-of-trade and day-to-day currency operations. Focusing on this criterion would, ironically, omit from discussion one of the most influential government-owned investment funds, the China Investment Corp, which was funded initially with the proceeds of a government bond sale, not out of China's prodigious reserves.

For all the discussion of the CIC's impact on the global stage, its footprint at home remains much more significant. When it was first created in 2007, the CIC allocated two-thirds of its initial USD200 billion to domestic, state-backed financial institutions; China, too, had balance-sheet holes to fill. The investments it made in Western financials—executed before the fund was formally constituted under Chinese law—have generated significant paper losses, exposing the CIC and Chairman Lou Jiwei to withering criticism from the public and intense pressure from political officials, which illustrates another interesting contrast: The CIC in early 2010 took on the appearance of an all-powerful investing force, rumored to be involved in the rescue of the US real estate market, SOE Dubai World, and Greece. At home, however, Lou and the CIC are subject to the same competitive pressures all bureaucrats in the People's Republic must endure. Never were the rivalries that define Chinese politics more defined than during the process that led to the CIC's creation.

In 2006 China surpassed USD1 trillion in foreign currency reserves held, and it was accumulating USD1 billion a day. At the time China required only USD700 billion to USD900 billion in reserve to satisfy daily needs; in addition to economists, policy makers and the Chinese public began to notice this excess. Soon a debate over the wisdom of diversifying away from traditional US Treasuries and other similar securities in search of greater returns on foreign reserves was underway. This debate exposed anew and intensified a longstanding rivalry between China's Ministry of Finance and the People's Bank of China (PBoC).

The Ministry of Finance was intent on sustaining its influence by gaining control of some of China's excess reserves and proposed a sovereign wealth fund in late 2006. The PBoC had opposed the creation of such a vehicle since 2003 because it saw no need to boost returns on reserves. Once the USD1 trillion threshold was broken, however, the PBoC was hard-pressed to justify the excess. The Ministry of Finance, under the leadership of Lou Jiwei, began to study the feasibility of an SWF in November 2006.[22]

Rising reserves provided the PBoC the wherewithal to fund the recapitalization of banks and other financial firms in 2005-06. The PBoC accomplished this through the Central Huijin Investment Company, which was formed in 2003 and invested more than USD700 billion in 20 state-owned financial institutions, including the four largest Chinese banks. The PBoC has another department, the State Administration of Foreign Exchange (SAFE), that manages foreign exchange reserves. Until November 2007 SAFE invested exclusively in bonds; the *Financial Times* reported on January 3, 2008, that a Hong Kong-based subsidiary, SAFE Investment Company, had invested in several publicly listed companies.[23] This move was widely perceived as a preemptive move against a new, MoF-backed sovereign fund. Nevertheless, finance minister Jin Renqing, at the March 2007 National People's Congress, announced, "The State Council has already made research into separating the management of normal foreign exchange reserves and a portion allocated for investment, this company is now under construction."[24]

In June 2007 the State Council did in fact approve the creation of the China Investment Corporation, using a special bond sale of USD200 billion to fund it. An initial bond sale raised USD80 billion to essentially buy Central Huijin. In total USD208 billion was raised,

USD27 billion through sales to the public, USD181 billion through sales to the PBoC. The bonds have a ten-year maturity and yield about 4.3 percent. The leadership of the CIC is in a difficult position because it must generate a double-digit return each year to satisfy its interest-payment obligation, maintain overhead, and keep up with any appreciation in the renminbi. It's not likely political considerations play much role in their investment decisions given the high return bar they have to meet.

In February 2010, the CIC filed a 13-F Holding Report with the US Securities and Exchange Commission (SEC), another action that reinforces the SWF's commitment to transparency and responsible citizenship in the global financial community. The SEC requires a 13-F HR to be filed by institutional investment managers with more than USD100 million worth of assets. For the year ended December 31, 2009, the CIC reported 84 positions in US-listed companies with a total market value of USD9.6 billion.

This filing is a positive from a public relations perspective and makes for good geopolitical optics. The real significance is what it suggests China can do with its USD2.4 trillion of foreign currency reserves. The CIC manages only a small sum relative to the total potential represented by this figure. Rumored to soon be receiving another USD200 billion to invest, the CIC's growth has significant implications for several asset classes and regions.

Despite the CIC's very public activities—in addition to actively participating in the International Monetary Fund-sponsored negotiations of a code of conduct for state-sponsored investment managers—the Chinese SWF is, like its peers, dogged by questions about ownership and intent. Equity ownership of publicly traded companies, among other asset classes, by what are essentially extensions of the state—the management and board of the CIC, for example, ultimately reports to the State Council of the People's Republic of China—has become anathema in the West over the last four decades. Suspicion about GCC SWFs is quelled by its aggregate half-century record of responsible participation in the global market; the CIC, in existence only since 2007 and created by what many fear is a serious threat to US hegemony in its own right, enjoys no such benefit of the doubt.

But the CIC never tried to lay low. The CIC's initial allocations, made even before it had a name or was even formally constituted under Chinese law, were high-profile investments in Morgan Stanley and the initial public offering (IPO) of The Blackstone Group. The CIC was seeking recognition as a responsible source of liquidity and stability when it made these moves. Lou Jiwei has stated from the CIC's founding in 2007 that the SWF wasn't interested in gaining control of the companies in which it invested. The focus from the beginning has merely been to generate long-term returns. These investments in US financials didn't work out as initially envisioned—the corrosiveness of subprime mortgages, credit default swaps, and synthetic securities had yet to be fully realized in late 2007—and the CIC has taken plenty of criticism at home for them.

According to some estimates, the USD9.6 billion reported on the 13-F represents just 10 percent of the CIC's total international portfolio. It also omits the Blackstone investment and the 2007 Morgan Stanley deal, though it does include a 2009 equity purchase. The CIC's stake in American Electric Power's wind energy unit wasn't included because the deal hadn't yet cleared all regulatory hurdles. The CIC also owns real estate, positions in private equity ventures, and fixed-income investments that wouldn't appear in a 13-F disclosure. Equity investments focused on foreign markets such as Kazakhstan, Mongolia, and Indonesia aren't included; such positions account for an estimated USD5 billion. But this glance at the CIC's portfolio reveals several broad trends, namely exposure to resources and financials, although the balance is shifting rapidly in favor of resources. The CIC got serious about deploying its capital in the second half of 2009, diversifying its exposure in terms of sectors and geography.

The CIC's largest single reported position is its enormously successful investment in Canada-based mining giant Teck Resources, which accounts for 38 percent of its "listed US" portfolio. This is the highlight of the CIC's heavy emphasis on resources, particularly metals and mining. The CIC also has significant gold exposure via miners and SPDR Gold Trust. The CIC bought 17.2 percent of Teck for USD1.5 billion in July 2009; by December 31, 2009, that stake was worth USD3.4 billion. Not only has the deal been financially successful, in economic terms, China has established access to one of the world's top producers of copper, metallurgical coal, and zinc as well as molybdenum and specialty metals, all of which it needs in great supply to sustain the growth necessary to satisfy a potentially restive population. The CIC will benefit from broad global demand for these metals; as prices rise, and assuming Teck continues to execute on the operational level, the value of the CIC's investment will continue to appreciate.

The 13-F confirms, too, the CIC's status as a passive investor; most of its US equity exposure comprises small stakes or positions in sector or geographic-focused exchange-traded funds. True to its stated aspirations, the CIC has snapped up small stakes in a number of companies and distributed funds to a number of outside managers for even broader exposure. Its Blackstone position was less than 10 percent of the investment manager's total shares, and the CIC agreed to a passive, nonvoting role. The CIC also agreed to hold the stake for a minimum of four years and to refrain from taking a position in another private equity firm for one year following the IPO.[25] The CIC opted out of board seats its 17.2 percent ownership stake in Teck would otherwise dictate. In November 2009 it bought 15 percent of US power producer AES Corp for USD2.2 billion. The CIC occupies one seat on AES's board, consistent with the SWF's oft-stated lack of interest in controlling companies.

Its initial investments in troubled US financial Morgan Stanley and in the high-profile Blackstone IPO resulted in significant losses and brought harsh scrutiny from Chinese officials and citizens down upon the CIC management, including Lou Jiwei. The post-March 2009 global market rally lifted the CIC to an impressive 2009 performance, which relieved domestic political pressure and set the SWF for a second infusion of USD200 billion.

Hardened and unbowed by its early experiences, the CIC has been among the most aggressive players on the global financial field since mid-2009. And most of that effort has been concentrated on diversifying its holdings away from Western financials toward commodities and other sectors considered important to China's long-term economic development. The company's investments in 2009 mainly focused on energy, including electric power and infrastructure. In this sense, the CIC—and other SWFs—are strategic investors; however, the long-term record suggests "strategy" for SWFs is about maximizing financial and economic as opposed to political returns.

The CIC acquired an 11 percent stake in a unit of Kazakhstan's state-run energy company in late September 2009, two weeks before purchasing 45 percent of Nobel Oil Group of Russia. The CIC was one of the major backers of Toronto-listed, Vancouver-based South-Gobi Energy Resources' late-January 2010 IPO. The CIC and Singapore's Temasek each agreed to buy USD50 million of stock in SouthGobi's equity sale, which raised USD394 million. The CIC also purchased USD500 million of SouthGobi's 30-year senior convertible bonds issued last year. Canada-based Ivanhoe Mines is SouthGobi Energy Resources' largest shareholder, currently owning approximately 65 percent of the issued and outstanding shares.

SouthGobi operates the Ovoot Tolgoi coal mine in southern Mongolia, 25 miles from the Chinese border. The company, which started production in 2009, will use the IPO funds to increase output, beef up the physical plant, and look for more coal; it's already at work on a three-year, USD800 million development plan implemented specifically to satisfy Chinese demand. Ovoot Tolgoi has been running 24 hours a day since July 2009, after it hit a monthly sales record of 231,556 tons the preceding June. The CIC also has a deal in place to invest up to USD700 million in Mongolia-focused Iron Mining International Ltd. Geographic proximity as well as its hunger for iron ore also led the CIC to negotiations with Australia-based Fortescue Metals Group.[26] Further indicating China's new willingness to explore markets well beyond East Asia, the CIC has had "early" talks for direct investments in Brazil, the world's second-biggest iron ore exporter, and Mexico, the No. 2 silver producer, Lou Jiwei said at the Asian Financial Forum in Hong Kong on January 20, 2010. It's safe to say that, given its positive experience thus far with Teck Resources and improving relations between Ottawa and Beijing, the CIC will revisit Canada in 2010. Teck is up nearly 70 percent since July 2009, and Canada has resources—and technologies and manufactured goods—the Middle Kingdom needs.

The CIC's asset allocation is as eclectic as the ADIA's. The SWF is also part of consortium (including the QIA) that bailed out Songbird Estates, the majority owner of Canary Wharf, a London office and shopping development.[27] *China Daily*, an English-language daily often characterized as an extension of the government, ran a report sourced to *Shanghai Securities News* in mid-January 2010 that the CIC was considering an investment in US high-speed trains.[28] Given the CIC's goal of accessing technologies with domestic relevance, this is entirely in line with its mandate.

Despite this flurry—Lou pumped about USD10 billion into commodity-related companies in the second half of 2009—the bulk of the CIC's assets remain locked up with domestic Chinese financials. This ongoing shift from financials, domestic and foreign, toward global resource companies will likely accelerate should the rumored second USD200 billion infusion of capital take place. China is in a position of incredible strength: In 2009 the Middle Kingdom actually added USD440 billion to foreign currency reserves; China's total reserves stood at USD2.4 trillion as of December 31, 2009, a total that has become, in the words of one prominent editorial-page economist, "a financial, economic and geopolitical reality of surpassing significance."[29]

East Is East

The term "Seidenstrasse" literally translated means "Silk Road." It was coined by German geographer Ferdinand von Richthofen in 1877 to describe the lucrative Chinese silk trade, which began during the Han Dynasty (206 BCE to 220 CE). The Chinese silk trade was the driving force behind the connection of trade routes into an extensive trans-Asian network.

Today these routes are in wide and increasing use. But the dynamic has changed. Now that the Middle Kingdom is rapidly growing, the vast petroleum reserves found on the Arab peninsula are of profound strategic value to it. As China's thirst for oil has grown, energy security has become a major consideration of its Middle East policy.[30]

Beijing once thought the Middle East too distant for significant direct investment; it limited its engagement to pushing Arab leaders to cut ties with Taiwan in favor of the People's Republic, instead limiting its efforts to convincing Arab capitals to sever their ties to Taiwan and establish diplomatic relations with the People's Republic.[31] But this view has changed dramatically in the last decade. In recent years commerce between East Asia and the Middle has intensified. In addition, Chinese officials are becoming more actively engaged with counterparts in the Arab world. Energy is the critical factor in the economic relationship, but this, too, is a two-way street. Beijing values the Middle East as a source of oil and as a huge potential market for China's oil services firms. In fact, Chinese labor services companies started working in the GCC in 1979. By 2001 China had signed almost 3,000 contracts in all six GCC states for labor services worth USD2.7 billion. China National Petroleum Corporation's construction unit entered Kuwait in 1983 and grew substantially when it won major oil storage reconstruction projects in the wake of the first Gulf War. Chinese services firms now operate in Egypt, Qatar, Oman, and other parts of the Middle East North Africa—or MENA—region.[32]

Trade between the GCC and China increased 40 percent between 1999 and 2004, spurring talks between the two parties about a comprehensive free-trade agreement in June 2004.[33] China and the UAE in April 2007 signed a memorandum of understanding in April 2007 for the purpose of deepening economic relations. In 2008 Dubai International Capital (DIC), a subsidiary of SOE Dubai Holding, and Chinese investment bank First Eastern Investment Group, formed a USD1 billion joint venture to invest in infrastructure, resource, and health care projects in China, with the long-term aim of listing these China-based companies on the Dubai Financial Market. This deal was an early effort in DIC's push to invest more than USD5 billion in Asia, the Middle East, and North Africa by 2011. Oil-based sovereign wealth is as interested in boosting its exposure to the Far East's economic boom as the Far East exporters are in exploring development opportunities in the increasingly relevant MENA region.

By September 2009, the GCC and China had concluded the first round of negotiations to establish a free-trade zone between the GCC and the Middle Kingdom.[34] In early 2010 a delegation of high-level Chinese officials met in Dubai with management of debt-burdened SOE Dubai World, the holding company whose assets include DP World.[35]

Discussions included potential Chinese investment in Dubai's transportation and logistics operations. DP World already has a presence in China, operating marine terminals in Shanghai, China's largest city; Shenzhen, location of the first and most successful Special Economic Zone; Tianjin, one of four municipalities with provincial-level status; and Qingdao, a major city in eastern Shandong province.

Chinese and GCC leaders played important roles in crafting the IWG's Santiago Principles. Their work not only preserved the long-term interests of their respective SWFs, it also demonstrated that Asian leaders could cooperate in a supranational context and produce a result acceptable to the West. Their ability to exert economic influence is unquestioned; this initial endeavor suggests East Asia and the Middle East are capable of participating with the US in the establishment of a 21st-century global economic and financial architecture.

Endnotes

[1] A long-term structural bull market for oil has benefitted countries beyond the Middle East. Norway's USD450 billion Government Pension Plan-Global has existed since 1990. It is the gold standard in terms of openness and transparency. And yet this SWF is avowedly political: Its charter includes a commitment to invest in "socially responsible" companies and funds. Russia, little more than a decade ago mired in (economic turmoil), rode high oil prices to a rapid accumulation of its own foreign-currency excess. The state responded by establishing the Russia Stabilization Fund. Later, the fund was split into two entities, one to preserve capital through low-risk fixed-income investments for use in case of fiscal emergency, one—the USD180 billion National Welfare Fund—to invest abroad for longer-term, macroeconomic purposes. Saudi Arabia, the world's largest oil producer, established its first SWF in April 2008. The kingdom has a much lower risk appetite than its Gulf Cooperation Council peers. Until April 2008 foreign reserves were managed by the Saudi Arabian Monetary Agency (SAMA), the kingdom's central bank. SAMA's nonreserve foreign holdings were estimated to exceed USD300 billion by 2008. Its reserves are valued at USD30 billion. In addition to these funds, SAMA manages nearly USD60 billion, including Saudi pension funds, on behalf of other government agencies. Its assets are mostly invested in liquid, low-risk bonds.

[2] Joshua Aizenman, "Reserves and the Crisis: A Reassessment," University of California, Santa Cruz, and the National Bureau of Economic Research, February 2009, http://econ.ucsc.edu/faculty/aizenman/Aizenman_CentralBanking.pdf (accessed September 03, 2009).

[3] Kuwait Investment Authority, "Kuwait Investment Office in London," Kuwait Investment Authority, 2008, http://www.kia.gov.kw/En/KIO/About/Pages/default.aspx (accessed August 11, 2009).

[4] Sheikh Abdullah's foresight served Kuwait well in 1991–92, when the country, now independent of the United Kingdom, had to rebuild following the first Gulf War. Not all uses of SWF managed accounts are so dramatic.

[5] Qatar Investment Authority, "Strategy," http://www.qia.qa/QIA/about.html#strategy (accessed September 3, 2009).

6 Landon Thomas, "Cash-Rich, Publicity-Shy, Abu Dhabi Fund Draws Scrutiny," *The New York Times*, February 28, 2008, http://www.nytimes.com/2008/02/28/business/worldbusiness/28fund.html?_r=2 (accessed September 3, 2009).

7 Sven Behrendt, "When Money Talks: Arab Sovereign Wealth Funds in the Global Public Policy Discourse," Carnegie Endowment for International Peace, October 2008, http://www.carnegieendowment.org/files/arab_sovereign_wealth_funds.pdf (accessed June 25, 2009).

8 Abu Dhabi Investment Authority, "Vision 2030," Abu Dhabi Investment Authority, 2009, http://www.investad.ae/en/AbuDhabi/Vision2030.aspx (accessed September 3, 2009).

9 Reuters, "Abu Dhabi Eyes China Fund for Co-Investment," January 25, 2010, http://www.gulfbase.com/site/interface/NewsArchiveDetails.aspx?n=123985 (accessed January 25, 2010).

10 Mubadala Development Company, "About Mubadala," Mubadala Development Company, 2010, http://www.mubadala.ae/en/category/about-mubadala/ (accessed August 11, 2009).

11 ArabianBusiness.com, "The Expat 50: The Region's Most Influential Expatriates," October 2009, http://www.arabianbusiness.com/expat-powerlist/profile/1189 (accessed November 11, 2009).

12 Ibid.

13 Michael Noer and Nicole Perlroth, "The World's Most Powerful People," *Forbes*, November 11, 2009, http://www.forbes.com/2009/11/11/worlds-most-powerful-leadership-power-09-people_land.html (accessed January 25, 2010).

14 Khalifa didn't make *Forbes's* most powerful list but did come in at No. 3 among the world's richest royals for 2009. Tatiana Serafin, "The World's Richest Royals," *Forbes*, June 17, 2009, http://www.forbes.com/2009/06/17/monarchs-wealth-scandal-business-billionaires-richest-royals.html (accessed January 25, 2010).

15 Abu Dhabi Investment Authority, "ADIA History," Abu Dhabi Investment Authority, 2008, http://www.adia.ae/En/About/History.aspx (accessed August 11, 2009).

16 Michael Backfisch, "Interview with HH Sheikh Ahmed Bin Zayed Al Nehayan, Managing Director of the Abu Dhabi Investment Authority," *Handelsblatt*, January 11, 2010, http://www.adia.ae/En/pr/Handelsblatt_Interview_110110.pdf (accessed January 25, 2010).

17 Stanley Reed and Emily Thornton, "Inside the Abu Dhabi Investment Authority," *Business Week*, June 6, 2008, http://www.businessweek.com/globalbiz/content/jun2008/gb2008065_742165.htm (accessed August 11, 2009).

18 Wolfgang Reuter and Bernhard Zand, "We Are Being Punished," Spiegel Online, May 19, 2008, http://www.spiegel.de/international/business/0,1518,554042,00.html (accessed June 25, 2009).

[19] US Dept of the Treasury, "Treasury Reaches Agreement on Principles for Sovereign Wealth Fund Investment with Singapore and Abu Dhabi," Press Release, March 20, 2008 http://www.ustreas.gov/press/releases/hp881.htm (accessed September 10, 2009).

[20] Abu Dhabi Investment Authority, "Investments," Abu Dhabi Investment Authority, 2008, http://www.adia.ae/En/Investment/Strategy.aspx (accessed August 11, 2009).

[21] HE Hamad Al Hurr Al-Suwaidi, Henry M. Paulson, Jr., and Tharman Shanmugaratnam, "Open Editorial," Abu Dhabi Investment Authority, October 13, 2008, http://www.adia.ae/En/pr/OpEd1310.pdf (accessed August 11, 2009).

[22] Amadan International, "The Creation of the China Investment Corporation," January 30, 2008, http://www.amadaninternational.com/reports/TheCreationofthe ChinaInvestmentCorporation.pdf (accessed September 9, 2009).

[23] Jamil Anderlini, Robin Kwong, and Justine Lau, "Chinese State Investor Buys Australian Bank Stakes," *Financial Times*, January 3, 2008, http://www.ft.com/ cms/s/0/c26ff650-ba2a-11dc-abcb-0000779fd2ac.html?nclick_check=1 (accessed September 9, 2009).

[24] Amadan International, "The Creation of the China Investment Corporation," January 30, 2008, http://www.amadaninternational.com/reports/TheCreationofthe ChinaInvestmentCorporation.pdf (accessed September 9, 2009).

[25] The Blackstone Group, "China's State Investment Company to Acquire Non-Voting Minority Stake in Blackstone," Press Release, May 20, 2007, http://www. blackstone.com/cps/rde/xchg/bxcom/hs/news_pressrelease_3282.htm (accessed September 3, 2009).

[26] Matt Chambers, "China Investment Corp Mulls $1bn Boost for Fortescue," *The Australian*, August 12, 2009, http://www.theaustralian.com.au/business/news/ china-investment-corp-mulls-1bn-boost-for-fortescue/story-e6frg90f-1225760419828 (accessed August 29, 2009).

[27] Helen Power, "China Investment Corp Bails Out Canary Wharf Owner Songbird Estates," *The Times of London*, August 29, 2009, http://www.timesonline.co.uk/tol/ money/property_and_mortgages/article6814331.ece (accessed August 29, 2009).

[28] Chunzhe Zhao, "China Investment Corp Likely to Invest in US High Speed Trains," *China Daily*, January 13, 2010, http://www.chinadaily.com.cn/china/2010-01/13/content_9316060.htm (accessed February 9, 2010).

[29] Robert Samuelson, "China's $2.4 Trillion Global Grip," *Washington Post*, January 25, 2010, http://www.realclearmarkets.com/articles/2010/01/25/chinas_24_ trillion_global_grip_97607.html (accessed January 26, 2010).

[30] Jin Liangxiang, "Energy First: China and the Middle East," *Middle East Quarterly*, Spring 2005, 3-10, http://www.meforum.org/694/energy-first (accessed December 19, 2009).

[31] Ibid.

[32] Ibid.

[33] Xinhua News Agency, "China to Seek Early FTA with GCC," February 12, 2009, http://w'ww.chinadaily.com.cn/china/2009-02/12/content_7471590.htm (accessed December 19, 2009).

[34] Joyce C. Abano, "GCC-China Free Trade Talks to Continue," *The Peninsula*, September 22, 2009, http://www.thepeninsulaqatar.com/Display_news.asp?section= Local_News&subsection=Qatar+News&month=September2009&file=Local_ News200909220566.xml (accessed December 20, 2009).

[35] Al Bawaba, "Dubai World Chairman Receives High Level Chinese Delegation," AlBawaba.com, January 24, 2010, http://www.albawaba.com/en/countries/UAE/ 259824 (accessed January 26, 2010).

4

Rumble in the Jungle

Africa is the last major geopolitical and economic frontier in the world. The continent is the ultimate destination for the long-term investor, and the place where politics and investing are interrelated. The governments of different countries will continue to play a great role in the investments made in Africa, and investors should understand this game in order to come out on top.

Africa is behind in economic and humanitarian terms but has huge natural resource exploration potential, and could gradually become a valid importing entity. On the other hand, there's no economic power that can legitimately claim to exert any political influence over it. What results is an endless chess game among the important global actors.

China is clearly becoming a major political force in Africa, something that's alarmed European and American leaders alike. Europeans, more accustomed to negotiation and discussion as the means to achieve their goals, with neither the ability nor the will to project military power, have been able to sustain an economic presence. The countries of the European Union have been fairly successful individually in helping their companies establish relevance in Africa, while at the same time making perfunctory observations about human rights and democratic values, a practice other Western powers have employed as well to shape up appearances of their Africa-focused development projects.

President Félix Houphouët-Boigny of Côte d'Ivoire ruled his country for 33 years, during which time it became one of the most prosperous nations in sub-Saharan Africa. In 1993 he reportedly said that the democratization of Africa over the preceding two years was a kind of fanaticism, and that starving people had no freedom because poverty and freedom were incompatible.[1]

Qian Qichen, one of the most important diplomats in China's modern history and Vice Premier of the State Council from 1993 until his retirement in 2003, once noted that during his visits to Africa he felt the "deep impression that the African countries were indignant at the political conditions attached to the financial assistance provided by Western countries."[2]

These observations and comments clearly illustrate an obvious fact of life: Not all parties dealing with an issue hold the same views about its proper handling. Ignorance of this simple reality, at least publicly, by many parties involved with the Africa question has hindered true development efforts for decades. Western powers, pleased with themselves for their infusions of cash and advisors, fail to see that Africans may not appreciate Western aid in the same light.

India provides an interesting case when it comes to international influence in Africa and the perception of who has it. It isn't among the usual names taken into account when commentators discuss moves made by emerging nations in Africa, or any other place. When India is mentioned it's rarely cast in a negative light—as you might expect for a country generally viewed as a rising but subdued power. And yet it was Indian companies, together with others from China, Canada, and Malaysia, that were first to collaborate with Sudan after US-led sanctions were imposed on the country in 1996. The collaboration helped produce Sudan's Greater Nile Petroleum Corporation (GNPC), which allowed Sudan to become a bona fide oil-exporting country.[3] India has also financed some USD600 million of energy infrastructure development in Sudan, including a 741 km oil pipeline and four 125 megawatt (MW) power plants and an associated transmission system.[4]

India's ruling elite, many observers tend to forget, are reputedly very good in negotiations—persistent yet subtle with broad, long-term vision. The country's representatives have generally achieved their goals on the international arena while easily shedding criticism of their actions in the domestic or South Asian political arenas.

On December 17, 1961, 30,000 Indian troops invaded the Portuguese colony of Goa, and India subsequently annexed the territory. The next day Adlai Stevenson, the US envoy to the United Nations, who had also helped found the institution, was the only representative of a major power to forcefully object at the UN assembly. India's representative L. K. Jha noted

> The use of force, in all circumstances, is regrettable but so far as the achievement of freedom is concerned, when nothing else is available, I am afraid that it is a very debatable proposition to say that force cannot be used at all.[5]

Although a resolution supporting India, and another demanding an immediate cease-fire, failed to be adopted, after the vote Ambassador Stevenson said

> [W]e have witnessed tonight an effort to rewrite the Charter, to sanction the use of force in international relations when it suits one's own purposes. This approach can only lead to chaos and the disintegration of the United Nations.[6]

Though Ambassador Stevenson's words were only partially prophetic, the point here is that while India was using force at home to consolidate its territory—Goa was not the only case—Indian Prime Minister Jawaharlal Nehru was traveling the globe advocating his version of "utopian internationalism." Most who heard him accepted his ideas. The prevailing attitude seemed to be that India, a democracy, deserved the benefit of the doubt. Yet, as Francis Pike noted

> At the end of his life, Nehru would learn belatedly that just as India's unity was established at the point of a gun, so power in the international arena resided with those countries that had the power to enforce their will.[7]

But history proves that geopolitics is a game; when Indonesia did to East Timor in December 1975 what India did to Goa, Indonesia was treated with contempt, some loud exceptions notwithstanding.[8]

Perception often differs from reality. Today, and only because of geopolitical interests, individual investors have been led to believe that whenever Russia or China pursues, for instance, greater access to natural resources, the global or regional political and economic ramifications will be dire. This argument finds receptive ears because China isn't a democracy, while Russia's democratic credentials are perceived with skepticism by the Western commentariat.

In this age of labels and pseudo politically correct attitudes, one definition that has been given to resource hunting is "resource nationalism," which defines nothing more than a pursuit that major powers throughout history have undertaken during times of strong economic growth: the time-honored attempt to control commodities. These assets are called "strategic" for a reason.

With the passage of years other industries have been identified as strategic, telecommunications, finance, and intellectual property among them. These industries came to prominence because of strong growth in developed economies, which was rooted in the capitalistic model of free enterprise and dominant access to the world's oil reserves. Their emergence allowed the West, led by the US, to surpass the rest of the world's economies and opened the door for a more sophisticated growth model.

Africa has endured a period when Europe- and US-based exploration and production companies used to take control of oil fields, offering their expertise—which they undoubtedly had and still possess—in exchange for a big slice of the energy pie. The same companies reigned supreme for decades in the Middle East. There's no material difference when China, Russia, or India, for that matter, devises strategies to do the same, though these emerging powers will never enjoy the advantage of literally dictating terms the major oil companies enjoyed in their heydays.

What it boils down to is the willingness of the Western powers to accept change that results in these countries behaving in the global market as they do. For obvious reasons initial reactions from Western officials have been generally negative, illustrated by an endless amount of literature addressing Chinese or Russian "aggression" or the transparency of SWF transactions and their structures. The rise of the SWFs, together with the increasing economic power of the sponsoring emerging economies, has raised the chorus of critics. Inevitably, however, the facts reveal that the objects of these critiques are operating within the rules, established by a fading geopolitical and economic order that nevertheless merits these meaningless lectures. These lectures certainly don't seem to resonate with the intended recipients. Mohamed El-Erian, then president and CEO of the Harvard Management Company, put it brilliantly in 2007:

History suggests that, in the vast majority of cases, the approach of debtors lecturing to creditors is not a very effective one. It does not help that such lecturing has materially intensified after some of the newer SWFs, including China, made the sensible decision to embark on a gradual diversification of hitherto excessively concentrated reserve holdings.

It is also inconvenient that such lecturing is coming on the heels of this summer's disruptions. After all, the systemic shock originated in the most sophisticated financial system in the world, involved the migration of activities outside the purview of adequate oversight, and led to disruptions at the very heart of the market system in industrial countries—be it in terms of segments (i.e., inter-bank, commercial paper, and money markets) or in terms of markets parameters (e.g., valuations, price discovery, and visibility).[9]

The truth of the matter is that emerging economies don't need SWFs in order to invest in another country's natural resource, banking, telecommunication, or other sectors. India, for instance, does not have an SWF but has been able to make strategic investments in Africa, the Middle East, and other places around the world for years. China, too, has created special vehicles that make state-sponsored investments in foreign assets. The China-Africa Development Fund, which opened its first office in South Africa in March 2009, is a good example of a non-SWF approach to foreign deployment of capital in Africa. It was created to support "Chinese companies to develop the cooperation with Africa and enter the African market." The Chinese government officially approved the establishment of the fund with first-phase funding of USD1 billion provided by China Development Bank; investable assets will eventually reach USD5 billion.[10]

The fund has signed projects with select Chinese companies such as China National Building Material Company, a cement, lightweight building materials, glass fiber, composite materials, and engineering services outfit, and Shenzhen Energy Group, a power generator and gas supply company.

In late 2007, the Industrial and Commercial Bank of China (Hong Kong: 1398, ICBC), a bank with strong ties to the state, bought a 20 percent stake in South Africa's Standard Bank, which operates in

18 African countries. The ICBC's strategy was two pronged: first, to expand in one of the relatively unspoiled retail banking markets in the world, and second, to do that while taking advantage of the weakness of the Western financial institutions. As 2008 unfolded this strategy seemed particularly sound, as buying into Western financial companies gradually became a game of indirect aid with no clear benefits. Again, this is not an SWF-related investment, but it most certainly has the state's blessings.

Although it's too early in the cycle to be absolutely certain of such an outcome, investors should look to the developing economies to take advantage of the positive long-term consequences that investments by SWFs will bring. Understanding the flow of capital to emerging economies will help investors realize superior long-term returns, not just because most SWF money will be invested there but because the majority of the recipient-country governments are now ready and able to support and contribute to their countries' economic potential.

China on the Lead

"I achieved more in my one-hour meeting with President Hu Jintao in an executive suite at my hotel in Berlin during the recent G-8 meeting in Heiligendamm," wrote President of Senegal Abdoulaye Wade in a column published in the *Financial Times* in early 2008, "than I did during the entire, orchestrated meeting of world leaders at the summit—where African leaders were told little more than that G-8 nations would respect existing commitments."[11]

President Wade's sentiment encapsulates the attitude of the majority of sub-Saharan governments toward Chinese investment overtures in the African continent, which, as China becomes more confident in its own economic strength, grow bigger and more influential by the day. One of the largest projects China ever developed in Africa, on an aid basis, was the 1860 km Tanzania-Zambia Railway. Construction started in 1970 and lasted for six years, during which time the Chinese government provided an interest-free loan of RMB988 million (USD145 million) and shipped about 1 million tons of equipment and materials. A total of approximately 50,000 technicians and workers were dispatched for the construction phase; during the peak period the number of Chinese workers was as high as

16,000.[12] Forty years later support for the region's "just struggle against imperialism, colonialism, and national liberation" is not expressed as a reason for Chinese to undertake projects in Africa. Although politics still play a significant role, economic motivations guide China's investment decision making. To understand the investments, however, you have to understand the politics.

China's foreign policy has generally followed five principles of peaceful coexistence: mutual respect for sovereignty, mutual nonaggression, mutual noninterference in internal affairs, equality, and mutual benefit. Historically the Chinese have considered respect for sovereignty and noninterference in each other's internal affairs as the most important of those principles. Although there are no altruistic motives behind these principles, the fact is that they resonate with governments around the world. More important, they play well in Africa, where a lot of governments and rulers do, for obvious reasons, prefer little scrutiny. The principle that holds everything together in the new century is mutual benefit, or the "win-win" approach, as it's come to be known. This, as much as its deep pockets, underlies China's willingness to contribute to a country's infrastructure needs. This so-called developmental approach has allowed it to slowly increase its influence in Africa over the past 15 years, even though historically China hasn't been an aggressive exporter of capital. Contrary to the norm during periods of aggressive Western investment, substantial amounts of money are now being allocated to infrastructure projects, some of which are connected to the specific resource investment, while others are not.

According to the Africa Infrastructure Country Diagnostic (AICD), among households in sub-Saharan Africa, 36 percent are without an improved water source, 73 percent are without improved sanitation, 37 percent are without electricity, and only 5 percent have a telephone. It comes then as no surprise that China's developmental approach, coupled with the cancellation of USD1.36 billion of African countries' debt nearly a decade ago and another USD1.3 billion in 2007, has become such a success.[13] The arrangement isn't perfect, as the Chinese, new to this game, often encounter political and social problems that they either hadn't considered in advance or, had they considered, preferred to ignore. Nevertheless, more positive things are taking place in Africa's infrastructure development these days than at any time in recent memory. If the present trajectory is maintained and

Africa enters a period of legitimate, sustainable growth, China's positive role here will resonate around the world. Its efforts, however, are
already being recognized; more countries are lining up to work with
China than are complaining about its ascendency. The World Bank's
pragmatic President Robert Zoellick, in a visit to Beijing in 2009, made
it clear that the institution he headed would welcome China's SWF
investment in its asset management company. He also noted that he
was hopeful that Chinese companies would start investing in the development of Africa's manufacturing capacity as well.[14]

There are three main ways through which China is engaged economically with Africa. The first is trade, which reached USD107 billion in 2008. China funneled USD5.5 billion in foreign direct
investment (FDI), the second method, to Africa in 2008. And the third
method is China's official development assistance (ODA) program
with Africa, used mainly to secure resource swaps, accounts for more
than two times investment flows.[15] The terms of China's ODA follow
principles established during then-Premier Zhou Enlai's visit to Africa
in the early 1960s: No conditions or demand for privileges can be
attached to ODA; China provides ODA in the form of grants, interest-
free or low-interest loans; and repayment will be rescheduled if necessary. China's aid program also includes technical assistance, with an
emphasis on agricultural technology and training in Chinese institutions. China's overall ODA program has focused on social and humanitarian projects, such as establishing hospitals, schools, low-cost
housing, sport venues, and library and government buildings, and
often is delivered in kind. ODA has also been used for infrastructure
construction and agricultural development.[16] Where infrastructure is
concerned, most Chinese funds are channeled to power-generation
projects and railways. According to a study by the World Bank

> By the end of 2007, China was providing at least USD3.3 bil-
> lion toward the construction of 10 major hydropower projects
> amounting to more than 6,000 megawatts (MW) of installed
> capacity. If completed, these schemes would increase the
> total available hydropower generation capacity in sub-Saha-
> ran Africa by around 30 percent....
>
> ...China has made a major comeback in the rail sector, with
> financing commitments on the order of USD4 billion for this

sector. They include rehabilitation of more than 1,350 kilometers of existing railway lines and the construction of more than 1,600 kilometers of new railroad. To put this in perspective, the entire African railroad network amounts to around 50,000 kilometers.[17]

The hunt for natural resources is the main reason for China's involvement in Africa, where China was a nonentity 15 years ago. Eighty percent of the more than USD22 billion worth of natural resources that it imports from Africa is oil, while timber and minerals cover the rest.

CNOOC Ltd (NYSE: CEO) is China's largest producer of offshore crude oil and natural gas and the company that leads the Middle Kingdom's oil ambitions in Africa. Africa holds the company's largest overseas net proved reserves, and CNOOC is active in 12 projects, with its main interests primarily located in Nigeria. The company paid USD2.7 billion in 2006 to acquire a 45 percent stake in the offshore oil mining lease OML 130 in Nigeria, where the main operator is France's Total. OML 130 is located in deep water and comprises four fields, AKPO, EGINA, South EGINA, and PROWEI. AKPO commenced production in March 2009, contributing around 11 percent of CNOOC's overall production. Less than a year after production at AKPO got underway, Total revised the field's plateau production volume upward by 28 percent to 225,000 barrels per day (bbl/d). Total also revised up by 33 percent the initial proved and probable reserves to 800 million barrels (bbl). The consortium plans to have the EGINA project up and running by 2015; initial estimates for proved and probable reserves are 600 million bbl.

Even considering these projects, China is still further behind in the Africa oil race than a casual look at the major media reports would have us believe. From 2001 to 2006 40 percent of Africa's oil production was exported to the United States, 17 percent to Europe; 14 percent went to China.[18] Although Africa is rapidly rising in importance to China, it is already critical to the US—it provides around 20 percent of the country's imported oil, and this share is likely to grow in the future. As Michael T. Klare has noted

The U.S. military, in particular, has been devoting special attention to Africa, often under the guise of the Global War

on Terror, but with an eye to the safety of offshore oil platforms in the Gulf of Guinea and the sea lanes that connect
these rigs with the eastern United States.[19]

The US still has hands-down the most important oil exploration
operations in Africa; other US-based businesses have significant
interests there as well. But its policies in the region have been an
exercise in bouncing between realism and utopian paternalism.
Either way the continent has become important enough that in 2007
President George W. Bush announced the formation of the US Africa
Command (AFRICOM), the nation's first foreign command to be
established since 1980.[20] AFRICOM describes its mission as follows:

> [I]n concert with other U.S. government agencies and inter-
> national partners, conducts sustained security engagement
> through military-to-military programs, military-sponsored
> activities, and other military operations as directed to pro-
> mote a stable and secure African environment in support of
> U.S. foreign policy.[21]

Nobody knows how China would act had it the power-projecting
capabilities the US currently enjoys. As things stand it seems China is
more committed to Africa, or at least is doing the right things to project such an image, than many other counties that have traditionally
done business there. Of the infrastructure projects China has
financed in sub-Saharan Africa, only 10 percent are directly linked to
natural-resource exploitation. The chart in Figure 4.1 depicts how the
rest of the funds have been invested.

Also interesting to note is the breakdown of Africa's trade pattern
(see Figure 4.2). The US and China are Africa's main trading partners. China has a more balanced relationship with the continent—its
trade deficit is much smaller than that of the US. In 2008 China
imported USD54.1 billion worth of goods, while its exports to Africa
totaled USD46.4 billion. The US imported goods worth USD110.4
billion, while exports were USD21.8 billion. The big difference is the
oil interests, which are big and well-established for the US, small but
growing for China. And because Africa's needs are a lot more basic
than the new version of a "killer" technology application, China has
been better able to bridge the gap with its lower-end manufactured
goods. The US trade position with Africa is informative for another

reason. We're constantly reminded of the US's deficit with China because the absolute size of the trading relationship almost cries out for big-headline treatment and desperate cries from politicians. But the deficit with Africa and other economic blocs are larger in percentage terms than the one with China.

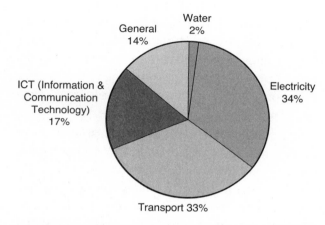

Figure 4.1 Confirmed Chinese infrastructure finance commitments in sub-Saharan Africa by sector, 2001-07.

(Source: World Bank Public-Private Infrastructure Advisory Facility)

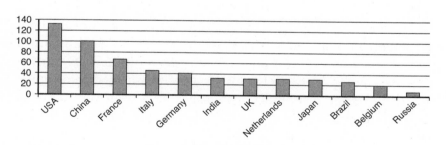

Figure 4.2 Africa's trade partners (2008) USD billions.

(Source: International Monetary Fund, United Nations)

Of Tigers and Bears

"Africa is our Mother Continent," said Prime Minister of India Dr. Manmohan Singh in 2008. "The dynamics of geology may have led our lands to drift apart, but history, culture and the processes of post-colonial development have brought us together once again."[22]

India is Africa's sixth-largest trading partner, and India-Africa bilateral trade increased from USD967 million in 1991 to USD30 billion in 2008.[23] In addition, 35 percent of Africa's meat imports, 30 percent of paper and pulp, 26 percent of dairy products, 23 percent of sugar and pharmaceuticals, and 20 percent of aluminum came from India in 2008. On the other hand, India's imports from Africa have been concentrated mainly in natural resources, with oil representing around 12 percent of these imports. According to the Energy Information Administration (EIA) Nigeria is the third-largest supplier of oil to India after Saudi Arabia and Iran.

Nigeria hopes to attract USD10 billion worth of investments from India in the next five years, in sectors such as telecom.[24] India's largest wireless operator, Bharti Airtel (Mumbai: 532454), has been the most eager of the Indian telecommunication companies to make a move into sub-Saharan Africa. In 2008-09 the company tried to buy South Africa-based telecommunications company MTN (OTC: MTNOY), which operates in 21 African countries. This deal fell through, but by early 2010 Bharti was considering a USD10.7 billion deal to acquire Kuwait's majority stake in Mobile Telecommunications' African assets, which include 40 million subscribers on the Zain mobile network.

Indian companies have traditionally entered the African continent through South Africa. The country received a large influx of Indians early on as they went to South Africa originally as workers imported by the British to the former Natal colony beginning in the 1850s. In recent years Indian companies have been very active in projects throughout Africa, and there have been years when they've closed more deals than any other emerging economy's representatives in the continent. The Tata Group of companies is a good example. The group is one of the oldest and biggest conglomerates in India and has its African headquarters in South Africa. Its Tata Motors (NYSE: TTM) division has been expanding in Africa since the 1970s and now operates in eight more African countries, including Senegal, Ghana, Nigeria, the Democratic Republic of the Congo, Uganda, Zambia, Mozambique, and Tanzania.

It is interesting to note that, as Figure 4.2 depicts, Russia is insignificant in Africa, engaging in only USD8 billion worth of bilateral trade. Only USD2.2 billion of this total was African exports in 2008, as Russia, self-sufficient when it comes to hydrocarbons, need not import oil and gas. But Russia has made a significant effort to reenter Africa in a more assertive way.

In an effort to increase his country's presence in the continent, Russian President Dmitry Medvedev visited Egypt, Nigeria, Namibia, and Angola June 22–26, 2009. This was the first visit by a Russian president to Nigeria, and the two sides didn't waste any time before signing nuclear- and natural gas-related agreements. The two main sets of expertise Russia has to offer to African countries are in the areas of exploration and production of oil and gas and in the development of nuclear technology.

It's well known that Russia wants to restore its status as a major player in Africa's economic and political chessboard. Although Russia's main foreign policy goals since the early 2000s have been to solidify its influence in Central Asia and expand its economic and political ties with China, its African ambitions shouldn't be underestimated. Russian investment in Africa has been slow to pick up, but the picture should be very different by 2015 (see Figure 4.3).

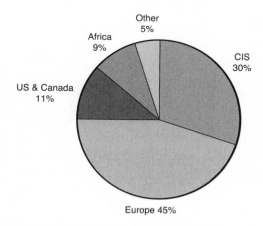

Figure 4.3   Russia's outward FDI (2008).

(Source: Standard Bank)

The natural gas deal signed by the two sides was not only the biggest during President Medvedev's trip, it was also the most important. Russian energy giant Gazprom (OTC: OGZPY) established a USD2.5 billion joint venture with the Nigerian National Petroleum Corporation (NNPC) for the building of refineries, pipelines, and gas power stations in Nigeria. As Gazprom's CEO Alexey Miller said at the time, "The joint venture will construct gas transport and power generation infrastructure in Nigeria, design and develop an associated petroleum gas gathering and processing system as well as subsequently build the Nigerian part of the Trans-Sahara gas pipeline."[25]

A few days after Medvedev's visit, Nigeria, Niger, and Algeria agreed to move ahead with the long-awaited construction of the Trans-Sahara gas pipeline (TSGP). The pipeline, subject of ten years of negotiations, is designed to bring Nigerian natural gas across the Sahara Desert to Algeria and then to be transported via existing underwater pipelines from Algeria to Italy and from Italy to the rest of Europe. The TSGP will be 4,400 km (2,734 miles) long and is expected to cost around USD13 billion. It should be ready five years after the start of construction, which could commence as early as 2010 or 2011. Besides Gazprom, many other energy companies will line up to get involved in this project. India's flagship natural gas company GAIL (Mumbai: 532155), France's Total SA, Italy's Eni SpA, and Anglo-Dutch giant Royal Dutch Shell are some of the major interested parties, illustrating again the multipolar world in which we live. Given the size and complexity of the project, a consortium of companies, the majority of them with strong governmental ties in their home countries, will work together to build the project and deliver the gas.

As has become customary the countries through which the pipeline will go will have ultimate control, but the companies involved, including Gazprom, will also have significant incentives to execute the project and, more important, for the natural gas to keep flowing into Europe. Such an arrangement will, in the long run, be more beneficial and productive to consumers in Europe and will serve as a strong answer to the analysts in assorted think-tanks worried about Europe's energy security and overreliance on Russian gas. Needless to say, Europe has been overrelying on Russian gas since the mid-

1970s with no material problems, and although Gazprom will control part of this new pipeline, the result will be the same: no substantive problem.

Endnotes

[1] Qian Qichen, *Ten Episodes in China's Diplomacy* (New York: Harper Collins 2005), 203.

[2] Ibid., 202-203.

[3] The UN imposed the sanctions on Sudan in 1996 to try to force the country to hand over several people suspected of involvement in a failed plot to assassinate Egyptian President Hosni Mubarak.

[4] Vivien Foster, "The Changing Landscape of Infrastructure Finance in Africa," Public-Private Infrastructure Advisory Facility, October 2008, 2.

[5] Thomas M. Franck, *Resource to Force: State Action Against Threats and Armed Attacks* (Cambridge, UK: Cambridge University Press, 2002), 116.

[6] Ibid.

[7] Francis Pike, *Empires At War: A Short History of Modern Asia Since World War II* (London: I. B. Tauris, 2010), 292.

[8] Contrary to the Goa incident, the US did not show any particular desire to condemn Indonesia. The then-US representative to the UN Daniel Patrick Moynihan wrote in his memoir later on regarding East Timor that "The Department of State desired that the United Nations prove utterly ineffective in whatever measures it undertook. This task was given to me, and I carried it forward with no inconsiderable success." Quoted in Christopher Hitchen's book *The Trial of Henry Kissinger* (New York: Verso 2001), 92.

[9] Mohamed A. El-Erian, "Towards a Better Understanding of Sovereign Wealth Funds," Discussant Comments on Peterson Institute Senior Fellow Ted Truman's Paper, "The Management of China's International Reserves," Presented at the Conference on China's Exchange Rate Policy Peterson Institute, October 19, 2007, 8.

[10] China-Africa Development Fund, http://www.cadfund.com/en/Column.asp?ColumnId=43 (accessed January 2010).

[11] Abdoulaye Wade, "Time for the West to Practice What It Preaches," Africa-China Trade Financial Times Special report, January 24, 2008.

[12] Ministry of Foreign Affairs of the People's Republic of China, "China's Assistance in the Construction of the Tanzania-Zambia Railway," http://www.fmprc.gov.cn/eng/ziliao/3602/3604/t18009.htm, November 11, 2000.

[13] Sub-Sahara Africa is the region of Africa to the south of the Sahara Desert that covers most of the continent's land and population.

[14] J. R. Wu and Andrew Batson, "China Discusses Investments in Africa," *The Wall Street Journal*, September 2, 2009.

[15] Dianna Games, "Emerging Commercial Rivalries in Africa: A View from South Africa," Policy Report, South African Foreign Policy and African Drivers Programme, South African Institute of International Affairs, February 2010, 2.

[16] Jian-Ye Wang, "What Drives China's Growing Role in Africa?," IMF Working Paper, October 2007, 9-10.

[17] Vivien Foster et al., "Building Bridges: China's Growing Role as Infrastructure Financier for Sub-Saharan Africa," World Bank/PPIAF, Washington, DC, 2009, Xiii.

[18] Ibid., 37.

[19] Michael T. Klare, *Rising Powers, Shrinking Planet: The New Geopolitics of Energy* (New York: Metropolitan Books, 2008), 148.

[20] Ibid., 149.

[21] United States Africa Command, Fact Sheet, http://www.africom.mil/getArticle.asp?art=1644 (accessed February 2010).

[22] Opening Address by Dr. Manmohan Singh, Prime Minister of India, at the Plenary Session-I of India-Africa Forum Summit Vigyan Bhawan, New Delhi, April 8, 2008.

[23] Dianna Games, "Emerging Commercial Rivalries in Africa," 2.

[24] Federation of Indian Chambers of Commerce and Industry.

[25] Statement by the Chairman of the Management Committee of OAO Gazprom Alexey Miller at the annual General Shareholders Meeting, June 26, 2009.

5

A New Oil Age

Few would debate the idea that global oil production will eventually peak. The only question is timing, and there's no way to know for sure when the actual peak will be attained. But data showing alarming declines from maturing fields outside OPEC coupled with production patterns from giant fields cast serious doubt on rose-tinted forecasts for global oil production capacity. The evidence strongly suggests that the world will never see more than 100 million barrels a day of oil production, as the Energy Information Administration (EIA) and other forecasters have suggested.

The most basic law of economics is that supply must equal demand, and price is the factor that balances the equation. A far more likely scenario is that with crude production limited, prices will need to rise to a level that rations demand.

In the summer of 1859, low on funding after more than a year of work, Edwin Laurentine Drake struck oil in a well drilled near Titusville, Pennsylvania.

Drake's effort wasn't man's first attempt to drill for oil. Nor was his well a prolific producer, yielding little more than 20 barrels of oil per day. But it was the first to be commercially successful. This simple well, drilled to a total depth of 69.5 feet (21 meters), sparked an overnight boom in Pennsylvania and established Drake as an unlikely pioneer of the global Oil Age.[1]

In recent years it's become fashionable to deride oil and other fossil fuels as expensive and unsustainable energy sources. But let's not forget history. In the 150 years since the self-proclaimed "Colonel" Drake drilled his Titusville well, the world has enjoyed an unprecedented wave of economic growth and human development that's lifted billions of people from poverty. This era of prosperity and the wealthy industrial nations it spawned were largely built on cheap energy derived from fossil fuels. The Oil Age hasn't unfolded without negative consequences, but it's dishonest to deny that affordable energy has meant a better quality of life for much of the world's population.

To modern ears it seems ridiculous to talk about cheap energy and crude oil in the same sentence. After all, when oil spiked to near USD150 per barrel in the summer of 2008, consumers all over the world experienced an energy shock unseen since the oil embargoes of the 1970s. But oil's ubiquity is based on its cost advantage; it's a versatile and concentrated source of energy. The oil era has made energy convenient in modern society and more available to a wider number of consumers than at any other time in human development. By any reasonable historical definition, crude oil is still a cheap source of energy—even at USD150 per barrel.

What was known as "rock oil" in Drake's day quickly became one of the most successful products in history. The first major market for oil was illumination. Although taken for granted in modern times, lighting wasn't commonplace in the middle of the 19th century; in fact, the ubiquity of public lighting was one of the most important factors separating nascent industrializing nations in Europe from the rest of the world. In that era, gas manufactured from coal was finding a growing market in street lighting but was not economic in all but the most densely populated areas.[2] Quality household illumination was also a luxury in the middle of the 19th century. Whale oil—a wax derived from the blubber of certain species of whales—burned brightly and produced little smoke and odor but was expensive and unaffordable for many. Camphene—a mixture of turpentine and alcohol—was cheaper than whale oil but highly explosive and volatile.[3] Around 1850 a Scottish chemist named James Young began the commercial manufacture of what he called "paraffine oil" (later paraffin), which was derived from coal. Widely known as coal oil at the time and in the Americas as kerosene, Young's invention quickly gained popularity. By the time Drake drilled his first well, there were already 50 to 60 plants in the US designed to convert coal into kerosene for use in lamps.[4]

But after Drake and other early drillers began producing oil in quantity in the 1860s, it quickly became apparent that synthesizing kerosene from rock oil was far cheaper than manufacturing the oil from coal. Some of the early US manufacturers of coal oil soon entered the petroleum industry, converting or shuttering coal oil manufacturing plants in favor of refineries to produce kerosene from crude.[5] Figure 5.1 is a comparison of the price of crude oil per barrel to that of sperm oil—the most prized type of whale oil—and crude whale oil from 1861 to 1900. It's not hard to see why crude quickly replaced whale oil as a source of light. Crude was the far cheaper product from the very dawn of the Oil Age.

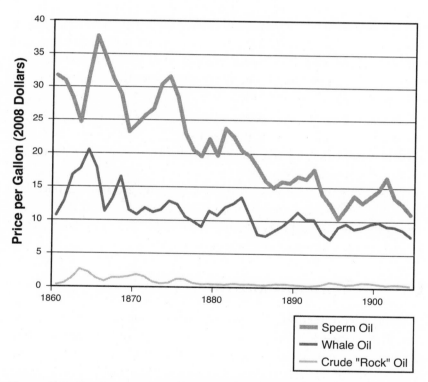

Figure 5.1   Crude oil and whale oil prices 1860–1905. Note: All prices rebased to 2008 dollars using implied inflation rate from BP Statistical data.

(Source: BP Statistical Review of World Energy 2008; Walter S. Tower, A History of the American Whale Fishery, Philadelphia: John C. Winston, 1907).

The increasing scarcity of whales forced the world's whalers—many based in Nantucket—to spend more time at sea to fill their holds with whale oil and bone, raising costs and cutting into profit margins. As a result the whaling industry began a gradual decline about ten years before Drake drilled his well. The outbreak of the Civil War in 1861 also caused significant damage to the industry. But competition with oil-derived kerosene clearly eroded whale oil prices after 1860 and accelerated the decline. At the height of the whaling industry in the mid- to late 1840s, more than 600 US whaling ships weighing a total of more than 230,000 tons plied the oceans; by the 1880s there were less than 100 whaling ships with total tonnage of just 30,000.[6]

Oil's capacity to drastically lower the price of energy for illumination was apparent by the latter half of the 19th century. At one point in the mid-1870s, sperm whale oil sold for more than USD30 per gallon (USD1,260 per 42-gallon barrel) compared to less than USD0.65 for crude oil. Kerosene meant that illumination was no longer a luxury. It became a staple of everyday life.

Perhaps even more important for the next chapter in the Oil Age was crude's abundance. Within a decade of the Drake well, crude was already America's fourth-largest export. By 1872 the North American oil industry was already producing about 7.6 million barrels of oil per year (320 million gallons) and exporting some 3.6 million barrels a year (151 million gallons), primarily to Europe.[7] At its height the American whaling industry produced a total of less than 325,000 gallons of sperm and whale oil combined per year.[8]

Oil for Transportation

Cheap illumination was the first use of crude oil in the 19th century. But the world's love affair with crude was only beginning. The big explosion in demand for oil came in the 20th century, as the automobile quickly moved from a curiosity for the wealthy to a mass-market consumer product.

The synchronous development of transportation and petroleum has since been inextricably intertwined. Just as crude oil made illumination cheap and affordable for the masses, oil has democratized global transportation. Personal horse-drawn carriages were a luxury at the turn of the 20th century; within just a few decades the personal automobile was taken for granted by many consumers in the developed world.

The development of the automobile in America came early in the 20th century. In 1950, by which time Americans owned 50 million cars, crude oil finally overtook coal as the nation's most important source of energy.[9] By the early part of the 21st century, there were more than 250 million passenger vehicles in the US.

And it wasn't just the number of cars in the US that exploded through the 20th century. The US Federal Highway Administration began keeping statistics on total vehicle miles traveled in 1960; the total number of miles US consumers drive each year has grown more than fourfold since.

Figure 5.2 shows the total amount of energy produced by crude oil consumed in the US, from the early days of the industry to the present. To make the figure comparable to the experience in other nations it's expressed in terms of per capita energy consumption—the amount of crude oil used per person.

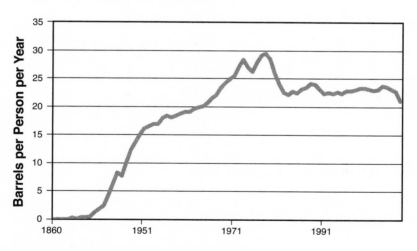

Figure 5.2 US per capita oil consumption.

(Source: Energy Information Administration Annual Energy Review 2008, US Census Bureau, US Bureau of Economic Analysis)

Figure 5.2 illustrates three clear phases of demand growth for crude in the 20th century. The first phase was the near-parabolic growth in demand for oil from 1900 to 1950 as cars became increasingly popular and affordable for consumers. This acceleration phase was followed by a slightly slower rate of growth from 1951 through the early 1970s as the automobile began to mature as a consumer product and the US market began to reach a saturation point.

Per capita crude oil consumption peaked in the early to mid-1970s. US dependence on oil imports grew steadily in the 1950s and 1960s, and domestic production peaked in the early 1970s. To make matters worse, just as demand for imports began rising the 1973 Organization of Petroleum Exporting Countries (OPEC) embargo cast doubt on the security and reliability of that supply. Crude oil prices spiked, and Americans began to drive more fuel-efficient cars to cut costs. The average US car in 1970 got just 12 miles per gallon compared to more than 17 miles per gallon in recent years, a 50 percent jump.[10] A final reason for the fall in US per capita crude consumption was crude's decline as a fuel for electric-power plants. In the mid- and late 1970s the US consumed more than 1.7 million barrels a day of crude and related products in the generation of electricity. By 2008 that figure had fallen to less than 200,000 barrels.[11]

The drop in crude oil consumption per capita in the final years covered by the chart also stands out. In 2008 the average American consumer used a little more than 21 million barrels of crude per day, the lowest since 1965. This is the result of the severe recession of 2007–09 that prompted consumers to pare back on driving and air travel.

The American Roadmap

Mark Twain once quipped that history doesn't repeat but it does rhyme. Alongside the developed European powers the US was among the first countries to see rapid economic development, the democratization of transport, and the accompanying surge in per capita oil demand.

In certain respects the US experience was unusual. Although America imported more oil as the 20th century progressed, relatively large domestic production encouraged consumption. The US remains the world's third-largest oil producer, behind only Saudi Arabia and

Russia. Neighboring countries in the Americas still account for around half of US oil imports.

But overall the US experience isn't unique. It can serve, too, as a roadmap for similar development in other countries. A classic example from the 20th century is Japan, which emerged from its devastation in World War II to become the world's second-largest economy in the span of just a few decades.

The time periods are different, but Figure 5.3 shows for Japan the same basic data and patterns as Figure 5.2 does for the US. Two lines are plotted on this chart; the first shows Japan's total primary energy consumption from 1960 to 2006 in terms of barrels of oil equivalent per capita. This data includes crude oil used for transportation as well as all other energy consumed in Japan, regardless of source or purpose. Primary energy includes, for example, electric energy produced from natural gas and nuclear power as well as energy made from coal in steel blast furnaces. The second line, covering data from 1965 to 2008, illustrates actual oil and related refined products consumed in Japan.

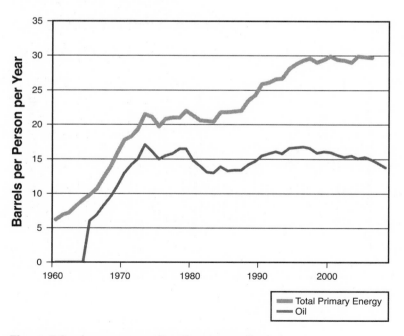

Figure 5.3   Japan per capita oil consumption.

(Source: BP Statistical Review of World Energy 2009, World Bank Development Statistics)

The rapid acceleration phase in oil demand growth for the US stretched from around 1900 to 1950. In Japan, a similar phase of growth occurred from shortly after World War II up until the early 1970s. Figure 5.3 depicts the final three decades of this ramp-up.

After 1973 there was in Japan, like in the US, a gradual drop-off in oil consumption per capita. Total energy consumption per capita has continued to rise over the entire period covered by Figure 5.3, but that growth was based primarily on the electrification of the Japanese economy. And as in most countries, oil isn't an important source of electric power in Japan. Much of the growth in Japanese energy consumption after 1973 has come from coal, nuclear power, and natural gas rather than oil. As was the case in the US after 1900, the rapid acceleration of Japanese oil and energy demand in the immediate post-World War II era corresponded to an accelerated phase of economic development and growth in per capita discretionary income.

Figure 5.4 illustrates what came to be known as the post-war Japanese economic "miracle."

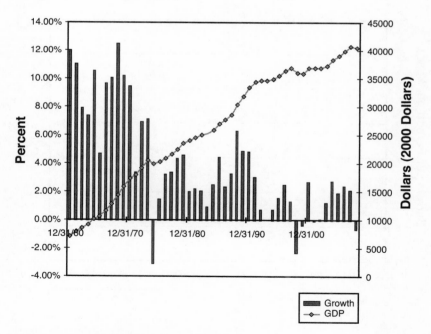

Figure 5.4   Japan GDP per capita.

(Source: Bloomberg Finance L.P.)

The dotted line plotted in Figure 5.4 shows Japanese per capita GDP in 2000 dollars. In 1960 Japan's GDP was just over USD7,000 per person, compared to around USD14,100 in the US and USD10,500 in the UK. Japan was an emerging market, not unlike the US in the early 20th century. US GDP in the mid-1920s was roughly equivalent to Japanese GDP per capita at the end of 1960. The bars illustrate the annual change in per capita GDP.

There are three clear phases for the Japanese economy over the time period covered by this chart: an accelerated phase of growth from 1960 through the early 1970s; a strong but more modest growth phase in the late 1970s through the 1980s; and finally a period of sub-par growth that's lasted from around 1990 to the present. The latter period—Japan's "Lost Decade"—occurred after the collapse of the Japanese equity and property bubbles circa 1990. The development of the Japanese economy and oil demand in the post-war era isn't identical to the US experience post-1900, but it follows the same basic pattern. As Japan's economy entered a phase of accelerated growth and disposable incomes rose, demand for transport and energy rose in tandem. It's only natural that as Japanese incomes rose, consumers looked to increase their standard of living by joining the Oil Age, just as their counterparts in the US and Western Europe had done decades before.

The New Oil Age

China, India, and other developing countries are now hitting the same development tipping point that the US, Western Europe, and Japan did decades ago. These emerging markets are entering the accelerated phase of oil demand growth so evident in the long-term charts of US and Japanese crude demand.

The patterns of oil consumption for the US and Japan we analyzed are based on per capita data. The immense population of today's emerging markets magnifies the impact of this per capita growth, putting an unprecedented strain on global oil supply. Yuwa Hedrick-Wong, chief Asian economist for MasterCard International, estimates that USD5,000 in annual pre-tax income is the tipping point for Asian consumers. When incomes reach this point, discretionary spending takes off; consumers spend as much as 60 cents out of every incremental dollar earned.[12] This estimate looks at least broadly consistent with the development of oil demand relative to GDP for Japan and the US.

Figure 5.5 shows Chinese GDP per capita and Chinese demand for oil on a per capita per year basis.

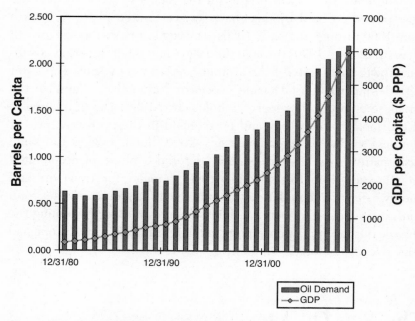

Figure 5.5   China GDP and oil consumption.

(Source: BP Statistical Review of World Energy 2009, Bloomberg Finance L.P., World Bank)

The relationship between GDP and oil demand is undeniable. Figure 5.5 also shows that as Chinese per capita GDP growth accelerated in the mid- to late 1990s, so, too, did per capita oil consumption. Some of the fastest growth of all has come since 2000, when Chinese GDP per capita surpassed the USD4,000 level.

Rapid growth in Chinese oil and energy demand has become something of a cause for consternation in the developed world. Environmental groups decry the pollution caused by China's growing dependence on energy produced by fossil fuels.

Some suggest that China should curb its rising demand or seek to utilize other, cleaner sources of energy rather than relying on oil. Unfortunately, developed-world critics all too often forget the central role oil and the cheap, concentrated energy it provides played in their countries' development. Chinese consumers want to reap the benefits of the Oil Age, as have their counterparts in the US, Japan, and Western Europe. Western sanctimony can't change the fact that China is following the same pattern of accelerated oil demand in direct response to rapid GDP growth that the US, Japan, and Western Europe experienced. If these experiences are any guide, China's accelerated phase will last for years to come.

Chinese oil demand currently stands at just over 2 barrels per person per year, compared to around 20 barrels in the US, 14 in Japan, and 11 to 13 across most of Western Europe. While China's demand on a per capita basis is already growing quickly, there's a great deal of upside before the nation reaches per person consumption levels equivalent to the developed world. With a population of more than 1.3 billion people, even a small increase in per capita oil consumption spells a major jump in petroleum demand. An increase of just a quarter of a barrel per Chinese consumer equates to around 1 million incremental barrels per day of demand on the world oil market.

China overtook the US to become the world's largest automobile market in early 2010. Despite a small drop-off in sales during the heart of the 2007-09 global recession and financial crisis, Chinese car sales show no signs of slowing down. In fact, sales appear to have accelerated in the immediate aftermath of the recession, as Chinese consumers who delayed purchases during the downturn resumed their erstwhile buying patterns. This implies still greater increases in individual energy consumption.

China gets most of the media attention, but it isn't the only demand-growth story for the oil market. Indians consume less than one barrel of crude oil per person per year, roughly equivalent to Chinese per capita consumption in the mid-1990s. India's per capita oil consumption growth has been steady though not quite as dramatic as China's. However, India's population growth has been roughly two times as fast as China's since 1980, so these per capita figures understate India's importance to the global oil market. And India's per capita GDP is also not as high as China's; it's not unreasonable to believe that the country's oil consumption will accelerate in coming years. With a population nearly as large as China's, Indian oil demand will be a force in global oil markets.

The Supply Constraint

Pressure from Western powers and environmental groups won't prevent China, India, and other emerging markets from following the well-worn path of near-parabolic oil demand growth in coming years. But there's a key difference between the US experience in 1900 and the current environment facing India and China: resource availability.

Despite record spending on exploration and the development of some promising new oil reserves, global oil production isn't likely to keep pace with accelerating demand. And there's one inevitable consequence of supply insufficient to meet demand: sharply higher oil prices.

The EIA disseminates an invaluable array of statistics on global energy use as well as projections as to future use and production. However, the EIA and other prominent forecasters have consistently overestimated the prospects for global oil production and underestimated the oil prices needed to make increased production economically viable. For example, in its 1999 International Energy Outlook under its most optimistic high oil price scenario, the EIA forecast crude oil prices would hover under USD30 a barrel in 2010. Under that scenario the EIA projected OPEC oil production of 36.6 barrels a day and non-OPEC production topping 53 million barrels a day.[13] OPEC production was expected to be lower under the EIA's high oil price scenario than under its low and reference price projections. The EIA quite logically forecast that higher oil prices would make non-OPEC oil projects more viable and tend to increase non-OPEC oil production; higher non-OPEC oil production spells lower demand for OPEC oil exports.

The reality is that oil prices entered 2010 at prices three times what the EIA projected, but even vastly higher-than-expected oil prices weren't enough to encourage growth in non-OPEC oil production. Non-OPEC oil production, excluding the former Soviet Union (FSU), has fallen steadily since the late 1990s, offset by an uptick in FSU production. The net gain in non-OPEC production is roughly

4 million barrels per day between 1999 and 2009, far less than the more than 12 million barrels a day forecast by the EIA back in 1999.[14]

Making specific long-term projections about something as tough to predict as global oil production is a thankless task; no matter how thorough, it's almost impossible to be entirely correct. But the bias of the EIA and other groups to overestimate production growth and underestimate prices illustrates a key point about global petroleum supply: The world's "easy" oil is dwindling. Readily accessed, cheap-to-produce oilfields are mature and generating flat or declining production. Oil prices must remain elevated in coming years to incentive the investment needed to maintain and grow production from more complex, expensive-to-produce fields.

In recent years the concept of "peak oil" has quickly gained popularity; myriad Web sites and popular pundits have espoused this view. Peak oil and the end of easy oil are related though not identical concepts. "Peak oil" is widely misunderstood. For one, its adherents don't claim that the world is literally running out of oil. And the concept has no direct connection to "proven oil reserves." Rather, "peak oil" refers to maximum output in terms of millions of barrels per day of production. Peak oil theorists believe that global oil production has or soon will top out and then begin to decline. Production from individual oilfields and major oil-producing regions typically follows a bell-curve pattern, where initial output is slow but then ramps up, plateaus, and begins to decline.

The North Sea's largest oilfields, including Norway's Ekofisk and the Brent and Forties fields in the UK, were discovered and put into production in the 1970s. Production ramped up quickly in the late 1970s and through the early 1980s. A brief production plateau in the late 1980s was followed by a renewed ramp-up in the 1990s.

But North Sea production peaked between 1999 and 2001 and has declined rapidly since. From a maximum of more than 6 million barrels a day total production has fallen by around a third in a decade.

Sometimes you'll hear the concept of peak oil called "Hubbert's Peak" and the bell-shaped production pattern as "Hubbert's Curve." Both are named for Marion King Hubbert, a scientist who produced the first extensive research modeling this production curve. In a now-famous 1950s paper, Hubbert predicted that US oil production would hit a peak between the mid-1960s or early 1970s; this prediction was derided by many at the time but proved spectacularly correct. US oil production hit a peak in 1971–72 and has fallen steadily ever since. This curve isn't just a random curiosity invented by scientists and mathematicians; there are real geological reasons production from conventional oil (and natural gas) reservoirs follows this pattern.

Oil does not exist underground in giant lakes or caverns. It isn't simply pumped to the surface. Oil and other hydrocarbons are actually found inside the pores and natural fractures of reservoir rock. A classic example is sandstone, a type of rock composed of sand-sized particles. Sandstone is an ideal medium because it contains many pores and cracks that hold oil, and those pores are often well connected, making it easier for hydrocarbons to flow through the reservoir rock and into a well.

Oil or gas in a reservoir exists under significant geologic pressure. This is what drives production—the pressure of the oil in the reservoir forces the oil through the reservoir rock into a well and to the surface. The oil is simply flowing from the high-pressure reservoir to the well, where pressure is far lower. This process is known as primary production.

A common image associated with the oil industry is a "gusher"— oil shooting from the ground like a giant fountain. The famous Spindletop Gusher struck in Texas in 1901 reportedly produced a column of oil that reached 150 feet into the air and took nine days to bring under control. This oil wasn't pumped to the surface. Natural geologic pressure created this effect at Spindletop. Gushers are dangerous, as oil and gas can ignite and cause fires. They're also wasteful; spilling valuable hydrocarbons is expensive. But gushers are rare in modern times because producers have learned how to control underground geologic pressures and prevent such events.

As a well is produced over time and hydrocarbons are removed, natural pressures ease, and production from the well begins to slow. Eventually, pressure declines to the point that it's no longer sufficient to drive hydrocarbons to the surface. This doesn't mean that all of the oil and gas in the field is gone; rather, depending on the field's characteristics, as little as 5 percent to 10 percent of the total oil in the field may have been recovered when primary production is exhausted.[15]

Producers rarely allow a well to reach the point where primary production ceases. Companies employ a wide variety of techniques to boost or attempt to stem the decline of reservoir pressures. Waterflooding is among the more commonly used techniques; it typically involves injecting water into a field to boost pressures, sweep oil toward wells, and stimulate production. Producers also routinely re-inject natural gas produced with oil back into the reservoir to keep pressures high.

As a field ages, producers can try even more techniques such as injecting CO_2 into the field. Unlike water, CO_2 is miscible with oil, and this helps it reach areas of the field untouched by waterflooding. And producers can also install pumps, either surface horsehead type pumps or so-called electric submersible pumps (ESP) that help the flow of oil to the surface when natural pressures decline.

In the case of the North Sea, the Norwegian Ministry of Petroleum and Energy estimates that the recoverable resources on the Norwegian continental shelf total 13 billion cubic meters of oil equivalent. Of that total the Ministry estimates that only 35 percent have been recovered and sold. Yet, even with close to two-thirds of expected total recoverable oil and gas still in the ground, Norway has experienced a steady decline in oil production since 2001, and those declines are expected to continue.[16] The UK faces a similar situation. BP recently estimated production from the UK's North Sea fields will drop by around 5 percent per year in coming years, and this could prove a conservative estimate if investment in the region isn't stepped up significantly.[17]

Another common misconception is that increased drilling activity can reverse the decline rate of fields once they've passed peak. Figure 5.6 shows the total number of wells drilled in the UK section of the North Sea going back to 1964.

Figure 5.6 breaks down the wells drilled by type. Exploration wells are wells drilled in the process of looking for new oil and gas fields, while appraisal wells are drilled to help confirm the size of a deposit. Development wells are drilled to actually produce oil and/or natural gas from a field. The number of wells drilled in the North Sea has remained relatively high in the years after production peaked in the play. In fact, drilling activity ticked higher from 2006 through 2008 amid rising commodity prices only to fall back in 2009 due to the global financial crisis. In other words, even though production from the North Sea began to fall sharply, producers continued to drill. Wells in the North Sea simply became less productive after the region saw its peak output.

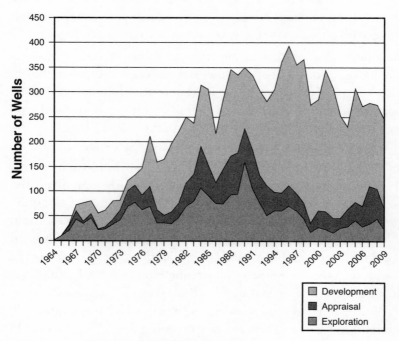

Figure 5.6   UK North Sea drilling activity.

(Source: UK Department of Energy and Climate Change)

North Sea oil production has peaked and will continue to fall in coming years—even though most of the recoverable oil in the region remains untapped. Production has fallen despite continued strong drilling activity and high commodity prices in recent years that have made targeting smaller pockets of oil in the region economic.

The Death of Cantarell

The North Sea is just one example of a major oil-producing region that's seen peak production. In even worse shape is Mexico, where production topped out at 3.4 million barrels per day in 2004 and declined to 3 million barrels per day in 2007 and 2.8 million in 2008.

According to Petroleos Mexicanos (Pemex), Mexico's state-owned national oil company, production will total just 2.5 million barrels per day in 2010, and exports will be in the neighborhood of 1.1 million barrels per day—down more than 40 percent from 2004. This is a major problem for Mexico's fiscal health, as roughly 40 percent of the government's revenue comes from oil exports. There are also significant implications for the US, as Mexico was, until recently, the second-largest oil supplier to its northern neighbor.

Mexico's two largest oilfields are Cantarell and Ku-Maloob-Zaap (KMZ), both located offshore in the bay of Campeche, part of the Gulf of Mexico. These aren't deepwater oilfields; the average water depth is 150 feet, so both Cantarell and KMZ can be drilled using simple jackup drilling rigs, a type of rig with legs that touch the seafloor. In 2008 these two fields combined accounted for roughly 63 percent of Mexico's total oil production.[18]

Cantarell is named after a fisherman who discovered the field in 1976 when he noticed a slick of oil floating on the surface of the bay of Campeche that was fouling his fishing nets. It's one of the largest fields ever discovered anywhere in the world and was for many years the most prolific producer in the Americas.

Table 5.1 ranks the largest oilfields ever discovered by estimated ultimate recoverable reserves (URR). On the basis of URR, Cantarell is the 12th largest oilfield ever discovered. It also ranks as the third largest field discovered outside the Middle East. Figure 5.7 illustrates the data on Cantarell's, KMZ's, and Mexico's total offshore production going back to 1981.

Much like production from the North Sea in the late 1980s, production from Cantarell began to level off in the late 1980s and early 1990s. To combat this process Pemex drilled more aggressively and upgraded many of the platforms, pipelines, and other basic infrastructure in the field's production. The de-bottlenecking efforts began to yield some uptick in production by the late 1990s. Then, Pemex undertook an even more ambitious development plan. The company built the world's largest nitrogen plant and began injecting the gas into the field in 1998.[19] This USD6 billion project worked: Cantarell production nearly doubled between 1996 and 2004.

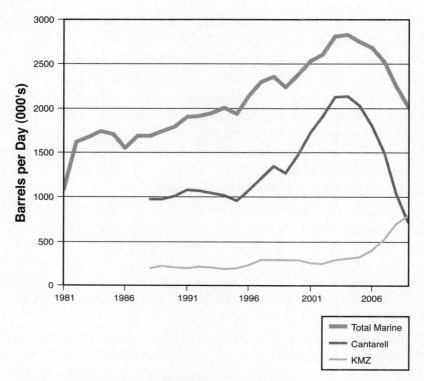

Figure 5.7   Mexican marine oil production.

(Source: Pemex Statistical Yearbook)

TABLE 5.1   Largest Oilfields Ever Discovered

Field Name	Country	Discovery Year	Production Start	Range of URR (billions of barrels)
Ghawar	Saudi Arabia	1948	1951	66–150
Greater Burgan	Kuwait	1938	1945	32–75
Safaniya	Saudi Arabia	1951	1957	21–55
Rumaila North and South	Iraq	1953	1955	19–30
Bolivar Coastal	Venezuela	1917	1917	14–30
Samotlor	Russia	1961	1964	28
Kirkuk	Iraq	1927	1934	15–25

TABLE 5.1   Largest Oilfields Ever Discovered

Field Name	Country	Discovery Year	Production Start	Range of URR (billions of barrels)
Berri	Saudi Arabia	1964	1967	10–25
Manifa	Saudi Arabia	1957	1964	11–23
Shaybah	Saudi Arabia	1968	1998	7–22
Zakum	Abu Dhabi	1964	1967	17–21
Cantarell	Mexico	1976	1979	11–20
Zuluf	Saudi Arabia	1965	1973	11–20
Abqaiq	Saudi Arabia	1941	1946	13–19
East Baghdad	Iraq	1979	1989	11–19
Daqing	China	1959	1962	13–18
Romashkino	Russia	1948	1949	17
Khurais	Saudi Arabia	1957	1963	13–19
Ahwaz	Iran	1958	1959	13–15
Gashsaran	Iran	1928	1939	12–14

(Source: Frederik Robelius, Giant Oil Fields—The Highway to Oil, [Uppsala, Sweden: Uppsala University, 2007])

But ultimately nitrogen injection can't counteract a field's natural decline. In the case of Cantarell, the project appears to have accelerated the long-run rate of decline. As of May 2009 production from Cantarell had dropped to barely 700,000 barrels per day, its lowest level since the early 1980s. Pemex plans to stabilize that decline, but these efforts will be expensive. At any rate nothing can reverse Cantarell's maturation and terminal production decline.

KMZ is smaller in terms of total reserves, but in 2009 it overtook Cantarell to become Mexico's most productive field. KMZ's history resembles that of Cantarell. It's been reported in energy industry media that KMZ is beginning to produce larger quantities of water and salt and less oil.[20] Higher water cuts suggest the water in the field has bypassed the oil; it's a good indication production has peaked.

Mexico plans to invest more in Cantarell and KMZ in an effort to mitigate the inevitable production declines. The country has also been pushing ahead with more aggressive development of some of its larger onshore fields such as Chicontepec with mixed results. But even if these efforts bear some fruit, Mexico is on pace to become a net importer of oil within a decade at the latest.

Fallen Giants

We know enough about the general patterns of oil production from individual fields and regions to know that it's inevitable that overall oil production will ultimately follow a similar path. But the oil-producing countries of the North Sea and Mexico are both outside OPEC. Some market observers argue that although non-OPEC oil production may not see much growth, OPEC's vast oil reserves will be enough to keep global oil production from peaking for years to come.

The bell-curve production pattern is only directly relevant for fields that are produced at more or less full capacity; non-OPEC countries typically try to maximize the production rate and ultimate recovery from fields. But OPEC fields are often voluntarily restrained and not produced at full capacity. For example, when OPEC cuts its official quota, member nations idle wells in their key fields to comply with the group's decision. Because production from fields inside OPEC is artificially restrained, it doesn't follow the same pattern as, for example, Cantarell. This doesn't mean, however, that there are no conclusions to be drawn from the experience of the North Sea and Cantarell. Ultimately, even at reduced production rates, OPEC fields also experience falling pressure and reduced production. Restraining production can create a longer plateau at the top of the bell curve but can't repeal the basic laws of geology and petroleum production.

In particular, as Table 5.1 details, 8 of the 20 largest fields ever discovered are located in Saudi Arabia. The Desert Kingdom is also one of the only countries in the world that has reliable spare production capacity; it has idle wells and fields that it can bring into production at any time. This additional output can be brought on-stream quickly and sustained for a prolonged period as needed to meet global demand. Saudi Arabia generally has 70 percent or more of the total spare capacity claimed by OPEC, and its spare capacity is considered far more reliable than any other OPEC nation. This swing capacity gives Saudi Arabia tremendous power in the global oil markets. And the country has projects in place to expand its spare production capacity over the next few years and solidify its position as the global swing supplier.

All told, Saudi Arabia's official production capacity will likely grow to around 12.5 million barrels a day over the next few years up from 10.5 million at the end of 2008. With massive investments under way, some believe that Saudi Arabia could, over time, push capacity up to as high as 15 million barrels a day. But there are two key points about the impact of these production capacity increases.

First, even if Saudi Arabia can achieve and sustain 12.5 million barrels a day of production capacity, the Desert Kingdom's spare capacity is likely to fall over time. Strong demand growth from emerging markets coupled with declining production from mature non-OPEC fields like Cantarell and the North Sea will boost the demand for OPEC oil; as the only real source of OPEC spare capacity, Saudi Arabia will need to dip into its excess capacity to balance global demand. The alternative: Saudi Arabia could pump less oil, allowing the price to rise and choke off demand. Second, several analysts have called into question Saudi Arabia's ability to actually meet and sustain its production goals. The main problem is that Saudi Arabia and Saudi Aramco are secretive about actual capacity and detailed production data from individual fields, including supergiants like Ghawar.

In his 2005 book *Twilight in the Desert*, Matthew Simmons analyzes evidence from a wide variety of sources, including technical papers from the Society of Petroleum Engineers (SPE). His conclusion: Supergiant fields in Saudi Arabia, including Ghawar, are rapidly maturing and soon will begin to see declining production—if that peak hasn't already occurred. Ghawar has at times produced more than 5 million barrels a day; it's the world's largest, most prolific, most important field. If Ghawar is likely to see significant production declines in coming years that would be a matter of paramount importance to global oil supply. Simmons also concluded that production from smaller fields won't be able to offset declines from the giants.[21]

Although it's unclear whether Simmons is correct, one point is certain: The world has historically relied extensively on production from a relatively small number of giant oilfields for the bulk of its production. The normal definition of what constitutes a giant field is any field with estimated URR of more than 500 million barrels; all of the world's 20 largest oilfields outlined in Table 5.1 are, of course, giants. The total number of giant fields discovered worldwide is small: As of 2005, only 507 oilfields, roughly 1 percent of all fields ever discovered, fit this definition.[22] However, it's estimated that 60 percent of global production and 65 percent of total global URR are found in these fields. The top 1 percent of oilfields exerts an outsized influence on global production. The wider implication is that if production from giant oilfields such as Ghawar and Cantarell is declining or nearing peak then so is global oil production as a whole. Moreover, it's unlikely that the development of smaller, nongiant fields will be enough to offset that decline.[23]

Unfortunately, data on production from the world's largest oilfields is spotty, but several researchers have managed to compile estimates of production from global giant fields. The general conclusion is that patterns of change in production from the world's 20 largest fields and 500 giant fields track total global production well; understanding where these fields are on the production bell curve is the key to understanding global oil production.[24,25]

A closer look at global giant field production reveals some alarming trends. Most of the world's existing giants are decades old, and fewer new giants are being discovered. The giant fields that have been discovered in recent years are smaller on average than giants discovered in decades past. Figure 5.8 offers a closer look at the pattern of giant field discoveries over time.

The 1960s were a golden age for giant field discoveries. In that single decade more than a quarter of all current reserves in giant fields were discovered. Since then the number and size of new giant field discoveries has waned at a rapid pace. What's striking is that many observers assume that the better technologies and equipment available today—such as seismic mapping, computer-aided simulations, and powerful drilling rigs capable of accessing deepwater fields—would accelerate the discovery of giant fields. But that's not the case. In the three decades since 1980, only around 12 percent of the world's giant oil reserves were found, less than half the amount discovered in the 1960s alone.

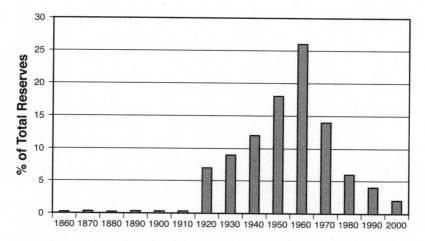

Figure 5.8   Giant field discoveries versus reserves. Note: Chart shows giant oilfield discoveries by decade as a percent of current total giant field reserves.

(Source: Wayne Kelley et al., "Proposition: Global Effort to Model Largest Oil Fields," Oil and Gas Journal, June 8, 2009.)

A quick glance at the details of the 20 largest oilfields presented in Table 5.1 shows that the giants of the giants have been in production for an average of more than 50 years. Of the 20 oil fields in Table 5.1 only Shaybah and Cantarell are less than three decades old, and the latter is known to be well past peak. In addition, Cantarell is the last oilfield discovered to produce at a rate of greater than 1 million barrels a day; in production terms, Shaybah is not as prolific.

Table 5.2 presents data on the actual production behavior of 261 giant oilfields worldwide that have passed their peak production levels.

TABLE 5.2   Production Behavior of Giant Oilfields

All Giants	Mean	Median
Depletion-at-peak	8.10%	7.20%
Decline rate	-6.50%	-5.30%
Cum. production/URR-at-peak	38.60%	38.30%
Discovery-to-first oil	5.2 years	3.0 years

TABLE 5.2   Production Behavior of Giant Oilfields

All Giants	Mean	Median
First oil-to-decline	17.7 years	13.0 years
Non-OPEC Fields		
Depletion-at-peak	9.10%	8.00%
Decline rate	-7.50%	-6.30%
Cum. Production/URR-at-peak	42.20%	41.40%
Discovery-to-first oil	5 years	3.0 years
First oil-to-decline	19.1 years	14.0 years
OPEC Fields		
Depletion-at-peak	6.30%	5.90%
Decline rate	-4.80%	-4.10%
Cum. Production/URR-at-peak	32.40%	31.60%
Discovery-to-first oil	5.6 years	3.0 years
First oil-to-decline	15.6 years	12.0 years

(Source: Mikael Hook, Bengt Soderbergh, Kristofer Jakobsson, Kjell Aleklett, Natural Resources Research, vol. 18, no. 1, March 2009)

Table 5.2 lists five key data points covering all giant fields, within OPEC and outside it. Depletion-at-peak is the rate of production compared to ultimately recoverable reserves (URR) in a field's peak year of production. Looking at the population of all giant fields, in the year of peak production the average field produces about 8.1 percent of total URR. The number is higher for non-OPEC than OPEC countries because within OPEC production is often restrained to comply with production quotas. In addition, the average giant oilfield peaks when 38.6 percent of its total estimated URR has been produced. Post-peak production declines at an average annualized rate of 6.5 percent. And it takes just under 18 years for the average giant field to go from first oil production to peak oil production.

When viewed in light of this data, the age of the world's largest oilfields is cause for alarm. Ghawar has been in production for nearly 60 years, more than three times the average time it takes for giant fields to hit peak production. Roughly 70 billion barrels of oil have been produced from Ghawar since it began yielding oil in 1951, and the highest estimates for total URR are around 150 billion barrels. Close to half the field's total reserves have already been produced, well above the average of 38.6 for all fields in Table 5.1. It's estimated that if Ghawar continues to produce at a rate of around 5 million barrels a day, each year the field yields another 1.9 billion barrels of oil. Undoubtedly, production from the field has been restrained since the 1980s to allow it to produce at a plateau level for a longer period of time. And the quality of the Ghawar reservoir is considered extremely high. However, the sheer age and maturity of the field lends a ring of truth to Simmons's conclusions that the field is near—or past—peak.

Global oil production is running on a treadmill—for producers to generate actual production growth they must first offset ongoing production declines from mature oilfields. The world needs a certain base level of drilling activity and new field discoveries just to maintain current production capacity. According to a study of 580 global oilfields conducted by the IEA, the average annual decline rate for post-peak oilfields is about 5.1 percent. The IEA estimates that with no additional spending on these older fields the natural annual decline rate would be closer to 9 percent.

Let's put that decline into perspective: If current production declines by 5.1 percent annually, global oil producers must find and develop new resources with total production equal to that of Saudi Arabia every three years just to maintain current production.[26,27] And the IEA believes the global decline rate is accelerating because of producers' increased focused on faster-declining offshore and smaller oilfields—speeding up the global oil treadmill. Producers will need to increase their investments in coming years just to offset accelerating natural declines in fields that are past their peak production. This will make it even harder to grow global production enough to meet demand.

The end of easy oil is a reality. Output from the large, cheap-to-produce giants that have been the mainstays of global production for decades is declining. Producers are turning to more expensive, difficult-to-produce fields.

Replacing easy oil production with hard-to-produce crude spells higher prices and myriad opportunities for investors.

Endnotes

[1] J. T. Henry, *The Early and Later History of Petroleum* (Philadelphia: Rodgers & Company, 1873).

[2] Ibid.

[3] Neil McElwee, "When Kerosene Was King," Oil 150, http://www.oil150.com/essays/2007/02/when-kerosene-was-king (accessed November 22, 2009).

[4] J. T. Henry, *The Early and Later History of Petroleum* (Philadelphia: Rodgers & Company, 1873).

[5] Ida M. Tarbell, *The History of the Standard Oil Company* (New York: McClure, Phillips, 1904).

[6] Walter S. Tower, *A History of the US Whaling Industry* (Philadelphia: John C. Winston, 1907).

[7] J. T. Henry, *The Early and Later History of Petroleum* (Philadelphia: Rodgers & Company, 1873).

[8] Walter S. Tower, *A History of the US Whaling Industry* (Philadelphia: John C. Winston, 1907).

[9] EIA Annual Energy Review 2008, http://www.eia.doe.gov/emeu/aer/append_e.html (accessed December 10, 2009).

[10] Bureau of Transportation Statistics, http://www.bts.gov/publications/national_transportation_statistics/html/table_04_09.html (accessed December 24, 2009).

[11] EIA Annual Energy Review, http://www.eia.doe.gov/emeu/aer/txt/ptb0513d.html (accessed December 21, 2009).

[12] Dominic Ziegler, "The Weakest Link," *The Economist*, February 6, 2003.

[13] EIA International Energy Outlook, 2009 http://www.eia.doe.gov/oiaf/archive/ieo99/oil.html (accessed December 31, 2009).

[14] BP Statistical Review of World Energy 2009, http://www.bp.com/productlanding.do?categoryId=6929&contentId=7044622.

[15] Charles F. Conaway, *The Petroleum Industry: A Nontechnical Guide* (Tulsa: PennWell, 1999).

[16] Ministry of Petroleum and Energy, "Norway's Oil and Gas Resources," http://www.regjeringen.no/en/dep/oed/Subject/Oil-and-Gas/Norways-oil-and-gas-resources.html?id=443528 (accessed January 4, 2010).

[17] Sam Fleming, "BP's Grim Warning over Growing Cost of North Sea Oil," Daily Mail, June 10, 2009, http://www.dailymail.co.uk/money/article-1192193/BPs-grim-warning-growing-cost-North-Sea-oil.html (accessed January 4, 2010).

[18] PEMEX Statistical Yearbook 2009.

[19] Offshore Technology, "Cantarell Oil Field, Gulf of Mexico, Mexico," http://www.offshore-technology.com/projects/cantarell/.

[20] Sam Fletcher, "Pemex, PDVSA, Petrobras: How Strategies, Results Differ," *Oil & Gas Journal*, August 3, 2009.

[21] Matthew R. Simmons, *Twilight in the Desert* (Hoboken: Wiley, 2005).

[22] Frederik Robelius, *Giant Oil Fields—The Highway to Oil* (Uppsala, Sweden: Uppsala University, 2007), http://uu.diva-portal.org/smash/record.jsf?pid=diva2:169774 (accessed January 5, 2010).

[23] Wayne Kelley, D. Ron Harrell, Richard S. Bishop, and Kirby Wells, "Proposition: Global Effort to Model Largest Oil Fields," *Oil & Gas Journal*, June 8, 2009.

[24] Ibid.

[25] Frederik Robelius, *Giant Oil Fields*.

[26] IEA World Energy Outlook 2008, http://www.worldenergyoutlook.org/docs/weo2008/chapter10.pdf, (accessed February 11, 2010).

[27] McKinsey Oil Supply-Demand presentation to the Society of petroleum Engineers April 15, 2009.

6

To the Ends of the Earth

From 2007 to 2009, as the US economy slowly sank into the most vicious economic downturn in three decades, demand for oil crashed. Exports of crude from Saudi Arabia fell below 1 million barrels a day for the first time in two decades. Plenty of market observers wondered aloud whether the US had seen peak demand for oil and predicted that crude oil prices would remain depressed for years to come as a result. Meanwhile, the Chinese economy bounced back more quickly than most economists dared hope at the beginning of the year. And even as Saudi Arabia's exports to the West plummeted, shipments to China soared above 1 million barrels a day. China overtook the US to become Saudi Arabia's largest oil export market.

This fundamental shift is symptomatic of a larger trend: The center of global demand for most commodities, including oil, is moving from the developed to the developing world. These countries are now reaping the benefits of the Oil Age just as their counterparts in the Western world did decades ago.

The quintessential example of "hard" oil is deepwater production and a massive global play that's been dubbed the Deepwater Golden Triangle.

The original Golden Triangle was the rough triangular region around Beaumont, Port Arthur, and Orange, Texas. On January 10, 1901, a group of drillers led by Pattillo Higgins and Captain Anthony Lucas struck oil just south of Beaumont. The well, drilled in a geologic formation known as the Spindletop salt dome, was a true gusher. The initial strike sent a geyser of oil 150 feet into the air and took nine days to bring under control. After the well was finally stabilized, it produced 100,000 barrels of oil per day, an unheard-of production rate in modern times.

The Spindletop well was so prolific it's referred to as "The Gusher." The discovery of the Spindletop oilfield set off an oil boom of epic proportions. The population of Beaumont alone tripled in the first three months after the discovery. The Spindletop discovery well was a simple vertical well drilled to a total depth of a bit more than 1,000 feet. The wells drilled in the flurry that followed were so prolific that the resulting glut of oil sent prices tumbling. In 2008 dollars, prices collapsed from over USD30 a barrel in 1900 to less than USD15 by 1905.[1]

Even today, more than a half century after oil production in the region finally ended, the Texas Golden Triangle remains a hub of the US petroleum, refining, and chemical industries.

The Deepwater Golden Triangle encompasses three major regions for deepwater exploration and development: Brazil, the Gulf of Mexico, and West Africa. The contrast between the easy-to-produce oilfields of the Texas Golden Triangle and the technically complex wells of the Deepwater Golden Triangle is telling.

Consider the case of the Tiber oilfield in the deepwater US Gulf of Mexico. British oil giant BP (London: BP, NYSE: BP) announced the discovery of the field in late 2009 after drilling a well in the Keathley Canyon Block 102, located roughly 250 miles southeast of Houston, Texas. The discovery well was drilled in water 4,132 feet deep. That's certainly deep enough to be considered a deepwater field but isn't remarkable in its own right; producers have successfully drilled wells in waters well over 10,000 feet deep. What's remarkable about Tiber is that the well BP drilled was 35,055 feet long, or more than 6.6 miles.[2] When the discovery was announced, the Tiber well was the largest, deepest well ever drilled anywhere in the world.

BP owns 62 percent of Tiber and is the operator of the field, while Brazilian national oil company Petrobras (NYSE: PBR) and US integrated giant ConocoPhillips (NYSE: COP) own 20 percent and 18 percent of the play, respectively. It will take considerable time for the Tiber partners to drill additional wells and accurately estimate the total size or recoverable reserves in Tiber. But BP did announce that it believes Tiber to be larger than its 2006 Kaskida find, located roughly 45 miles from Tiber. Workers at Kaskida encountered an

800-foot thick column of oil and natural gas that's estimated to contain more than 3 billion barrels of oil equivalent. If Tiber is larger than Kaskida, the field is, in all likelihood, a true giant.[3]

The technical complexity of drilling a well like Tiber is immense. In fact, until Chevron (NYSE: CVX) successfully drilled its Jack discovery in the Lower Tertiary Gulf in 2006, many pundits felt that actually drilling a well in these conditions and successfully producing oil was technically impossible. Pressures in deepwater fields like Tiber can top 10,000 pounds per square inch (PSI), roughly 700 times atmospheric pressure on Earth at sea level. Pressures that extreme can damage pipes and equipment or simply cause a well to collapse, rendering it unproductive. To produce oil (or natural gas) from such a well requires the use of specialized equipment and techniques. Hiring the rig powerful enough to drill a deepwater well can cost upward of USD600,000 per day.

To make matters worse, oil located that far below the seafloor exists at extreme temperatures; it's estimated that the oil in Tiber is more than 250 degrees Fahrenheit (121 degrees Celsius).[4] Meanwhile, the temperature at the seafloor, where the well is produced, is just above freezing. When superheated oil hits a pipeline running through ice-cold water it creates tremendous stress on equipment. Moreover, the extreme temperature shifts can cause oil to thicken or solidify, restricting production. Simply drilling an ultra-deepwater well of that length is a challenge. Many deepwater oilfields, including Tiber, are found in rock layers located beneath a thick layer of salt. Because the salt located deep beneath the seafloor is at high temperatures, it's constantly shifting, putting tremendous strain on pipes and equipment. And wells drilled through salt have a tendency to collapse, threatening productivity.

A productive deepwater development involves a great deal more than drilling a few wells. Producers must build floating production platforms to handle and process output from deepwater wells and design subsea pipelines and equipment to control and transport oil from subsea wells to these floating platforms. Building out the infrastructure to produce these fields takes years; for example, Chevron's Tahiti field in the Gulf was discovered in 2002 but didn't see first production until 2009, and the project cost Chevron and its partners USD2.7 billion.[5]

Several of the larger fields discovered in the Deepwater Golden Triangle over the past three years won't reach peak production until 2020 or later. Producers are aggressively targeting deepwater plays simply because that's where the world's remaining major concentrations of hydrocarbons are to be found. The easy oil is largely gone.

Many investors want to know just how expensive it is to produce oil from deepwater fields. The truth is no one can tell you with any degree of certainty because deepwater oil production is still a relatively new, cutting-edge technology. Estimates range from USD30 to more than USD70 per barrel. Costs vary widely by region; moving equipment and labor into place in the Gulf of Mexico, for example, is easier than offshore Africa. Rather than seek inaccurate estimates of the cost of deepwater production, focus on what happened to capital spending on global oil projects when crude tumbled from close to USD150 per barrel in the summer of 2008 to less than USD40 by the end of the year. According to estimates from Douglas-Westwood and Barclay's, total offshore capital spending declined by 6 percent to 9 percent in 2009 from 2008 levels.[6] That's despite the fact that crude oil prices only remained depressed for roughly six months before recovering to over USD70 a barrel.

According to Douglas-Westwood, global deepwater production accounted for just 2 percent of total world oil output as recently as 2002, but by 2015 it's expected to account for around 12 percent. To support this growth in production, total offshore capital and operating expenditures will grow dramatically, from USD260 billion in 2008 to USD360 billion by 2013. Douglas-Westwood sees spending on deepwater drilling alone at around USD30 billion annually by 2013, when total offshore spending on drilling will reach USD89 billion a year. Offshore operations and maintenance spending is forecast to total USD330 billion between 2009 and 2014.[7] The growing importance of tough-to-produce deepwater fields as a source of oil production growth implies higher oil prices for the foreseeable future.

In spite of all these complexities, the deepwater is one of the only regions of the world where producers are discovering giant and supergiant oilfields. That means deepwater will continue to see development, and producers with strong positions in the best deepwater regions will benefit by producing more oil in an environment of rising demand and higher prices.

To play the coming rise in global oil demand and the end of easy oil, seek exposure to the world's few remaining sources of rising hydrocarbon production and the firms that facilitate their development.

Brazil: King of the Deep

Brazil is currently the second-largest oil producer in South America, behind Venezuela. But there's a big difference between these two nations. Brazil's production has been rising steadily in recent years, while Venezuela's output has plummeted.

According to the *BP Statistical Review of World Energy*, from 1998 through 2008, Brazilian oil production increased 90 percent, or roughly 900,000 barrels per day. Meanwhile, Venezuelan production plummeted by more than a quarter, about 920,000 barrels per day. This trend is forecast to continue. There's considerable promise in Venezuela's heavy oil Orinoco Belt, but the Chavez government's antagonistic policy toward foreign companies operating in Venezuela has hampered investment.

The contrast between Brazil's national oil company (NOC), Petroleo Brasileiro (Petrobras) (NYSE: PBR), and Petroleos de Venezuela SA (PDVSA) couldn't be more stark. Petrobras and the Brazilian government have allowed contracts to be structured so that they encourage foreign investment in Brazilian fields. Without that investment and the technical know-how offered by foreign producers, it wouldn't be possible to produce Brazil's prolific fields. Brazil is almost unique among global producers in that the vast majority of its oil production comes from offshore fields. Petrobras accounts for more than 95 percent of Brazil's total oil production and close to 90 percent of its output is from offshore fields. The importance of offshore production to Brazil's total output has grown steadily over time from around half in the early 1980s to 75 percent in the mid-1990s. With most of Brazil's production growth slated to come from offshore fields, the percentage contribution should continue to rise.[8]

Historically, most of Brazil's offshore production has come from a region known as the Campos Basin, located east of Rio de Janeiro. In 2009, for example, Campos Basin production accounted for more than 82 percent of the nation's total oil output. But the Santos Basin, an area located offshore south of Rio, has yielded some of Petrobras's largest discoveries in recent years and will account for much of Brazil's production growth going forward.

The most exciting finds in Brazil have come in ultra-deepwater pre-salt fields. Most of the deepwater Gulf of Mexico finds in recent years, including Tiber, are also found beneath a layer of salt that complicates drilling. Petrobras's pre-salt finds are some of the largest discovered anywhere in the world in decades, and as the company ramps up development of these finds it will generate some of the most impressive production growth of any major oil company in the world. As Figure 6.1 shows, Petrobras plans to ramp up crude oil production from around 2 million barrels per day in 2009 to nearly 4 million in 2020, largely thanks to strong growth from pre-salt fields.

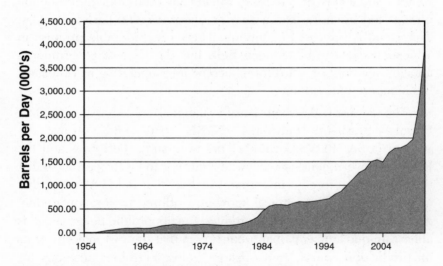

Figure 6.1   Petrobras total oil and NGL production.

(Source: Petrobras Operational Highlights, Petrobras 2009-2013 Strategic Plan)

Four of the most exciting Brazilian pre-salt finds are Tupi, Iara, Guara, and Carioca. Petrobras began announcing that it had made a major oil find in the deepwater Santos Basin in 2006. The company formally announced the discovery and initial analysis of Tupi in late 2007 after its second successful well test in the region. The field is located in waters 6,000 feet deep in the Santos Basin. The field itself is between 9,000 and 12,000 feet beneath the seafloor under a layer of salt as much as 2 kilometers thick. The company has since conducted additional appraisal drilling and believes the field to contain 5 to 8 billion barrels of oil. Many believe Petrobras is being conservative about the size of the find and will upgrade estimates as it completes extended well tests. But even if reserves estimates remain unchanged, Tupi is a giant find, the largest in the Americas since Cantarell in the 1970s. Petrobras envisions total production from Tupi reaching over 1 million barrels a day in 2020.[9]

Petrobras has a 65 percent stake in Tupi, while BG Group (London: BG/, OTC: BRGYY) holds a 25 percent stake and Portuguese operator GALP Energia (Lisbon: GALP) the final 10 percent. BG Group has partnered with Petrobras on some of its largest finds and is even more bullish than the Brazilian NOC on the prospects for Tupi.

The Petrobras extends beyond Brazil. The NOC operates nearly a quarter of the world's deepwater production—it has as much or more experience in the deep than any other company in the world. Petrobras has become a natural partner on deepwater projects all over the world, including the other two legs of the Deepwater Golden Triangle, the Gulf of Mexico, and offshore West Africa. Petrobras is the premier global deepwater play, and the partly state-owned firm has preferential access to Brazilian deepwater finds.[10]

BG Group, Petrobras's partner on many of its key finds, is another interesting play on deepwater Brazil. BG is also one of the world's top plays on natural gas and liquefied natural gas (LNG).

China also clearly recognizes the importance of Brazil's deepwater oil finds. During the heart of the global credit crisis in late 2008 and early 2009, there was considerable speculation that Petrobras would have trouble funding its ambitious 2009-to-2013 investment plan. Some pundits felt the country would delay development of key fields until commodity prices rebounded. China saw that as an opportunity, and in early 2009 the China Development Bank agreed to loan USD10 billion to Petrobras. Although that might not seem a huge sum, at the time even the strongest, most creditworthy companies in the world had trouble getting credit. As part of the deal Petrobras agreed to sell as much as 100,000 barrels of oil per year to Chinese energy giant Sinopec (NYSE: SNP).[11]

The Deepwater Gulf

US oil production peaked in the early 1970s at close to 11 million barrels a day and has fallen steadily to less than 7 million barrels a day in recent years. One of the few bright spots for US production is the deepwater Gulf of Mexico.

Total US deepwater production is slated to soar from less than 2 percent of US production in 1990 to around one-third of total output this decade.

The largest field discovered in the US Gulf of Mexico to date is BP's Thunder Horse. Discovered in 1999, the field finally achieved maximum production in 2009, at least four years behind BP's original schedule, due to a series of delays in the construction of infrastructure to support production. Thunder Horse is estimated to contain nearly 3 billion barrels of oil, while the Thunder Horse North section of the field contains another 691 million barrels.[12]

Thunder Horse is located in the Mississippi Canyon of the Gulf of Mexico in waters of 5,600 to 6,500 feet deep. At full capacity Thunder Horse produces 250,000 barrels of oil a day and 200 million cubic feet of natural gas, making it the second-largest producing field in the US behind Alaska's Prudhoe Bay. Underground pressures in the field are as high as 18,000 PSI, and temperatures reach 275 degrees Fahrenheit (135 degrees Celsius).[13] BP has a 75 percent interest in the field, while Exxon Mobil (NYSE: XOM) owns the remaining 25 percent stake. In addition to Thunder Horse, BP also operates the Atlantis, Dorado, and King South Fields. The company is the largest producer in the deepwater Gulf and has the largest acreage leased in the region.

BP is also the leader in a number of major new discoveries, including the Tiber and Kaskida fields in the Lower Tertiary Gulf that may rival or exceed Thunder Horse in terms of total reserves. Although these new discoveries won't contribute to production for years to come, they should help cement BP's leading position in the deepwater Gulf over time.

US oil giant Chevron (NYSE: CVX) also has an attractive position in the deepwater Gulf. The company's Jack and St. Malo fields, discovered in 2004 and 2003, respectively, are each projected to contain nearly 400 million barrels of oil and should see first production by 2014. On 2009 Chevron started work at its Tahiti field, where total production is designed to ramp up to around 125,000 barrels a day.[14]

BP and Chevron both have attractive positions in the deepwater Gulf, but they are far from pure plays on the region. Both companies are major integrated oils with diversified exposure across many different regions. That said, both Chevron and BP have solid exposure to deepwater production globally and represent good, safety-first plays on the expanding importance of deepwater fields in global oil production.

US-based Anadarko (NYSE: APC) stands out among the smaller independent oil companies with exposure to the deepwater Gulf. The company produces around 150,000 barrels of oil equivalent per day in the deepwater Gulf, with around half of that coming in the form of oil and natural gas liquids (NGL). In most cases, Anadarko isn't the operator of these deepwater fields but has stakes in the production.

The April 2010 explosion at a BP-owned rig that caused the leakage of an estimated 25,000 barrels per day into the Gulf will almost certainly lead to tighter regulation of offshore drilling in the U.S. Other jurisdictions are likely to take note of the environmental impact and the economic devastation to local tourism and fishing industries on the Gulf. The cost of drilling offshore will increase as the result of this disaster, as will the price of oil.

West Africa

Nigeria and Angola are the largest deepwater producers in Africa.

Most of Angola's production is from offshore fields. The country's NOC, Sonangol, divides the offshore regions in a series of blocks covering shallow-water, deepwater, and ultra-deepwater regions. The blocks are jointly owned by the NOC and various foreign oil companies. Among the most prospective plays, Deepwater Block 14 contains 11 significant oil discoveries. Sonangol has a 2 percent stake, while Chevron, which owns 31 percent, is the operator. Italy's Eni (NYSE: E) and France's Total (NYSE: TOT) each hold 20 percent stakes, and Galp Energia (Lisbon: GALP) has a 9 percent share. The largest producing project in Block 14 is the Benguela, Belize, Lobito, and Tomboco play, which hit peak production of about 200,000 barrels a day in 2008.[15]

A series of new projects is due to come on-stream in Angola through the middle of the decade. The list includes the 200,000 barrels per day Pazflor development operated by Total that's due to hit peak production after 2011. And a series of BP discoveries in Block 31 located in about 6,000 feet of water are due to hit peak output of around 300,000 barrels a day after 2012. All told, planned megaprojects in offshore Angola due to come on-stream between 2009 and 2014 are expected to yield peak output of more than 1.4 million barrels per day.[16]

Angola overtook Nigeria in 2009 to become Africa's largest oil producer, but that was primarily because of political instability in the latter nation's primary oil-producing region, the Niger Delta. Nevertheless, Nigeria contains some attractive deepwater oilfields. The largest is Agbami, located just 70 miles off the coast in water that's roughly 5,000 feet deep. Chevron operates the field and owns a 68.15 percent stake, with Statoil and Petrobras holding 18.85 percent and 13 percent stakes, respectively. The USD5.4 billion project saw first production in 2008 and in 2009 hit its full output of 250,000 barrels per day of oil and 450 million cubic feet of gas.

Chinese firms have made significant investments in offshore energy assets in West Africa. In mid-2009 Sinopec agreed to a USD7.2 billion deal to purchase Canada's Addax Petroleum. Addax had significant exposure to fields in offshore Nigeria. Also in 2009 China National Offshore Oil Company and Sinopec bought Marathon Oil's (NYSE: MRO) 20 percent stake in offshore Block 32 in Angola for USD1.3 billion.[17]

Although Nigeria and Angola dominate current production volumes, some of the largest and most promising discoveries in recent years have been farther to the west off the coasts of Ghana, Liberia, Côte D'Ivoire, and Sierra Leone. Better still from an investor's standpoint, many of the most attractive fields in this emerging region have been discovered and are being developed by smaller, independent producers that offer far more leverage to production upside than producers like Chevron and Exxon Mobil.

London-based Tullow Oil (London: TLW, OTC: TUWOY) announced the discovery of the Jubilee field of the coast of Ghana in the summer of 2007. The field is located in two different offshore license blocks, the Deepwater Tano and the West Cape Three Points, in waters roughly 4,000 feet deep.

What's even more interesting about deepwater plays in Ghana is that Anadarko and other producers believe they may just be a small part of a much larger play that extends westward more than 1,000 kilometers to offshore Sierra Leone. This theory gained additional credence when Anadarko announced it encountered hydrocarbons at its Venus exploration well in 5,900 feet of water offshore Sierra Leone in September 2009. The subsea rock structures and characteristics are similar to what producers have encountered in Ghana, suggesting the entire region between Venus and Jubilee is prospective for oil.

Anadarko owns 40 percent of the Venus prospect and is the operator. Australian giant Woodside Petroleum (Australia: WPL, OTC: WOPEY) and Repsol each own 25 percent, Tullow the remaining 10 percent. Anadarko holds interests in a total of 8 million acres encompassing ten offshore blocks in Sierra Leone, Liberia, Côte D'Ivoire, and Ghana and is the operator on seven of those ten blocks. If the theory holds true, Anadarko would be the leading acreage holder in this emerging West African play.

Going Unconventional

Outside deepwater, unconventional oil and liquids are likely to grow considerably in coming years.

"Unconventional" is a broad term that refers to any liquid fuel that isn't produced using conventional well technologies. Examples include the oil sands of Canada, biofuels such as ethanol, biodiesel, and extra-heavy crude oil. Figure 6.2 details US Energy Information Administration (EIA) estimates for total global unconventional field production in 2030 as compared to 2006.

Three sources of unconventional liquids production stand out: oil sands, extra-heavy oil, and biofuels.

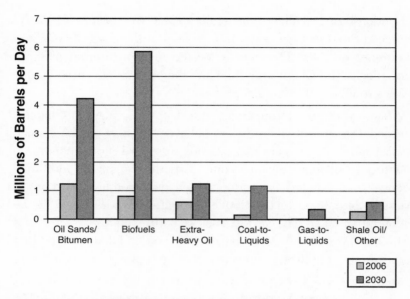

Figure 6.2   World production of unconventional liquid fuels.

(Source: Energy Information Administration)

Oil sands are nothing more than a solid or semisolid hydrocarbon known as bitumen that's mixed with sand, dirt, and water. This bitumen can be processed into refined products, including gasoline and diesel fuel, though the process requires additional steps compared to refining conventional crude. While oil sands have been mined in other countries around the world, Canada is the center of the global industry and is far and away the leading producer and the largest bitumen-reserve holder.

There are two main oil sands production methods: strip mining and in-situ production. Strip mining involves simply scooping large quantities of oil sands and heating them to remove the bitumen from debris. This is practical only for oil sands resources located reasonably close to the surface. In-situ mining is used to produce oil sands located farther under the surface. One common sort of in-situ mining is known as steam-assisted gravity drainage (SAGD). In SAGD, producers drill two horizontal wells. Into one well the producer pumps superheated steam that literally melts the bitumen from the sands. As the bitumen melts, it flows (via gravity) to the lower horizontal well and can be pumped to the surface. It's estimated that roughly 80 percent of Canada's oil sands reserves are located too far under the surface to be produced via strip mining.

The oil sands are a classic resource play—widely distributed with little exploration risk. For surface mining operations, the largest costs are upfront. Most surface mining operations under way or planned in Canada are relatively large-scale projects that also call for building and running an upgrader used to process the bitumen into synthetic crude oil. The synthetic oil can be sold to refiners just like light sweet crude, the highest-value product in the marketplace. But upgraders are expensive and require massive upfront investment so are only economically attractive for relatively large projects.

In-situ projects tend to be smaller. Although some larger projects do have upgraders, that's not often the case. This presents two problems. First, the producer has to find a source of natural gas liquids or synthetic crude oil to use as a diluent; basically, the producer has to mix the bitumen with other products so it will flow through a pipeline. Second, the final product is bitumen, which is priced more like heavy oil than light sweet crude. Not all refineries have upgraders and facilities designed to handle heavy crude. Bitumen trades at a discount to light sweet crude oil or synthetic crude. The advantage of an in-situ operation is that the upfront costs of developing are lower because you don't need to pay for an expensive upgrader.

Operational costs are another big issue for the sands. In in-situ operations, steam is used to heat the bitumen so it can flow into a well. The problem is most steam is produced using natural gas. Producing steam is an energy-intensive process; producing in-situ oil sands requires a large amount of natural gas. Although surface mining operations don't use steam to heat the bitumen for mining purposes, steam is often used to separate bitumen from sand. And natural gas is an important commodity for many upgraders. Hydrogen produced from natural gas, for example, is used to turn bitumen into synthetic crude.

Producing a barrel of crude can require moving two tons of sands. The fuel to power the giant earth-moving equipment used in such operations is diesel. Obviously diesel and natural gas prices are an operational cost.

With nearly a half century's experience in the region, Suncor Energy (TSX: SU, NYSE: SU) is the premier pure play on the Canadian oil sands. As of early 2010, Suncor's annual production from its oil sands properties totaled 350,000 barrels per day, but the company's resources are vast—proved and probable reserves exceed 6 billion barrels of oil equivalent, with potential upside to more than 22 billion barrels on existing properties. Suncor uses both mining and in-situ technology to produce its oil sands reserves.

There's considerable confusion about the actual cost of producing oil sands. The reason is that much of the actual cost is upfront capital associated with building upgraders and other key infrastructure. Suncor's operating costs are roughly USD35 to USD40 per barrel—the company can continue to produce oil from its existing properties even at low prices. However, prices of USD35 to USD40 are far too low to justify investment in new oil sands developments. Based on Suncor's decision to postpone several key projects in late 2008 and early 2009, it appears that oil sands producers need sustained crude prices above the roughly USD70 to justify the massive investments required to build out their capacity.

Chinese firms have been significant investors in Canadian oil sands assets. In 2009 China National Petroleum Company and its subsidiary PetroChina (NYSE: PTR) bought a 60 percent stake in Athabasca Oil Sands Corporation's Mackay River and Dover oil sands projects for USD1.9 billion. Also in 2009, Total (NYSE: TOT) sold a 10 percent stake on the Northern Lights oil sands project to China-based Sinopec, making the two firms 50 percent partners in the USD10.7 billion venture. Sovereign wealth fund China Investment Corp (CIC) bought a 17 percent stake in metals producer Teck Resources (NYSE: TCK), which, in turn, has an interest in the Fort Hills oil sands project.

From a purely geological and reserves standpoint, Venezuela's massive heavy oil reserves in the Orinoco Belt are a highly attractive unconventional oil resource. The Orinoco Belt likely rivals the Canadian oil sands in terms of total resources. But recent moves by the Venezuelan government to nationalize the oil industry and renegotiate contracts with foreign companies operating in the nation have resulted in the exodus of several key producers.

The outlook for PDVSA and Venezuelan energy policy remains highly uncertain, but the nation does contain an impressive resource, and a number of companies have been willing to ignore the obvious political risks to maintain a presence there. With Venezuelan government finances in shambles due to weak production growth, it's likely that some foreign investors are simply seeking a foothold in the South American nation in anticipation of the day when energy policies change.

Nearly three-quarters of Venezuelan oil exports went to the US in 2007. Although the Chavez government has made it a priority to diversify exports away from the US, that's a tough challenge because much of Venezuela's output is heavy sour crude that's tough to refine. US refineries are among the most technically complex in the world, and many have been set up to handle heavy sour crude, making the US the only logical export market for much of PVSA's output.

China and Chinese energy firms have been actively investing in Venezuela. In late 2009 the two countries signed five separate agreements related to the energy industry. China National Offshore Oil Company and Sinopec both announced deals to partner with PDVSA on two separate blocks in the Orinoco Belt. And the two countries also signed an export agreement that could result in greater oil exports from Venezuela destined for the Chinese market.[18]

In early 2010 PDVSA announced the formation of joint ventures (JV) targeting additional blocks in the Orinoco Belt. One JV, covering the Carabobo block, is led by Chevron, the only American firm that's maintained a significant presence in Venezuela since 2007. The second JV, covering the Carabobo 1 Centro and Carabobo 1 Norte blocks, includes several Indian energy firms, headlined by an 11 percent stake for Oil & Natural Gas Corporation (ONGC) (India: ONGC, OTC: ONGCF) and 3.5 percent stakes each for both Oil India Limited (India: OINL) and Indian Petroleum.[19]

Russia has also entered Venezuela. During the President Chavez's two-day visit to Moscow in 2009, PDVSA and Russian companies signed a series of energy agreements. The first was a memorandum of understanding to cooperate in the Orinoco Belt. The initial investment needed in this venture will be more than USD600 million.[20]

The same partners also signed a second deal to develop the Junin-6 block in Orinoco, which would require the investment of as much as USD30 billion over the next 25 years. Russia's monopoly oil transport pipeline company, Transneft (Russia: TRNF, OTC: TRNFF), also plans to partner with PDVSA on the construction of a 1,300 kilometer (800 mile) pipeline to transport oil from Junin-6.[21]

Oil from the Orinoco Belt—the region that's getting the most attention from foreign firms investing in Venezuela—is a classic example of "hard" oil. Oil from the region is extremely heavy, more akin to the oil produced from the oil sands region of Canada than conventional crude. Just like oil from the sands, it doesn't flow naturally into wells and must be extensively upgraded and refined. Much of it is also sour oil, meaning that it has high sulfur content and is extremely corrosive to pipes and equipment.

Russia, Iraq, and Iran

Three traditional major oil producers that have garnered significant interest in recent years are Russia, Iraq, and Iran.

Russia surpassed Saudi Arabia to become the world's largest oil producer in 2009, pumping more than 10 million barrels of crude oil per day in the final months of the year and setting a new post-Soviet era production record.[22] Surging by roughly one-third between 2000 and 2010, Russia's oil production growth has been impressive, and the country will remain among the world's most important producers and exporters for years to come.

That said, growth in Russian production isn't quite as sensational as it first appears. First, the only reason Saudi Arabian output was lower is because of cuts to OPEC quotas put in place to stabilize oil prices after the 2008 commodity price collapse; Saudi Arabia still has the capacity to produce more oil than Russia if demand for that oil were sufficient. More important, the surge in oil production toward the end of the past decade was largely due to the faster-than-anticipated startup of the giant Vankor oilfield operated by Russian energy giant Rosneft.

Vankor is a 900-million barrel field located in located in the western part of what is considered Eastern Siberia. Historically, most of Russia's production has come from Western Siberia, the region closer to Russia's population centers. However, most of the big fields in the western part of the country, such as Russia's largest oilfield, Samotlor, have matured beyond their peak production.

To make up for the decline in the west, Russian producers are turning to remote and inhospitable Eastern Siberian fields such as Vankor and the Sakhalin Island projects. These projects, located amid Arctic conditions, are another example of "hard" oil. The startup of Vankor in late 2009 obscured the continuing decline in production from Western Siberia. But with that startup in the rearview mirror, Russian output is likely to at best remain stagnant in coming years.

China has aggressively pursued deals with its northern neighbor to secure supplies of both oil and natural gas. In early 2010 the two countries reached a USD25 billion long-term deal that will result in more Russian oil going to China. Oil producer Rosneft and pipeline monopoly Transneft will split USD25 billion in loans from the China Development Bank in exchange for around 300,000 barrels a day of increased oil exports over a 20-year period. The exact terms of the deal haven't been disclosed.[23] Rosneft (Russia: ROSN), Transneft, and Lukoil (Russia: LKOH, OTC: LUKOY) are the prime plays on Russia's oil resources, and all three are also active investing in international resources.

As Figure 6.3 shows, Iraq once produced more than 3 million barrels of oil per day, back in the early 1980s, but since that time geopolitical events have hampered the nation's output.

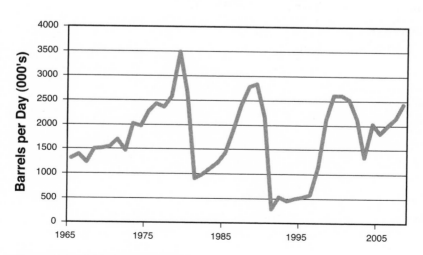

Figure 6.3   Iraq oil production.

(Source: BP Statistical Review of World Energy 2009)

In 2010 Iraqi oil production is finally approaching its pre-war levels of 2.5 million barrels a day, though it's still under its early 1980s high. That's despite the fact that, unlike most regions of the world being explored today, Iraqi oilfields are relatively easy-to-produce, prolific onshore fields. Some analysts believe Iraq's total reserves may approach those of Saudi Arabia; the difference in experience between the two countries in terms of production history is largely the result of Iraq's ongoing instability.

The Iraqi government awarded a series of contracts in 2009 with the goal of boosting the nation's output to as high as 12 million barrels per day. That goal is largely seen as unrealistic, though there's real potential for Iraq to boost production to around 6 million barrels per day in coming years if the country can address "above-ground" security threats that hamper investment in the fields and make it tough for companies to operate. According to a recent study, getting Iraq to 6 million barrels a day of output would require a total investment of USD28 billion to USD43 billion, a tremendous investment in a short period of time.[24]

Table 6.1 details the results of Iraq's first and second major bidding rounds for oil contracts.

TABLE 6.1   Iraq Oilfield Licensing Results

Round 1 (1 of 8 Bids Accepted)	Consortia	Award Plateau
Rumaila	BP/China National Petroleum	1.85 million barrels a day
Round 2 (7 of 10 Bids Accepted)		
Majnoon	Shell and Petronas	1.8 million bbl/day
Qaiyarah	Sonangol	120,000 bbl/day
West Qurna (phase 2)	Lukoil and Statoil	1.8 million bbl/day
Garraf	Petronas/Japex	230,000 bbl/day
Badra	Gazprom/Kogas/Petronas/TPAO	170,000 bbl/day
Najmah	Sonangol	110,000 bbl/day

(Source: Iraq's Official Petroleum Licensing Round Web site [http://www.pcld-iraq.com/index.php])

No major American integrated oil companies won contracts in Iraq, though European giants BP, Royal Dutch Shell, and Statoil all have stakes in various fields. But state-owned and state-sponsored NOCs are setting up to be big players in Iraq, as evidenced by licensing wins for China National Petroleum Corporation, the parent of PetroChina (NYSE: PTR), Malaysia's state-owned Petronas, and Angola's Sonangol.

The better direct investments in Iraq are the oil services firms such as Schlumberger (NYSE: SLB) and Weatherford International (NYSE: WFT), both which stand to benefit from the massive investment needed to meet the production plateau targets that are part of the Iraqi contracts.

Iraq's neighbor, Iran, produces nearly 4.5 million barrels a day, down from a high of more than 6 million barrels a day in the 1970s but up from around 500,000 barrels a day since 2000. Iran's giant oilfields were discovered between the mid-1930s and the late 1960s and are mature. Many observers believe these fields peaked before the 1979 Islamic Revolution, though geopolitical turmoil in the wake of this upheaval undoubtedly hurt production. Nonetheless, the country is still an important producer and with better infrastructure, and more extensive investment could see increased production in coming years.

Strained relations among Western powers and Iran have opened up opportunities for Chinese firms to invest with little real competition. Table 6.2 offers a rundown of recent major deals and investments by Chinese firms in Iran.

TABLE 6.2   China's Oil Deals in Iran

Company (Stake)	Project
China National Petroleum (70%)	$2.25 billion project to develop the South Azadegan oilfield
China National Petroleum (40%)	$4.7 billion to develop South Pars gas field
China National Petroleum	$5.76 billion in two-phase development of North Azedegan oilfield
Sinopec	$2 billion for the development of Yadavaran oilfield

(Source: Paula Dittrick, "Chinese Oil Companies Invest Heavily Abroad," Oil & Gas Journal, *February 8, 2010)*

Beyond the Producers

The combination of rising oil demand and constrained supply spells an end to the era of cheap oil prices. Commodity prices will need to remain elevated to encourage the development of complex oilfields. And high prices will also help ration oil use, particularly in the developed world, to accommodate the relentless growth in demand from emerging market consumers with fast-growing disposable incomes.

Exploration and production (E&P) firms with the scope to actually grow their output in this environment stand to benefit handsomely. Some, such as Petrobras, have preferential access to key reservoirs, while others, such as Anadarko and Tullow, are potential takeover targets for larger producers looking to expand into fast-growing oil-producing regions.

However, companies that produce oil and gas aren't the only plays on rising oil prices and the end of easy oil. The most direct beneficiaries of these trends never produce a drop of oil or a cubic foot of natural gas but have the technical know-how and make the advanced equipment required to unlock the world's increasingly complex fields.

That's largely the province of the oil services, drilling, and equipment industry. The group is the best-placed of all over the long term to benefit from the new normal for global energy markets.

Schlumberger is far and away the world's largest oilfield services company and is among the best diversified geographically, with operations in 80 countries and exposure to just about every imaginable oil or gas-producing region of the world. The company is also considered a technological leader in many key service lines, making it a partner of choice for firms seeking to develop complex fields in regions like the deepwater. This technical leadership is supported by a USD800 million research and development (R&D) budget, far higher than any of its peers. Schlumberger is also known for maintaining a steady stream of acquisitions, often motivated by a desire to fill out a key service line and add more technical depth.

Weatherford International is far smaller than Schlumberger but is expanding rapidly and is developing a strong presence in key international markets such as Russia and Iraq. Weatherford is perhaps best known as an expert provider of services related to mature oil-fields. Traditionally, Weatherford has had a strong presence in North America, particularly in Canada. North American oilfields have been extensively developed for decades and, in some cases, over a century. North America has been a proving ground for all sorts of technologies that squeeze oil from older fields. An example is underbalanced drilling, a technique that prevents damage to mature fields.

Dril-Quip (NYSE: DRQ) has two divisions: drilling equipment and services. The former accounts for about 85 percent of revenue and is the main division of interest from an investing standpoint. The company's drilling equipment segment mainly manufactures subsea products used primarily in deepwater offshore field developments. Dril-Quip is a market leader in subsea wellheads. Wellheads are devices installed on top of a subsea well to control underground pressures and prevent oil or gas from gushing through the top of the well. Casing, the thick metal pipe used to line a well, is also suspended from the wellhead.

Cameron (NYSE: CAM) and FMC Technologies (NYSE: FTI) are larger plays on subsea equipment. Cameron and FMC manufacture the same basic types of equipment as Dril-Quip, and both have been market leaders in key product lines such as subsea trees and oil and natural gas separation equipment at times over the past five years.

National-Oilwell Varco (NYSE: NOV) is an oil services and equipment firm that operates in three basic businesses: rig technology, petroleum services, and supplies and distribution services. The rig technology segment is the jewel in National Oilwell's crown and accounts for about two-thirds of the company's total operating profits.

Acergy (Norway: ACY; NSDQ: ACGY) and Subsea 7 (Norway: SUB; OTC: SBEAF) are both leaders in the subsea engineering and construction business. One of the most important business lines for both firms is known as SURF—subsea umbilicals, risers, and flowlines.

Umbilicals are nothing more than electrical and hydraulic cables that connect a surface-based platform to subsea wells. Risers are flexible steel pipes that connect underwater pipelines or wells to surface-based floating production platforms. Risers actually carry oil and/or gas from subsea developments to the surface. Flowlines are smaller-diameter pipes used to transport oil and gas underwater.

All subsea developments require the installation of SURF. Subsea engineering and construction companies design and construct these systems on behalf of producers. Just as with the subsea equipment manufacturers, rising interest in deepwater exploration and development in key markets such as Brazil and West Africa spell rising demand for SURF and other engineering and construction services related to subsea projects.

Tenaris (NYSE: TS) is one of the world's largest manufacturers of oil country tubular goods (OCTG). OCTGs are essentially pipes and casing that are used in the construction of wells. Casing for example, is a thick, large-diameter pipe that's cemented in place underground to prevent undesirable liquids, such as water, from seeping into a well and to prevent the well from collapsing. Although manufacturing pipe might seem like a low-tech, low-margin business, that's not the case. Drilling in deepwater environments exposes pipes and casing to extreme temperatures and pressures that can cause pipes to fail.

Shifting East

Energy investors eagerly await the US Energy Information Administration's weekly petroleum report; they hope to use the data to discern the latest trends in US oil demand and inventories. This US-centric bias is an anachronism, a holdover from a time when conditions in the US and Western Europe were critical to predicting the future path of crude prices.

But times are changing, and unfortunately, far too many investors have failed to recognize the change. Politicians in the West spout populist rhetoric about market manipulation and greedy speculators even as data released by the Commodity Futures Trading Commission (CFTC) suggest that speculators in the oil futures markets have little long-term impact on prices.

Others accuse the big oil companies of artificially inflating prices, even as the very same companies struggle to find attractive new reserves. Most promising fields are held by state-owned national oil companies. Even the largest big oil company, Exxon Mobil, controls less than 3 percent of global oil production, making it far from a monopolist.

While the Western world looks for scapegoats, China, India, and other burgeoning consumer nations have recognized the changes afoot and are quietly buying access to supplies of oil and natural gas. Strong growth in demand for oil from emerging markets coupled with constrained supply spell an end to the era of cheap energy prices.

Individual investors would be wise to follow the strategy of the developing world by allocating capital to the companies with the potential to see real production growth in coming years and the services and equipment firms with the technological know-how to produce those plays.

Endnotes

1 *BP Statistical Review of World Energy 2009.*

2 "BP Announces Giant Oil Discovery in the Gulf of Mexico," BP Press Release September 2, 2009, http://www.bp.com/genericarticle.do?categoryId= 2012968&contentId=7055818 (accessed February 11, 2010).

3 "BP's Tiber One of Industry's Deepest Wells," September 2, 2009, http://www. ogj.com/index/article-display/3139514532/articles/oil-gas-journal/exploration-development-2/discoveries/2009/09/bp_s-tiber_one_of.html (accessed February 15, 2010).

4 "BP Finds 'Giant' Oil Source Deep Under Gulf of Mexico," *The Washington Post*, September 03, 2009 http://www.washingtonpost.com/wp-dyn/content/article/ 2009/09/02/AR2009090203560.html (accessed February 16, 2010).

5 "Chevron Announces First Oil from Tahiti Field in Gulf of Mexico," Chevron press release May 6, 2009, http://www.chevron.com/news/Press/release/ ?id=2009-05-06 (accessed February 13, 2010).

6 Douglas-Westwood Global Deepwater Prospects Presentation February 2010, http://www.dw-1.com/files/files/520-Global%20Deepwater%20Prospects% 20-%20DOT%20-%202010%20Feb.pdf (accessed February 19, 2010).

7 Ibid.

8 Petrobras Operational Highlights, http://www2.petrobras.com.br/portal/frame_ ri.asp?pagina=/ri/ing/index.asp&lang=en&area=ri (accessed February 15, 2010).

9 Petrobras Strategic Plan 2009 - 2013, http://trade.gov/td/energy/PETROBRAS% 20Strategic%20&%20Business%20Plan%202009-2013%20OTC%2020091.pdf (accessed January 17, 2010).

10 Ibid.

11 Iuri Dantas and Jeb Blount, "Petrobras Gets $10 Billion China Loan, Sinopec Deal," Bloomberg.com, February 19, 2009, http://www.bloomberg.com/apps/ news?pid=20601207&sid=aUcQstVre0Po (accessed February 9, 2010).

[12] Energy Information Administration, "Assumptions to the Annual Energy Outlook 2009," http://www.eia.doe.gov/oiaf/aeo/assumption/oil_gas.html (accessed February 1, 2010).

[13] Uchenna Izundu, "BP Ramps Up Thunder Horse Production," April 17, 2009, http://www.ogj.com/index/article-display/359580/articles/oil-gas-journal/drilling-production/production-operations/articles/bp-ramps-up-thunder-horse-production.html.

[14] *Oil & Gas Journal* Special Report, "Drilling and Production Major Projects," August 10, 2009, http://www.ogj.com/index/article-display/0711973246/articles/oil-gas-journal/volume-107/issue_30/Drilling___Production/Special_Report__Major_projects.html.

[15] EIA Country Analysis Brief: Angola http://www.eia.doe.gov/emeu/cabs/Angola/Oil.html (accessed January 28, 2010).

[16] *Oil & Gas Journal* Special Report, "Drilling and Production Major Projects," August 10, 2009, http://www.ogj.com/index/article-display/0711973246/articles/oil-gas-journal/volume-107/issue_30/Drilling___Production/Special_Report__Major_projects.html.

[17] Paula Dittrick, "Chinese Oil Companies Invest Heavily Abroad," *Oil & Gas Journal*, February 8, 2010, http://www.ogj.com/index/article-display/3061413046/articles/oil-gas-journal/volume-108/issue-5/general-interest/chinese-oil_companies.html (accessed February 20, 2010).

[18] Eric Watkins, "China, Venezuela Sign New Round of Energy Agreements," *Oil & Gas Journal*, December 30, 2009 (accessed February 14, 2010), http://www.ogj.com/index/article-display/7053340949/articles/oil-gas-journal/general-interest-2/2009/december-2009/china_-venezuela_sign.html.

[19] Eric Watkins, "Venezuela Awards Carabobo Blocks to Two Consortia," *Oil & Gas Journal*, February 11, 2010, http://www.ogj.com/index/article-display/6351691277/articles/oil-gas-journal/drilling-production-2/production-operations/unconventional-resources/2010/02/venezuela-awards_carabobo.html.

[20] Eric Watkins, "Russia, Venezuela Agree on Energy Agreements Package," *Oil & Gas Journal*, September 11, 2009.

[21] Ibid.

[22] Reuters, "Russia September Oil Output Hits Record 10 Million bpd," http://www.reuters.com/article/idUSTRE5912PI20091002 (accessed January 15, 2010).

[23] David Winning and Shai Oster, "China, Russia Strike $25 Billion Oil Pact," *The Wall Street Journal*, February 18, 2010.

[24] Sam Fletcher, "Iraq, Nigeria Oil Output Increasing," *Oil & Gas Journal*, December 14, 2009, http://www.ogj.com/index/article-display/1645249597/articles/oil-gas-journal/exclusive-online-features/market-journal/2009/12/iraq_-nigeria_oil.html (accessed February 11, 2010).

7

Natural Gas: The 21st-Century Fuel

The 19th century was the century of coal, the 20th the age of oil. The 21st century is shaping up to be the century for natural gas. Natural gas has three powerful advantages over oil: It's more widely available, it's cheaper, and it's environmentally friendly.

The rapid development of the global liquefied natural gas (LNG) market has turned gas from a regional market limited by a rigid pipeline network into a global market much like crude oil. Consuming countries with LNG import terminals can now obtain their gas from a variety of different regions of the world, diversifying their supply base and lowering the risk of disruption. LNG has also unlocked vast "stranded" gas supplies—giant gas fields in places like Australia previously considered worthless because they're too remote and too far away from pipelines.

The shift in sentiment surrounding the North American gas market has been swift and dramatic. At the turn of the century most market observers felt the US would need to import an ever-increasing volume of LNG to make up for declining gas production at home and falling production and imports from Canada. A decade later, the US overtook Russia to become the world's top producer of gas, and the surfeit of natural gas is so dramatic there's serious talk of exporting US gas abroad as LNG or promoting policies that would encourage greater domestic use of the fuel.

More recently producers in North America have pioneered the production of natural gas from so-called unconventional fields such as shale and tight sands. This technological advance has unlocked a veritable ocean of natural gas that can be produced at reasonable prices.

Unconventional natural gas production was pioneered by smaller independent producers. But the big US and European oil companies are jumping into the market with increasing enthusiasm, acquiring the technology and know-how needed to produce shale gas. North America doesn't have a lock on unconventional gas; the big producers have plans to develop shale fields located in Europe and across Asia as well. Developing these fields will take time but holds the promise of making gas an even more viable fuel for meeting the inexorable rise in demand for energy in the developing world.

Electricity and Industrial

Primary energy consists of energy used for all purposes, whether it's oil for transportation, gas for heat, or electricity produced from a wind turbine. Primary energy consumption is typically measured in British thermal units (Btu), the amount of energy needed to heat a pound of water by 1 degree Fahrenheit. Roughly speaking, it's about the amount of energy released from striking a match. A Btu represents a tiny amount of energy, so when we speak of energy consumption on a national or international scale, primary energy is measured in quadrillions of Btu, or simply "quads."

Primary energy consumption is a useful gauge of the relative importance of different energy sources regardless of end-use. Figure 7.1 illustrates global primary energy consumption by fuel type.

Natural gas is a member of the energy Big 3—oil, natural gas, and coal currently account for 85 percent of global energy use. Contrary to popular belief, that's not projected to change much in the coming two decades. According to Energy Information Administration (EIA) projections, more than 83 percent of global energy consumption will come from the same three fuels in 2030. But oil, natural gas, and coal don't serve identical end-markets.

Crude oil is the world's transportation fuel. Thirty years ago, when oil supplies were far more plentiful, many nations around the world used oil to produce power. But that's no longer the case; today only 4.5 percent of global power is generated by crude.[1]

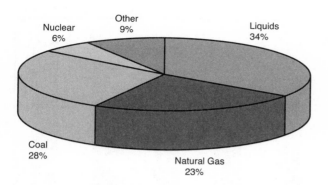

Figure 7.1 Global primary energy consumption by fuel.

(Source: Energy Information Administration International Energy Outlook 2009)

The other major use of oil is in heavy industries. Roughly 30 percent of industrial demand for energy comes from the chemicals industry, for example, the manufacture of plastics from chemicals derived from oil or natural gas. The iron and steel industry makes up another 20 percent of global industrial energy demand, while the nonmetallic minerals and paper industries account for 10 percent and 6 percent of industrial use, respectively.[2] Taken together, these two end-markets—transport and industrial—account for more than 85 percent of the oil consumed globally.[3]

In contrast, natural gas is not yet an important global transportation fuel, though over time transport is likely to become a more important market. Instead, the key end-uses for natural gas are industrial demand, electric power, and residential and commercial heating.

As Figure 7.2 illustrates, electric power and industrial are also projected to remain the two dominant uses for the fuel in coming decades. Of the two, electric power will be the faster growing market for gas, though the fuel is also well-positioned to grab market share from oil in heavy industry.

The case for rising global electricity consumption is much the same as for rising oil demand. Just as with crude oil, the primary driver of growth in global electricity use is the emerging markets. Between 2010 and 2030 electric-power generation in countries outside the Organization for Economic Cooperation and Development (OECD), a proxy

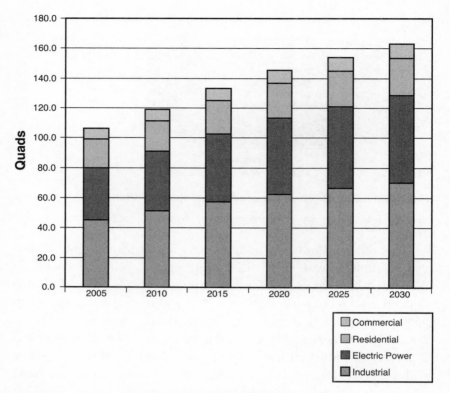

Figure 7.2   World natural gas consumption by end-use.

(Source: Energy Information Administration International Energy Outlook 2009)

for the emerging markets, is projected to jump by 85 percent, more than three times the pace of the developed world.[4]

The growth in electricity demand from developing countries is nothing short of spectacular. As recently as 1980 OECD countries consumed more than twice as much power as non-OECD countries. In 2012, the developed and developing world will consume roughly the same amount of power, and in 2030 non-OECD countries are projected to consume 40 percent more power than the entire developed world.[5] The driver of this increased demand is the same as for oil: higher disposable income. As consumers become wealthier they're able to afford appliances such as air conditioners, television sets, refrigerators, and personal computers (PC)—all of these products consume electricity.

And there's plenty of room for upside in electricity use. The average person in China consumes 2,041 kilowatt-hours (kWh) of electricity per year compared to more than 7,100 kWh in Germany and a whopping 13,500 kWh in the US. But China is rapidly closing that gap—per capita electricity use more than doubled between 2000 and 2006.[6]

While non-OECD growth in electricity demand will outpace that in the developed world, the entire world is undergoing a process of electrification. Electricity is becoming a more important source of total energy consumption in both the developed and developing world. Figure 7.3 depicts the growth in electric-power consumption and total global energy consumption starting in 1990, with projections out to 2030. Over this time period total global energy consumption roughly doubles, while electricity use rises by nearly 180 percent. Electricity is the fastest-growing end-use for energy in the world over this time period.

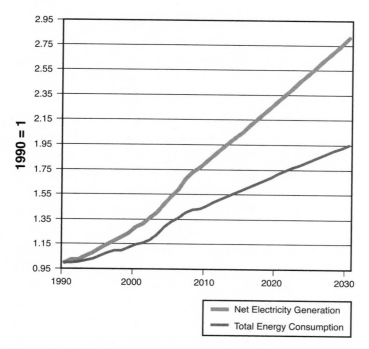

Figure 7.3   World electricity consumption versus total energy consumption 1990–2030.

(Source: Energy Information Administration International Energy Outlook 2009)

A powerful reason for this trend is simply the proliferation of power-hungry household devices such as PCs, mobile telephones, and kitchen appliances and the increased use of heat pumps and air conditioners. Air conditioning alone accounts for some 16 percent of US household electricity consumption, kitchen appliances make up another 27 percent, and laundry equipment 7 percent.[7] The infrastructure that supports a high-tech economy such as data centers and server farms is similarly energy-intensive. Developing countries are still far behind the US and other parts of the developed world in terms of the prevalence of basic household appliances.

The Gas Choice

The two main sources of demand for natural gas are electric-power generation and industrial applications. The key question is why companies would choose to use gas to produce electric power, as an industrial fuel, or as feedstock rather than coal and oil.

In markets where natural gas competes with oil, gas's main advantages are that it's more readily available and cheaper. Figure 7.4 shows the price of crude oil compared to US and UK natural gas prices.

Natural gas is considered a regional fuel. The US, for example, has obtained its gas from a combination of domestic production and imports from Canada via pipeline. Although gas imported from further afield in the form of LNG has become a more meaningful component of North American supply in recent years, it's still a relatively small part of the supply mix. Similarly, Europe has traditionally obtained most of its gas from North Sea production and via pipeline from Russia.

As a result, natural gas prices can differ widely between regions of the world. To reflect this, Figure 7.4 depicts prices for both US NYMEX-traded natural gas futures and UK-traded ICE futures. ICE futures are traded in terms of British pence per therm, while US gas futures are traded in US dollars per million Btu (USD/MMBtu); Figure 7.4 converts ICE futures and oil prices to USD/MMBtu for ease of comparison.

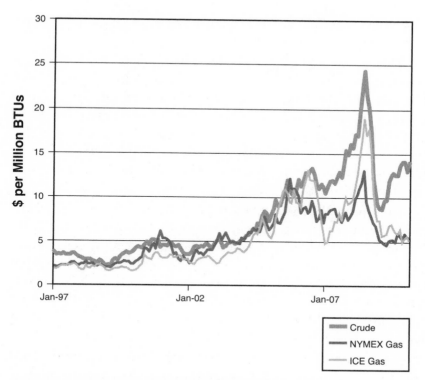

Figure 7.4 Crude and natural gas prices. Chart assumes 5.8 million Btu in a barrel of crude oil.

(Source: Bloomberg Finance L.P.)

For most of the period covered by this chart, oil and US/UK natural gas prices were closely correlated, though crude typically traded at a slightly higher price than gas. But starting around 2006 the close correlation completely broke down—oil has consistently traded at a much larger premium to natural gas and, in some cases, the two commodities don't even move in the same broad direction. This shift is largely structural rather than temporary. Global oil supplies are likely to remain constrained as older, mature fields see declining output and producers turn to more remote, technically complex and expensive-to-produce fields to fill the supply gap.

Supply bottlenecks in the global gas market are far less onerous. The rapid development of unconventional gas reserves has vastly improved the supply picture in the US. Meanwhile, several large LNG projects have come on-stream in recent years, adding to global supply and allowing consuming countries to diversify their supply from traditional pipeline sources.

The greater availability and reliability of supply mean natural gas prices will remain relatively cheap compared to oil. From 1996 through 2006 the ratio of US oil to US natural gas prices on an energy-equivalent basis averaged 1.2-to-1. From 1996 through the end of the decade, the ratio jumped to nearly 2-to-1. It's likely that the recent experience will continue and the oil/gas ratio will remain high for years to come, encouraging the substitution of gas for oil where possible.

Enterprise Products Partners LP (NYSE: EPD) is one of the largest operators of natural gas processing and fractionation facilities in the US. When raw natural gas is produced, it consists primarily of methane but also contains a large number of other hydrocarbons collectively known as natural gas liquids (NGL). Some gas, known as "wet" gas, is naturally higher in NGLs, while other fields produce almost pure methane, known as "dry" gas. NGLs include propane, butane, natural gasoline, and ethane.

Toward the end of 2009 and into early 2010, US petrochemical companies were retooling their facilities to allow them to produce more ethylene from gas-derived ethane and propane rather than oil-derived naphtha. As of the end of 2009, Enterprise Products estimated that petrochemicals producers had added 100,000 barrels a day (bbl/d) of new capacity to crack ethane and propane to make ethylene; in many cases this was done by modifying their naphtha equipment.[8]

Ethylene is among the most important and most fundamental petrochemicals. The fact that chemical manufacturers are spending the money needed to revamp their plants to use ethane rather than naphtha strongly suggests that the higher crude-to-gas ratio is seen as a fundamental shift in the market, not a temporary change.

None of this means natural gas will completely replace oil in industrial markets. However, it is likely to gain market share, particularly in markets with plentiful supply. This list includes the US, where strong production growth from unconventional natural gas fields will sustain a large cost advantage for gas over oil for the foreseeable future.

Also, the Middle East is projected to see a large increase in industrial natural gas demand. Petrochemical production is far and away the dominant source of industrial demand for gas in the Middle East, and ethane-based ethylene and propylene from countries like Saudi Arabia and Kuwait have massive cost advantages over ethylene produced from naphtha in Asia. Total Middle East ethylene capacity is expected to grow from 16.9 million metric tons per year in 2008 to 28.1 million in 2012, while propylene capacity will increase from 3.5 million tons per year to 7 million over the same period.[9] Much of that chemicals production is destined for Asian markets.

While natural gas looks likely to gain significant share from oil in the industrial market, the transportation market is more complex. Compressed natural gas (CNG) is routinely used to power vehicles, including passenger cars, buses, and taxis. Alternatively, larger vehicles can run efficiently on LNG; liquefying gas allows vehicles to carry more fuel and increase their range. But transportation is currently a tiny market for the fuel in the US. The American transportation sector consumes around 0.04 trillion cubic feet (tcf) of natural gas per year compared to the 4.77 tcf consumed in residential applications, 6 tcf for industrial uses, and 6.9 tcf for electricity generation.[10]

Globally, it's estimated that there are more than 7 million vehicles running on natural gas either in the form of CNG or LNG, up from less than 2 million in 2001.[11] This represents a tremendous rate of growth and sounds like a lot of vehicles until you consider that there are more than 200 million passenger vehicles in the US alone and an estimated 600 million to 700 million globally.

Although the US has an abundance of natural gas, it's not a leading market for natural gas-powered vehicles. Argentina is the world leader with 1.7 million natural gas vehicles, while neighboring Brazil has 1.56 million; South America accounts for nearly half the world's natural gas vehicle market, with many operating as taxis in major metropolitan areas. Outside South America, Italy is the leader in Europe, while CNG and LNG are also relatively popular in Russia, Iran, and India. The US, by comparison, has only around 120,000 such vehicles on the road today.[12]

Transport is a huge potential growth market for natural gas. The US consumes around 9 million bbl/d in the form of motor gasoline alone. On an energy-equivalent basis that's more than 50 billion cubic feet (bcf) of natural gas equivalent per day. When you consider that total current US consumption is around 60 bcf per day, replacing even a small part of the gasoline market with natural gas would imply an enormous increase in total natural gas demand.

There are more than 200 million passenger vehicles on the road in the US alone; replacing or retrofitting even a small percentage of that total would be expensive and take years. Similarly, refueling infrastructure in the US, EU, and other major gasoline-consuming markets is set up to distribute liquid fuels through a vast network of gas stations. There are well over 100,000 stations in the US alone. Converting these stations to offer CNG fuel would be a mammoth undertaking. There are only 339 CNG fueling stations in the US open to the public.[13]

Nevertheless, it's likely there will be greater use of gas as a transport fuel in coming years. The first markets to be penetrated significantly are fleet vehicles such as buses, taxis, and garbage trucks. Refueling such vehicles requires building only one or a handful of centralized refueling stations in a particular area. In 2006 about 15 percent of US transit vehicles were powered by natural gas, and that was estimated to save around 109 million gallons of diesel fuel annually. Penetration of fleet vehicles in other countries such as Argentina is even higher.[14]

Besides cost, another advantage of using CNG in fleet vehicles is emissions. The US Environmental Protection Agency (EPA) estimates that vehicles using CNG cut carbon monoxide emissions by 90 to 97 percent, nearly eliminate particulate emissions, cut nitrogen oxide (NOX) emissions by 35 percent to 60 percent, and reduce carbon dioxide (CO_2) emissions by 25 percent.[15] Cutting emissions of NOX and particulate matter provides significant near-term benefits such as reducing smog. Reducing pollution isn't just a developed world issue, as some of the world's most polluted cities are found in emerging markets; reduction of inner-city pollution caused by diesel engines has been a major motivation for countries such as India and China to encourage natural gas vehicles.

The true game-changing market for natural gas vehicles isn't personal passenger cars or fleet vehicles but freight trucks. Building out infrastructure for truck refueling is a simpler matter than for passenger cars; a handful of stations located along key routes would suffice. And this is a far larger potential market than fleet vehicles. It's estimated there are around 8 million trucks on US highways burning around 2.5 million barrels of oil per day.[16]

The most direct play on rising use of natural gas as a transportation fuel is Clean Energy Fuels (NSDQ: CLNE), the largest provider of LNG and CNG in the US and Canada. Clean Energy builds CNG and LNG fueling stations on behalf of fleet operators and then earns an ongoing revenue stream by selling the CNG and/or LNG fuel needed to power those fleets. The company was founded by billionaire T. Boone Pickens, and the oil magnate remains on Clean Energy's board of directors.

Electricity generation is the fastest-growing major end-use for natural gas. Table 7.1 illustrates some of the cost factors involved with building and operating new power plants in the US.

The data for Table 7.1 are the EIA's assumed costs for a long list of different types of power plants put into service in 2016. Note that these costs are in 2008 dollars per megawatt-hour and apply solely to the US; although costs will differ in other countries, the table still offers a useful look at overall trends.

Gas is used both as a source of baseload power—run the facilities on a near-constant basis to meet ongoing power demand—and for peaking power, to feed additional electricity onto the grid during times of peak demand. Gas is ideal as a peaking-power source because plants can be started and stopped quickly, whereas it takes time to start a coal plant and heat the boilers to a sufficient temperature to produce power.

Capital costs are ultra-low for gas plants because they're simple and quick to build. It takes roughly two years to construct and bring a new gas plant online, compared to four years for a coal plant and six or more for a nuclear facility.[17] And it's far easier to get permits to build a new gas facility than it is for coal or nuclear plants.

TABLE 7.1 Cost of US Power Plants

	Plant Type	Capacity Factor (%)	Levelized Capital Cost	Fixed O&M	Variable O&M (Including fuel)	Transmission Investment	Total System Levelized Cost
Coal	Conventional Coal	85	69.2	3.8	23.9	3.6	100.4
	Advanced Coal	85	81.2	5.3	20.4	3.6	110.5
	Advanced Coal with CCS	85	92.6	6.3	26.4	3.9	129.3
Natural Gas	Conventional Combined Cycle	87	22.9	1.7	54.9	3.6	83.1
	Advanced Combined Cycle	87	22.4	1.6	51.7	3.6	79.3
	Advanced CC with CCS	87	43.8	2.7	63.0	3.8	113.3
	Conventional Combustion Turbine	30	41.1	4.7	82.9	10.8	139.5
	Advanced Combustion Turbine	30	38.5	4.1	70.0	10.8	123.5
Nuclear/ Renewables	Advanced Nuclear	90	94.9	11.7	9.4	3.0	119
	Wind	34.4	130.5	10.4	0.0	8.4	149.3
	Wind—Offshore	39.3	159.9	23.8	0	7.4	191.1
	Solar PV	21.7	376.8	6.4	0.0	13.0	396.1

TABLE 7.1 Cost of US Power Plants

Plant Type	Capacity Factor (%)	Levelized Capital Cost	Fixed O&M	Variable O&M (Including fuel)	Transmission Investment	Total System Levelized Cost
Solar Thermal	31.2	224.4	21.8	0	10.4	256.6
Geothermal	90	88.0	22.9	0.0	4.8	115.7
Biomass	83	73.3	9.1	24.9	3.8	111.0
Hydro	51.4	103.7	3.5	7.1	5.7	119.9

(Source: Energy Information Administration Assumptions to Annual Energy Outlook 2010)

Operating costs for gas-fired facilities are higher than for coal plants. This is mainly the result of higher fuel prices—gas is more expensive than coal on an energy-equivalent basis. But this is heavily dependent on your assumptions for future gas prices; gas has traditionally been a volatile commodity with wild seasonal price swings. Natural gas futures traders call the market "the widow-maker," as its legendary price swings can produce some epic losses. But new supplies coming on-stream—both new access to LNG and unconventional reservoirs—promise to reduce volatility in this market and make the fuel a more attractive option.

Finally, like coal plants gas plants require no major investment in transmission technology because it fits well with the existing grid.

A quick glance at the table shows that on a total system cost basis in the US, the economics of gas are compelling compared to coal, even though coal is the cheaper fuel on a Btu basis. Low capital cost, quick lead times, and ease of grid integration are all major benefits for gas.

Also, note that gas is also competitive with all other energy sources included in the table. Wind and solar—the two alternative energies that get significant attention in the popular media—aren't competitive on a pure cost basis. This is mainly due to low capacity factors, high fixed maintenance costs, and required massive transmission investments.

In countries like China and Germany, where gas prices are higher than in the US, the economics of gas would likely be less attractive. But Table 7.1 shows that you can't simply look at fuel prices to determine a power source's economic viability. And, regardless of fuel prices, gas has some compelling advantages.

The other major driver of growth in the use of gas as a fuel in power plants is the environmental attraction of the fuel. The average US natural gas-fired power plant produces half as much CO_2, less than one-third the NOX, and 1 percent as much sulfur dioxide (SOX) as a coal plant to produce an equivalent amount of electricity.[18] And coal plants also emit mercury and particulate matter; emissions from gas plants for both pollutants are negligible.

In developing countries such as China and India the more immediate concern is emissions of NOX, SOX, and particulate pollution.

Acid rain caused by sulfur emissions damages crops, and NOX emissions cause smog in addition to respiratory illness. Meanwhile, mercury emissions have been linked to birth defects and a wide range of maladies in adults. Only around 1 percent of Chinese city-dwellers breathe air that would be considered safe in the European Union.[19]

The Chinese government has taken steps to address this issue. Efforts include shutting down older, coal-fired power plants and high-polluting factories. Many of these facilities weren't fitted with the sort of scrubbers used to control emissions in the West. China is also diversifying away from coal, boosting the share of its power that comes from less polluting sources such as nuclear power and natural gas.

Much of the debate about reducing carbon emissions centers on making greater use of renewables. This would be a huge mistake. Natural gas actually has a long track record as a quick, cheap way to reduce carbon emissions. And gas is far cheaper than wind, solar, or any other alternative.

Figure 7.5 shows the history of UK electric-power generation going back to 1970. Total power generation over this time period is up nearly 28 percent due to general growth in the UK economy and increased electrification. Despite this growth, total CO_2 emissions from UK power plants have actually fallen by more than 19 percent since 1970.[20]

Many investors' first reaction is that this must be due to increased use of solar, wind, tidal, or some other alternative energy source. But Figure 7.5 shows that's not the case—UK carbon emissions have fallen largely because the nation has substituted natural gas-fired plants for oil- and coal-fired facilities.

In light of its cost and environmental benefits, natural gas is well-placed to gain market share in industrial, transportation, and electricity generation in coming years. The key to realizing all these benefits is obtaining sufficient supply at a reasonable cost.

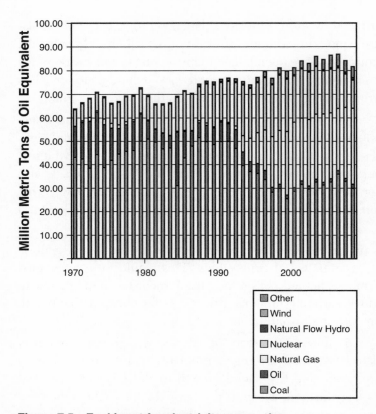

Figure 7.5   Fuel input for electricity generation.

(Source: UK Department of Energy and Climate Change)

Liquid Energy

There's nothing magical about LNG. It's nothing more than a super-cooled version of natural gas. When gas is cooled to around minus 260 degrees Fahrenheit (minus 162 degrees Celsius), it condenses into a liquid.

Better still, as gas cools it takes up less space; LNG takes up roughly one-six-hundred-and-tenth the volume of gas in its natural gaseous state. To put that into context, a beach ball-sized volume of gas shrinks to the size of a standard ping-pong ball when it's converted to LNG. This is a key consideration when it comes to transport.

LNG frees gas from the pipeline grid. If you're able to turn natural gas into a liquid, it can be loaded onto tankers just like crude oil and transported anywhere in the world. Gas reserves once considered stranded and useless can be exploited using LNG technologies. The LNG supply chain is simple. The gas is produced the same way as if it were to be transported by pipeline to the consumer. This raw natural gas is then transported by pipe to a liquefaction facility. These liquefaction facilities are located in the gas-exporting country.

The liquefaction facility represents the largest single cost center in the LNG supply chain. Basically, the gas is treated to remove some of its impurities, such as corrosive sulfur, CO_2, and water, and is then fed into a gas liquefaction unit known as a train. Most liquefaction facilities are made up of multiple trains. After the gas is liquefied, it's loaded onto specialized LNG tanker ships. These tankers' storage units are designed with multiple layers of insulation to keep the LNG cool during transport. Nonetheless, even with multiple layers of insulation, LNG cargo does warm up slightly during the course of a voyage—typically around 0.15 percent of the cargo boils each day. This is called boil-off gas. If the boil-off gas were allowed to build up too much, pressure inside the tanks would increase. In modern LNG tankers, it's actually removed from the storage tanks and used to help propel the tanker ship.

LNG tanks are never really fully emptied; a small quantity of so-called heel gas is retained. This gas helps to retain the LNG tanks at super-cooled temperatures during their journey back to pick up another load of LNG.

The final step in the LNG supply chain is the regasification terminal. These terminals are located in the importing country. Natural gas is reheated to more normal temperatures and then injected into the pipeline network to be used just like normal gas.

In 2008 total global trade in LNG was 226.51 billion cubic meters (bcm), while total world consumption of natural gas was 3018.7 bcm.[21] Table 7.2 offers a detailed look at the world's largest LNG exporters and importers in terms of total volume.

TABLE 7.2   World's Largest LNG Exporters and Importers

Global LNG Trade Exporters	Quantity (bcm)	Importers	Quantity (bcm)
Qatar	39.68	Japan	92.13
Malaysia	29.40	South Korea	36.55
Indonesia	26.85	Spain	28.73
Algeria	21.87	France	12.59
Nigeria	20.54	Taiwan	12.07
Australia	20.24	India	10.79
Trinidad & Tobago	17.36	US	9.94
Egypt	14.06	China	4.44

(Source: BP Statistical Review of World Energy 2009)

Japan and South Korea currently dominate the market for LNG imports, accounting for roughly half of the world total. Japan, in particular, has a long history as an importer of LNG because the country has almost no domestic sources of oil or natural gas and has long been almost totally dependent on imports.

Some might be surprised to see the US on the list given the fact it's the world's largest gas producer. But natural gas storage capacity typically consists of depleted natural gas fields; companies pump gas into these underground fields and then withdraw it as needed. Because the US has a large number of depleted fields, it also has more capacity to store natural gas than most other countries in the world. The US can take shipments of natural gas during the summer months, when it's in low demand, and store it for future use.

China and India are becoming ever-more important consumers of LNG. China commissioned its third LNG receiving terminal in late 2009 and has more such terminals under construction, including the massive Ningbo LNG project that's due for startup in 2012.[22]

Qatar is by far the largest producer of LNG. The country's North Field, estimated to contain about 900 trillion feet of gas, is the largest nonassociated natural gas field in the world. (Nonassociated simply means that the gas isn't found dissolved in oil, as it is in many fields.) Qatar's domestic LNG sector is dominated by two companies, Qatar LNG (Qatargas) and Ras Laffan LNG Company (RasGas).[23] The former is a joint venture between Qatar's national oil company

(NOC), Qatar Petroleum, Total (France: TOT, NYSE: TOT), Exxon Mobil (NYSE: XOM), Mitsui, Marubeni, ConocoPhillips (NYSE: COP), and Shell (London: RDSA, NYSE: RDS/A). The Rasgas consortium is 30 percent owned by Exxon, with Qatar Petroleum owning the majority stake of 70 percent.[24]

Qatar plans significant further expansion of its LNG projects. The RasGas 3 project, capable of producing 7.8 million metric tons of LNG per year, equivalent to about 10.6 bcm, started up its seventh train in February 2010. And Qatargas 2 train 5, capable of producing 7.8 million metric tons of LNG per year, started up in late 2009.[25]

The northern part of the North Field stretches across a maritime border into Iran, where it is known as the South Pars field. The Iranian side of the field is also under development; China National Petroleum Company owns a 40 percent stake in the play and has invested USD4.7 billion in its development.

Indonesia has also been expanding its already considerable LNG export capacity. The Tangguh project in the province of Papua is operated by British Petroleum (London: BP, NYSE: BP) and owned by a consortium that includes BP, with a 37.16 percent stake; China National Offshore Oil Company (NYSE: CEO), with a 16.96 percent share; Mitsubishi, with 16.3 percent; Nippon Oil, with 12.23 percent; KG, with 10 percent; and LNG Japan, with 7.35 percent. The first part of the project went into service in 2007, the second in July 2009 with an inaugural shipment of LNG to China.[26] The Tangguh project is backed up with long-term supply arrangements, including deals to supply gas to the Fujian LNG project in China and Korean steelmaker POSCO.

Australia is another country that's likely to become a more important supplier of LNG, particularly to Asia, in coming years. The greater Gorgon LNG development, led by Chevron (NYSE: CVX), will supply 15 million metric tons of LNG per year from three trains and is scheduled to go into service in 2014. Chevron's Wheatstone LNG project, due to come online after 2014, will also supply an additional 4.3 million metric tons per year from two trains.[27]

Another major player in Australia and a more direct play on LNG generally is Woodside Petroleum (Sydney: WPL, OTC: WOPEY). Woodside operates the largest oil and gas development in Australia, known as the North West Shelf (NWS) development.

Oil Search (Sydney: OSH, OTC: OISHY) is traded in Australia but was founded in Papua New Guinea in 1929 and operates all of Papua's major oil and gas projects. The local government owns 17.6 percent of the company. Oil Search holds a 30 percent interest in the Papua New Guinea LNG project that's operated by oil giant Exxon Mobil. That project is scheduled to begin its first sales of LNG in 2013 or 2014 and will have a maximum capacity of around 6.6 million metric tons of LNG per year. There's potential upside because the Papua New Guinea project likely has additional gas reserves suitable for production via LNG.

Another producer with direct leverage to LNG is Britain's BG Group (London: BG, OTC: BRGYY). The company has operations in all legs of the LNG supply chain, including liquefaction capacity, LNG sales agreements, LNG trading operations, regasification terminals, and LNG tankers. In Australia, the company's Curtis Island project in Queensland is due for first LNG production in 2014 and is expected to ramp up to full capacity of 8 million metric tons per year. BG has already sold most of that production under long-term agreements to customers in China, Chile, and Singapore.

Looking beyond the producers, Dresser-Rand (NYSE: DRC) manufactures and provides parts and maintenance for compressors and turbines. Turbines and compressors have myriad uses at all stages of the energy business, but the LNG industry is one of Dresser's top-end markets.

Finally, Chart Industries (NSDQ: GTLS) manufactures and sells a variety of cryogenic equipment and engineered parts. Chart manufactures these products for a variety of uses, primarily in the energy and medical industries. However, roughly 60 percent of revenue comes from energy-related businesses, and 85 percent of the company's backlog is related to energy.

Unconventional Boom

On December 14, 2009, Exxon Mobil offered to purchase US exploration and production (E&P) firm XTO Energy in a USD41 billion deal. The mega-merger highlights a sea-change in the North American natural gas markets.

XTO Energy's core competence has long been the production of natural gas from unconventional fields such as the Barnett Shale located near Fort Worth, Texas, and the Haynesville Shale of Louisiana.

Oil and natural gas don't exist underground in giant lakes or caverns but in the pores and cracks of a reservoir rock. When a well is drilled into that reservoir rock, the natural geologic pressures drive the oil or gas through the reservoir rock into the well and to the surface. Unconventional reservoirs are a different story. Although there's often natural gas or oil contained in these rocks, the rocks are impermeable—the pores and cracks in the rock that contain the gas aren't well connected, so there's no way for it to flow through the reservoir and into the well. Many of the most prolific unconventional reservoirs are shale, a fine-grained sedimentary rock composed of layers of clay or mud particles.

Producers have known that natural gas exists in shale fields such as the Barnett for decades and drilled some wells in the play as far back as the 1950s. But most wells produced a quick rush of gas and quickly died; only the gas located immediately adjacent to the well was able to flow. George Mitchell, now widely considered the pioneer of the shale industry, was considered a laughingstock in the 1980s for drilling wells in the Barnett, which is now recognized as one of the most prolific fields ever discovered in the US.

Two key technologies have revolutionized the shale gas industry: horizontal drilling and hydraulic fracturing. Shale reservoirs in the US are often found as much as 8,000 to 14,000 feet under the surface of the Earth in layers a few hundred feet thick. By drilling down to the shale layer and horizontally through the shale itself, producers expose a longer portion of their wells to the productive shale layer. In contrast, a simple vertical well, drilled straight through the shale layer, would only be productive over the short segment of the well exposed to the shale.

Hydraulic fracturing involves pumping a liquid into the reservoir under tremendous pressure. This actually breaks the rock, creating cracks for the gas to flow through the formation and into a well. In short, fracturing improves the permeability of the field.

Producers also introduce what's known as proppant—typically sand, sand coated with resin, or ceramic material—into the fracturing fluid. The proppant actually enter the cracks caused by the fracturing and holds—or "props"—these cracks open. This prevents the newly formed cracks from closing as soon as pressure is removed.

The combination of these two technologies has unlocked a massive North American unconventional gas resource. Figure 7.6 shows US marketed production of natural gas going back to the mid-1980s.

US natural gas production appeared to start a decline after 2001, and Canadian production soon began to falter as well. With US and Canadian conventional gas production in decline, most thought North America would become increasingly reliant on LNG imports to meet gas demand. But breakthroughs in unconventional production after 2005 drove US gas production to new all-time highs by 2007-08. US imports of LNG fell after 2007, and the US faced a glut of gas by the end of the decade.

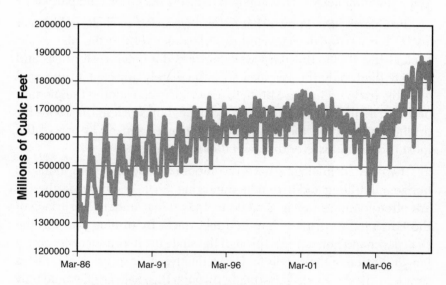

Figure 7.6   US marketed natural gas production.

(Source: Energy Information Administration)

Excess natural gas supplies in storage depressed natural gas prices after the middle of 2008 but have completely changed sentiment surrounding the fuel. Without unconventional gas production, it wouldn't be possible to hold serious discussion about expanding the use of gas as a source of electric power or as a transportation fuel.

Although producers are unlikely to be able to produce gas economically at USD4 to USD5 per MMBtu long term, several have noted that prices in the USD6 to USD7 per MMBtu range would be sufficient to incentivize further production growth. The promise of plentiful, relatively inexpensive gas is creating the potential for new markets for the fuel.

If investors needed any further confirmation of the potential of this resource, Exxon provided it when it agreed to buy XTO in its largest deal in years. Exxon isn't the only super-major to have taken an interest in North American shale gas plays. BP, Total, and Statoil, among others, have partnered with US unconventional gas producers to develop plays in the US or have purchased stakes in key plays on their own. There's little doubt North American unconventional gas is a world-class play. And there's significant potential for the development of unconventional plays outside the Americas as well. China's Sinopec (NYSE: SNP) has announced it's in talks with BP to collaborate on shale gas fields in China. And in November 2009 Royal Dutch Shell and PetroChina announced a deal to co-develop shale resources in China.

It will take time to develop international shale gas. It's no accident that the first major shale fields to be developed are those located in the US, where significant infrastructure to produce and store gas already exists.

The biggest winners in the unconventional shale boom are US producers with significant exposure to unconventional shale plays. All are now takeover targets for international companies looking to follow Exxon's lead. The services and equipment firms with the technologies needed to produce shale will also be in high demand. Range Resources (NYSE: RRC) is a leading player in the red-hot Marcellus Shale in Appalachia. Range actually drilled the first commercial well in the play back in 2004.

Petrohawk Energy (NYSE: HK) has solid acreage positions in three key US shale plays, the Fayetteville Shale of Arkansas, the Haynesville Shale of Louisiana, and the Eagle Ford Shale of southern Texas. The Haynesville Shale dominates Petrohawk's production, accounting for more than 40 percent of its total output. The firm has around 345,000 net acres of land in this region and estimates that the property could hold some 15.7 tcf in total resource potential.

Along with the much larger Chesapeake Energy (NYSE: CHK) Petrohawk is one of the biggest landholders in the Haynesville. The company's average well in the Haynesville showed an initial production (IP) rate of more than 18 million cubic feet of gas per day. This high IP rate indicates that Petrohawk's wells are being drilled in the highest-return part of the play; the company has assembled prime acreage—not low-quality properties near the periphery of the Haynesville.

Contract drilling giant Nabors Industries (NYSE: NBR) owns a fleet of the most modern rigs, which allow it to drill these complex wells. Nabors leases these rigs to operators for a daily fee known as a day-rate. The company has purpose-built many of its rigs for particular operators looking for a customized rig; these rigs are normally secured by long-term contracts that essentially finance the cost of construction.

Finally, oil service giant Baker Hughes (NYSE: BHI) garnered significant leverage to unconventional gas development when it purchased BJ Services, a US-based firm that specialized in hydraulic fracturing. Unlike BJ, Baker has a large existing international presence. That means it will be able to market BJ's expertise in hydraulic fracturing abroad to develop international shale gas fields.

The Conventional Choice

Amid all the excitement about LNG and unconventional gas, don't forget about traditional producers, Russia in particular. Although the US recently overtook Russia to become the world's top producer, the country is a close No. 2 and remains a key supplier of gas to both Europe and, increasingly, Asia.

Traditional definitions of proved reserves don't properly capture unconventional resources; however, based on conventional reserves, Russia remains No. 1 with an estimated 43.3 trillion cubic meters.[28]

The must-own firm for playing Russian gas production is Gazprom (Moscow: GAZP, OTC: OGZPY), the partially state-owned firm that's responsible for 84 percent of Russia's gas production. In addition to producing both gas and oil, Gazprom owns the world's largest network of pipelines, a total of 159,000 kilometers, and owns power-generation assets in its home country. Russia's strategic goal is to boost gas production from 664 bcm in 2008 to 885 to 940 bcm by 2030. As the largest player Gazprom will be responsible for most of that upside. The company has a number of new developments in the works to meet these targets.

Russia currently supplies most of its gas under long-term arrangements to Europe. However, Asia is clearly becoming a big priority. Gazprom sees Chinese natural gas demand growing rapidly and believes the Middle Kingdom will need to import more than half its supply by 2025. Gazprom and China National Petroleum Corporation signed basic agreements covering increased gas supply in 2009. Although commercial terms remain vague, Gazprom has noted that volumes under discussion are comparable to China's total current gas consumption.[29]

Crude oil tends to dominate the headlines and remains first in most investors' minds. That's a huge mistake: Natural gas is cheaper, cleaner, and more widely available than oil and is price-competitive with coal in many markets. These advantages make it likely that gas will grab market share from other fuels in industrial, electric power, and even transportation markets in coming years.

US energy giant Exxon projects that gas will be the world's fastest-growing fossil fuel through 2030. Use of natural gas will grow by 1.8 percent per year, compared to 0.5 percent for coal and 0.8 percent for oil. This would make gas a more important source of power than coal by 2030.

Exxon backed that prediction with a USD41 billion long-term bet on gas when it purchased XTO Energy in December 2009. Investors would do well to follow Exxon's lead.

Endnotes

[1] Energy Information Administration International Energy Outlook 2009, http://www.eia.doe.gov/oiaf/ieo/graphic_data_electricity.html (accessed January 24, 2010).

[2] Ibid.

[3] Ibid.

4   Ibid.

5   Ibid.

6   World Bank Data Finder, "Electric Power Consumption," http://datafinder.worldbank.org/electric-power-consumption (accessed February 25, 2010).

7   EIA, http://www.eia.doe.gov/emeu/reps/enduse/er01_us_tab1.html (accessed January 5, 2010).

8   Enterprise Product Partners Fourth Quarter 2009 Conference Call February 1, 2010.

9   "Looming Mideast Olefin Production May—or May Not—Spell Oversupply," *Oil & Gas Journal*, March 23, 2009, http://www.ogj.com/index/article-display/356853/articles/oil-gas-journal/volume-107/issue-12/processing/looming-mideast-olefin-production-maymdashor-may-notmdashspell-oversupply.html.

10 Annual Energy Outlook 2010, http://www.eia.doe.gov/oiaf/aeo/aeoref_tab.html (accessed February 27, 2010).

11 Nina Rach, "Special Report: Natural Gas Vehicles Gain in Global Markets," February 16, 2009, *Oil & Gas Journal*, http://www.ogj.com/index/article-display/353339/articles/oil-gas-journal/volume-107/issue-7/general-interest/special-report-natural-gas-vehicles-gain-in-global-markets.html, (accessed February 14, 2010).

12 Ibid.

13 Ibid.

14 Ibid.

15 NaturalGas.org, "Natural Gas and the Environment," http://www.naturalgas.org/environment/naturalgas.asp#pollution (accessed February 17, 2010).

16 Bob Tippee, "TIPRO Uses Convention to Push Increased Gas Use," *Oil & Gas Journal*, February 25, 2010 (accessed February 25, 2010).

17 EIA Annual Energy Outlook 2010, http://www.eia.doe.gov/oiaf/aeo/electricity_generation.html (accessed February 17, 2010).

18 US Environmental Protection Agency (EPA), "Clean Energy," http://www.epa.gov/rdee/energy-and-you/affect/air-emissions.html (accessed February 25, 2010).

19 Joseph Kahn and Jim Yardley, "As China Roars, Pollution Reaches Deadly Extremes," *The New York Times*, August 25, 2007, http://www.nytimes.com/2007/08/26/world/asia/26china.html (accessed January 26, 2010).

20 UK Department of Energy and Climate Change, http://www.decc.gov.uk/en/content/cms/statistics/climate_change/gg_emissions/uk_emissions/2008_final/2008_final.aspx (accessed February 12, 2010).

21 BP Statistical Review of World Energy 2009, http://www.bp.com/productlanding.do?categoryId=6929&contentId=7044622.

22 Leena Koottungal, "Special Report: Construction Survey Shows Delay in Completion Dates," *Oil & Gas Journal*, November 16, 2009, http://www.ogj.com/index/article-display/9676765680/articles/oil-gas-journal/volume-107/Issue_43/General_Interest/Special_Report__Construction_survey_shows_delay_in_completion_dates.html.

23 EIA, Qatar Country Analysis Brief, http://www.eia.doe.gov/cabs/Qatar/Background.html.

24 Ibid.

25 "Special Report: Major Oil and Gas Projects," *Oil & Gas Journal*, August 10, 2009, http://www.ogj.com/index/article-display/0711973246/articles/oil-gas-journal/volume-107/issue_30/Drilling___Production/Special_Report__Major_projects.html.

26 EIA Country Analysis Brief: Indonesia, http://www.eia.doe.gov/cabs/Indonesia/NaturalGas.html.

27 "Special Report: Major Oil and Gas Projects," *Oil & Gas Journal*, August 10, 2009, http://www.ogj.com/index/article-display/0711973246/articles/oil-gas-journal/volume-107/issue_30/Drilling___Production/Special_Report__Major_projects.html.

28 BP Statistical review of World Energy 2009.

29 "Gaining Momentum" Gazprom Investor Day Presentation February, 2010, http://www.gazprom.com/f/posts/74/811580/investor_day_2010_presentation.pdf.

8

Coal: The World's Workhorse

Investors all too often dismiss coal as an anachronism, a relic of the 19th century. For many environmental groups, coal is public enemy No. 1 because of its reputation as the dirtiest of the fossil fuels. Coal will remain an important part of the global energy mix in the 21st century, just as it was in the 18th and 19th centuries.

Countries like China and India will continue to pursue natural gas, nuclear, and other sources of electric power, but coal remains the cheap choice in both nations and will still be the largest source of power in 20 years.

Coal doesn't get enough respect. The mobile telephones, personal computers (PC), and flat-panel televisions that are the trappings of modern life in a high-tech economy are all powered by electricity, and chances are electricity is derived from coal. More than 42 percent of global electricity generation comes from coal, double the contribution from natural gas, the next most important source of power.[1]

The US gets more than half its power from coal; Germany and Denmark, two nations often hailed for their investments in renewable power sources, derive 49 and 51 percent of their power from coal, respectively.[2] Coal is even more important in the developing world, supplying 81 percent of China's electricity and 68 percent of India's.

Coal is cheap, plentiful, and widely distributed geographically; it's second only to oil in terms of global primary energy consumption. The US Energy Information Administration (EIA) projects coal's share of global primary energy consumption will rise slightly by 2030.

Steam and Met

The term "coal" actually refers to two different commodities used for very different purposes. Just as with oil and natural gas, coal serves two end-markets: industrial energy and electric power generation.

Steam coal is used in power plants to produce electricity. As is the case with crude oil, not all steam coals are exactly alike. Some steam coal naturally contains a large amount of sulfur. When burned, the sulfur in this coal bonds with oxygen in the air to form sulfur dioxide (SOX), a dangerous pollutant that causes acid rain. Because most countries in the developed and developing world alike have tightened emissions standards for SOX, burning high-sulfur coals typically requires the use of flue gas desulfurization (FGD) units, commonly known as scrubbers. Advanced modern scrubbers are capable of removing more than 95 percent of the SOX in exhaust gas from a power plant.[3]

Steam coals also differ due to their heat content. For example, a typical steam coal produced in the Central Appalachian region of the Eastern US would contain 12,500 British thermal units (Btu) per pound and about 1.2 percent sulfur. Meanwhile, coal from the Illinois Basin in the US tends to have relatively high Btu content but is also high in sulfur; standard Illinois Basin coal as defined by the EIA has 11,800 Btu per pound and sulfur content of about 5 percent.

Metallurgical coal—typically known simply as met or coking coal—is used to make steel in blast furnaces. Metallurgical coal is high in energy and carbon content, low in ash content, and low in sulfur. Met coal is fed into a furnace and heated to around 1,000 to 1,100 degrees Celsius (2,000 degrees Fahrenheit) in the absence of oxygen to make what's known as coke. Coke is a dense, nearly pure form of carbon that burns at an extremely high temperature.[4]

Because met coal must be higher in energy content and lower in impurities than steam coal, it also typically trades at a higher price per ton. At the end of 2009, for example, US met coal traded around USD117.52 per short ton (0.91 metric tons) compared to USD51.22 per ton for Central Appalachian coal and USD9.30 per ton for Powder River Basin coal.

The drivers of growth in coal demand are, therefore, twofold: growth in demand for electricity and world steel production in blast furnaces. Global demand for electricity is rising quickly, particularly in the developing world. But even in developed countries electricity demand is growing at a faster pace than energy demand generally. Coal is the dominant source of electric power globally and therefore stands to gain from the broader growth in demand for electricity. The main advantage of coal over other fuels is that it's widely available in some of the world's fastest-growing consuming countries, notably China. Availability of supply translates into lower costs. This advantage alone will be enough for coal to maintain its market share in global electricity generation.

As Figure 8.1 illustrates, China is both the world's largest producer and largest consumer of coal.

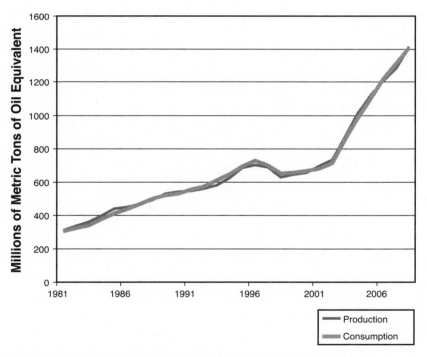

Figure 8.1   Chinese coal consumption and production.

(Source: BP Statistical Review of World Energy 2009)

Figure 8.1 shows Chinese coal production and consumption in terms of millions of metric tons of oil equivalent from 1981 through 2008. On this basis China produces more than two times as much coal as its nearest competitor, the US.

As the Chinese economy began to experience accelerating growth in the late 1990s, electricity demand began to rise sharply, and the country aggressively built out its power-generation capacity. Much of this growth came in the form of new coal plants. In recent years China has opened a new large-scale, coal-fired power plant every seven to ten days.[5] What's most interesting about Figure 8.1 is that as Chinese demand for coal ramped up after 1998, domestic coal production was able to keep pace.

In 2009 China imported record-setting quantities of coal. However, it's fair to say that China is far less dependent on imports for its coal supply than is the case for other fossil fuels such as oil and natural gas. Given the country's massive production base and its cache of the third-largest coal reserves in the world behind the US and Russia, China's relative self-sufficiency in coal is likely to persist for the foreseeable future. This gives coal a structural advantage over other potential power sources.

At first blush projecting a sharp rise in demand for both coal and natural gas in China's energy mix seems incongruous. But natural gas accounted for only about 3 percent of China's primary energy consumption in 2006; this share of the Chinese energy mix will rise sharply due to a strong expansion in gas-generating capacity and greater industrial use of the fuel. But the increase in gas's share of the grid is coming from a relatively low base.[6]

Meanwhile, coal's share of total electricity generation and of primary energy consumption will drop slightly but remain dominant. The EIA projects that coal will remain the preeminent source of power for China for years to come.[7]

China is far from the only growth story when it comes to steam coal. India is forecast to see stronger growth in coal demand for power generation in coming years due to a policy of rapidly building out such capacity. The Central Electric Authority (CEA) and the Confederation of Indian Industry (CII) compile a white paper every five years that offers targets for the amount of electric generating capacity India will need to meet demand. The current plan, the 11th in this series, runs from 2007 through 2012 and targets the addition of total capacity of 78,577 megawatts (MW) over the planning period. Of that total, nearly three-quarters of the added capacity, a total of nearly 53,000 MW, is projected to come from coal-fired plants.[8]

Figure 8.2 provides a detailed breakdown of the planned timing of these power-capacity additions. It's clear that coal plants dominate this plan, and installations are expected to accelerate in the final three years of its execution. In addition, the white paper notes that preliminary estimates for capacity additions in the 12th plan, covering the following five years, call for an additional 40,200 MW of thermal capacity.

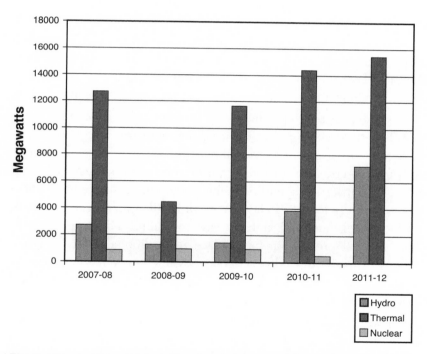

Figure 8.2   India projected power capacity additions. Note: Thermal capacity technically includes coal, natural gas, and liquid-fuel capacity but is roughly 90 percent coal-fired.

(Source: Central Electric Authority, Confederation of Indian Industry [CII])

During implementation of India's 10th plan, from 2002 through 2007, the country added only 12,114 MW of thermal capacity and 21,180 of total MW—the 11th plan represents considerable acceleration in planned coal-fired capacity build-out. India has a mixed record of actually fully meeting its plans; actual achievement under the 10th plan was only about 52 percent of the target. But most of the shortfall was due to supply constraints on the part of equipment manufacturers, in particular Bharat Heavy Electricals.

India's planned heavy reliance on coal-fired capacity to meet growing demand for electricity suggests the fuel is the most economic choice for the country, just as it is for China. But there's one key difference between China and India: India is far more reliant on imports of coal, and this has broad implications for key exporting nations such as Australia.

China is the key country to watch when it comes to rising industrial coal demand. Steel blast furnaces require coke made from metallurgical coal. China is the world's largest steel-maker, producing more than four times as much as its nearest competitor, Japan.

It's also possible to produce steel by using an electric arc furnace to melt scrap steel. This method uses electricity for energy and doesn't require the use of coke as in a blast furnace. However, economic use of an electric arc furnace requires substantial supplies of scrap metal. Countries such as the US have enough scrap metal to make electric arc furnaces—also known as mini-mills—an economic way to produce steel, but that's not the case in China.[9] Ninety percent of Chinese steel production takes place in traditional blast furnaces. Although this share will likely decline given China's massive demand for steel, blast furnaces will remain the primary production method for some time to come.

Figure 8.3 shows the projected growth in coal demand for both the developed (OECD) and developing world (non-OECD) out to 2030. Both regions of the world will see growth in coal demand, but a whopping 93 percent will come from developing countries.

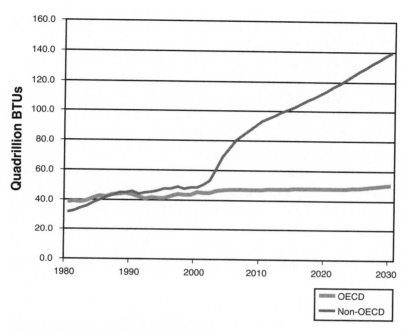

Figure 8.3   Global coal consumption.

(Source: Energy Information Administration International Energy Outlook 2009)

Environmental Issues

The most common charge leveled against coal is that it's a dirty fuel. This characterization is largely true. The list of harmful pollutants includes particulate matter, or soot, SOX, nitrous oxide (NOX), and mercury. However, the use of modern scrubbers and new, more advanced plant designs are helping to clean up coal plants.

Plant operators use a device known as a flue gas desulfurization (FGD) unit, or scrubber, to remove sulfur from power-plant flue gas. FGD units are simple. Flue gases exiting a plant boiler travel through a tower and are sprayed with a liquid that contains limestone sorbents. These sorbents actually absorb the sulfur in the gas.[10] Other ways of controlling sulfur emissions include burning low-sulfur coals such as those from the Powder River Basin of the Western US or pre-washing coal before it's burned.

Tackling NOX is more complex. One way NOX emissions can be controlled is through so-called low-NOX burners, where the coal is burned in stages and the amount of oxygen in each stage is carefully controlled. This technique reduces NOX emissions by 40 to 60 percent. Another technique is similar to that used to remove sulfur. Flue gasses are passed through an ammonia-based spray that converts NOX to harmless byproducts including nitrogen and water.[11]

Mercury is tougher to remove. Although it occurs in only minute quantities in coal, it can accumulate over time and pose a significant hazard. Some existing scrubber and precipitator technologies have been shown to reduce mercury emissions, and research is under way on chemicals that could be sprayed into flue gas to strip out more mercury.[12]

Scrubbers and similar equipment are useful ways of stripping most pollutants from coal-fired-plant emissions. But the focus of the environmental debate surrounding coal is the issue of carbon dioxide (CO_2) and greenhouse gas (GHG) emissions.

Figure 8.4 illustrates that burning coal produces far more carbon emissions than burning oil or natural gas. Given the importance of coal in the global energy mix, the fuel is also far and away the world's most significant source of energy-related GHG.

There are a number of ways to control the carbon emissions of coal-fired power plants. One of the simplest is to employ the most efficient modern plants possible. Table 8.1 details the emissions profiles for three different types of coal-fired power plants.

Generating efficiency is a measure of how effectively a plant converts energy in coal to electricity; the higher the number, the more efficient the plant. All pulverized coal (PC) plants work in the same basic manner. Coal is ground into a powder of roughly the same consistency as talcum powder. This powder is then injected into a boiler and ignited; the heat created is used to produce steam that, in turn, drives a turbine. Older, subcritical plants run at lower pressures and temperatures than newer, supercritical and ultra-supercritical plants. The higher pressures and temperatures of newer plants make these facilities more efficient.

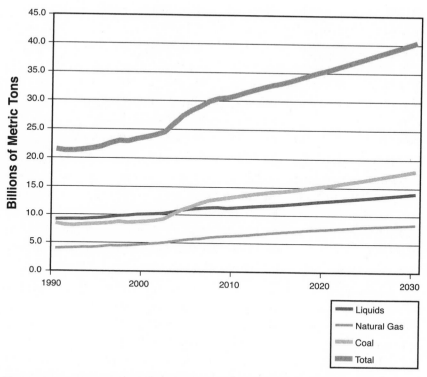

Figure 8.4   Global emissions of carbon dioxide by fuel type.

(Source: Energy Information Administration International Energy Outlook 2009)

TABLE 8.1   Cost and Emissions of Coal Plants

	Subcritical PC	Supercritical PC	Ultra-Supercritical PC
Generating Efficiency (HHV)	34.3	38.5	43.3
Coal Feed (Kg/Hr)	208,000	185,000	164,000
Carbon Dioxide Emitted (Kg/Hr)	466,000	415,000	369,000
Total Plant Cost (USD/KW)	1,280	1,330	1,360

(Source: The Future of Coal: Options for a Carbon-Constrained World, Massachusetts Institute of Technology (MIT), 2007 http://web.mit.edu/coal/The_Future_of_Coal.pdf?kloc=NONE)

Note: Based on a 500 megawatt coal plant

The difference between older, subcritical PC plants and the most modern, ultra-supercritical plants is large. The efficiency ratio is nearly 10 percentage points higher. Modern plants consume far less coal to produce the same amount of energy. The ultra-supercritical, 500 MW plant consumes 44,000 kilograms (97,000 pounds) less coal per hour than the referenced subcritical plant. The most efficient plant in Table 8.1 produces nearly 100,000 kilograms (220,000 pounds) less CO_2 per hour than an older, subcritical plant.

This is exactly the path China has been taking to reduce emissions and improve efficiency. In 2007 the Chinese government embarked on a plan to ensure the closure of 50 gigawatts (GW) of older, inefficient, coal-fired power plants by 2010 and to close any 100 MW generators that have been in use for 20 years or more. For example, the government required any company wanting to build a new 600 MW modern facility to close down 420 MW of older capacity.[13]

Although China has made efforts to modernize its plants, the same can't be said of Europe and the US. The average coal plant in Europe is close to three decades old, while in North America this average is closer to 35 years. Plants built that long ago can have average efficiencies a full 10 percent or more below the current state of the art.[14] It's become fashionable for activists in the West to fight the construction of new coal-fired facilities. In some cases, environmental activists go to extreme measures such as physically impeding the movement of people, vehicles, and equipment. Ironically, these efforts, coupled with uncertainty surrounding the future of climate change policy, are increasing emissions of all sorts of pollutants, a classic tale of unintended consequences. Operators unable to build new plants are simply running older, more inefficient plants instead. Over time, natural gas, nuclear, or some other, cleaner fuel may be able to replace these aging coal facilities, but this transition will take years. By refusing to allow construction of a new generation of coal plant, it's inevitable that the average efficiency of Chinese coal installations will surpass those in the West.

Looking a bit further into the future, there's considerable promise in a technology called carbon capture and sequestration (CCS). Most proposals for CCS involve capturing CO_2 and storing it in natural underground rock formations. In a natural reservoir gas doesn't escape to the surface because there's an impermeable cap rock above the formation that won't allow the gas to pass through. CCS would involve injecting CO_2 into similar formations. CCS is already being done on a commercial scale, though not to trap power-plant emissions. Norway's Sleipner field in the North Sea contains natural gas mixed with unusually large quantities of CO_2. Norway imposes a tax on carbon emissions, so the operator of the field, Statoil, can't simply separate and flare the CO_2. Instead the company uses a technique known as amine scrubbing to remove and isolate the CO_2; this process involves mixing the gas with liquid amine, a chemical that absorbs gaseous CO_2. The amine solvent and CO_2 can then be separated using heat, and the amine can be reused. Statoil injects the separated CO_2 into a shallower rock formation located above the gas-producing Sleipner field, which contains mainly salt water. This formation is sealed, so the gas can't escape, and Statoil monitors the formation to ensure that none is accidentally released. Sleipner captures a total of about 1 million tons of CO_2 annually, and the rock formation used for sequestration has enough volume to store decades' worth of produced CO_2 safely. Although Sleipner involves capturing less carbon than the average coal plant, it's still a valuable illustration of CCS's potential.

One play on cleaning up coal is Alstom (France: ALO, OTC: AOMFF). The company builds and supplies parts for modern natural gas, coal, hydropower, and even nuclear power plants. In addition, Alstom performs maintenance and upgrades to existing facilities, which makes it a direct beneficiary of the desire to upgrade power-plant efficiency. Alstom is capable of building the newest, most efficient coal plants.

Alstom has been working on one of the world's first true carbon-capture pilot projects, a 30 MW plant located in Germany that utilizes a technology known as Oxy-Combustion to capture CO_2 up to 75,000 metric tons per year. In Oxy-Combustion, the coal is burned in the presence of nearly pure oxygen and recycled flue gas rather than normal air. The product of burning coal in this environment is almost purely CO_2 and water vapor; the pure stream of CO_2 is easier to separate and sequester than the diluted CO_2 produced in a normal coal plant.

Supplying the Demand

Many of the world's largest coal consumers are far more self-sufficient in coal than in other fossil fuels. For example, the US is the world's second-largest coal consumer behind China, but it produces plenty of both steam and metallurgical coal to meet domestic demand. Blessed with the world's largest coal reserves, the US is likely to export it in larger quantities in coming years.

But Chinese demand for coal has outstripped supply. In 2009, imports, including both met and steam coal, soared to a record of more than 126 million metric tons. Given the planned build-out of India's coal-fired generation capacity, the country is set to be the world's fastest-growing importer of steam coal.

The EIA projects total steam coal exports to surge 32 percent between 2007 and 2030 and met coal exports to rise 28 percent. Table 8.2 offers a list of the largest exporters for both steam and met coal in both years. One country truly stands out: Australia, which will soon surpass Indonesia to become the world's largest exporter of steam coal. It's already the established leader in met coal exports. Close to two-thirds of total global metallurgical coal exports come from Australia, which exports roughly five times as much coal as each of its nearest competitors, the US and Canada.

The key to Australia's continued dominance of the coal trade is its massive expansion of coal port export capacity. Australia has nine coal-loading terminals with a total capacity of more than 330 million metric tons per year. The largest ports in Australia include the Port of Newcastle in New South Wales, which has total capacity of more than 100 metric tons of exports per year, and Gladstone Bay and Dalrymple Bay in Queensland, with capacities of 75 and 68 million tons per year, respectively.[15]

The only country that really challenges Australia in terms of exports is Indonesia, and that's only for exports of steam coal. Indonesia ramped up its production and exports of coal because it's able to load coal directly onto river barges and transport it to larger vessels moored offshore. This eliminated the need to construct much of the advanced infrastructure Australia has in place to export coal.[16] But export growth is starting to hit a wall. Indonesia's domestic-power demand is ramping up, and the government has made noises about limiting growth in exports to maintain more of the resource for domestic consumption. Meanwhile, the bottlenecks in export capacity that have plagued Australia for years are being resolved by port expansions. This is allowing Australia to overtake Indonesia in steam-coal exports.

TABLE 8.2   Largest Exporters of Steam and Met Coal

Steam Exporters	2007	2030
Indonesia	201.5	202.6
Australia	126.5	241.7
South America	80.5	166.7
Southern Africa	75.3	110.5
Eurasia	67.8	90.1
USA	27.0	24.4
Met Coal Exporters	**2007**	**2030**
Australia	151.3	204.4
USA	32.2	23.7
Canada	29.4	38.0
Indonesia	22.6	21.6

(Source: Energy Information Administration International Energy Outlook 2009)
Note: All figures in short tons (1 short ton = 0.9 metric tons)

The strategic importance of Australia's vast coal resources and export potential hasn't gone unnoticed in China. In 2009 Chinese coal mining giant Yanzhou Coal Mining (NYSE: YZC) acquired Australia's Felix Resources in a deal worth USD3.2 billion. Felix Resources was attractive because it had significant coal production growth opportunities.

In China, Yanzhou owns six mines, all producing steam coal. Total production from those six mines is around 33 million metric tons per year. These plays are all located in Shandong Province in Eastern China, a populous coastal area where coal is in high demand. It's also a relatively easy area from which to transport coal because of its proximity to key railway lines. Yanzhou's main mines are mature—the oldest of the core six plays was discovered in 1966 and put into production in 1973, while the youngest was put into production in 2000. Although there are years of production ahead for these mines, this relative maturity is one reason the miner is branching out and buying reserves in Australia.

In addition to the core six mines, Yanzhou also has three newer mines, a steam-coal mine, a met-coal mine, and combination steam-coal/met-coal mine. Annual coal capacity from all three mines should ramp up to more than 5 million tons over the next few years.

The Felix takeover was a large deal, but it's far from China's sole attempt to gain access to coal reserves. China spent USD8 billion in coal-related acquisitions in 2009 alone.

US-based coal mining giant Peabody Energy (NYSE: BTU) has dramatically shifted its operational focus in recent years from the US market to Australia and, to a lesser extent, other regions within Asia. In 2009 Peabody exported 9.6 million short tons (8.7 metric tons) of steam coal and 6.9 million short tons (6.3 million metric tons) of met coal from its Australian mines.

By 2014, through a series of major mine expansions, Peabody believes it can expand its thermal capacity to between 15 million and 17 million short tons per year (13.7 million to 15.5 million metric tons) and its met coal capacity to around 12 million to 15 million short tons (11 million to 13.7 million metric tons). That would represent production growth of 77 and 117 percent, respectively.

Elsewhere in Asia, Peabody has expressed interest in projects in Mongolia, a country that's likely to be a key supplier to neighboring China. It'll take years for Mongolia to become a significant part of Peabody's revenue base, even under the most optimistic scenarios. But management has highlighted the nation as a significant opportunity going forward. In the US, Peabody's exposure is primarily to coal from the Powder River Basin and the Illinois Basin. Powder River Basin coal typically can be mined from the surface rather than deep underground, so it's cheaper to produce.

Macarthur Coal (Sydney: MCC, OTC: MACDF) is a Queensland, Australia-based coal miner that's 22.4 percent owned by CITIC Group, a China-based investment fund that has interests in a long list of commodity plays. Steel plays ArcelorMittal (NYSE: MT) and

POSCO (NYSE: PKX) own 16.6 percent and 8.3 percent stakes in the firm, respectively.

Macarthur owns a 73.3 percent share of a joint venture that controls the Coppabella and Moorvale mines in Queensland, which combined produce 6.3 million metric tons of coal annually. In addition, the company owns a 74.6 percent share of the Middlemount Mine Project. Larger, more diversified plays on Australian coal mining include BHP Billiton (Sydney: BHP; NYSE: BHP) and Xstrata (London: XTA; OTC: XSRAY). The former is the world's largest mining concern with operations in nickel, copper, iron ore, uranium, and diamonds, among other markets.

As a percentage of revenue BHP's largest market is iron ore, but it also derives more than 16 percent of revenue from metallurgical coal and 13 percent from steam coal. Though its business is diversified, BHP ranks among the world's largest exporters of both commodities.

London-based Xstrata's biggest market is copper, which accounts for more than 40 percent of revenue. The company also derives a quarter of its revenue from thermal coal and 5 percent from coking coal. Xstrata has 30 operating coal mines in Australia, South Africa, and Columbia, and ranks as among the top exporters of thermal coal in the world.

Bucyrus (NSDQ: BUCY) manufactures mining equipment used to produce all sorts of metals and minerals. But far and away its top end-market is coal, which accounts for more than three-quarters of the firm's business. Another important end-market for Bucyrus is equipment used to produce oil sands; this machinery accounts for less than 10 percent of new equipment sales.

The company sells new equipment and provides after-market parts and services. Roughly half of its revenue comes from new equipment, the other half from after-market services. Sales of new equipment tend to perform best during strong coal markets, while recurring maintenance revenue shines in weaker markets.

Although environmental factors will remain a concern for coal plants for the foreseeable future, more efficient modern plants and the adoption of modern scrubber equipment can make coal a cleaner source of power. And companies are just beginning to examine the potential of carbon capture technologies. Investors should resist the idea that environmental concerns will bring an overnight change to US or global electric supply. It's easy to forget the scale of the electric grid. Building the coal plants that now supply half of America's power and 42 percent of global electricity took decades, and these facilities generate a massive amount of power. Closing and replacing these plants would require a rebuild of one of the most complex and expensive pieces of infrastructure on Earth. And it would take decades to accomplish.

Investors in the developed world must also recognize that the energy equation is different in a country like China or India than it is in the US. Every developed-world country, including the US and Japan, has gone through a rapid, accelerated phase of energy demand growth at some point in the history in its development. The fact is that a rise in personal disposable income and rapid energy demand growth go hand-in-hand. Developing markets will remain focused on supplying these energy needs. Although countries like China have and will continue to take steps to lessen the impacts of their rapid growth on the environment, it's unreasonable to expect drastic changes that would stunt economic growth.

Endnotes

[1] EIA International Energy Outlook 2009, http://www.eia.doe.gov/oiaf/ieo/index. html (accessed January 26, 2010).

[2] International Energy Agency Country Statistics, http://www.iea.org/stats/ electricitydata.asp?COUNTRY_CODE=DE (accessed January 27, 2010).

[3] Duke Energy, "Sulfur Dioxide Scrubbers," http://www.duke-energy.com/environ-ment/air-quality/sulfur-dioxide-scrubbers.asp (accessed February 21, 2010).

[4] World Coal Institute, "Coal & Steel," http://www.worldcoal.org/coal/uses-of-coal/ coal-steel/.

[5] Keith Bradsher and David Barboza, "Pollution from Chinese Coal Casts a Global Shadow," *The New York Times*, June 11, 2006, http://www.nytimes.com/2006/06/ 11/business/worldbusiness/11chinacoal.html (accessed February 22, 2010).

[6] EIA International Energy Outlook 2009.

[7] Ibid.

[8] CEA and CII White Paper on Strategy for 11th plan, http://www.cea.nic.in/ planning/white%20paper.pdf (accessed February 26, 2010).

[9] World Coal Institute, http://www.cea.nic.in/planning/white%20paper.pdf.

[10] Department of Energy, "Coal Becomes a Future Fuel," http://www.netl.doe.gov/KeyIssues/future_fuel.html.

[11] Ibid.

[12] Ibid.

[13] "China to Require Swap of Old Coal Plants for New," January 31, 2007, http://uk.reuters.com/article/idUKPEK24451620070131?pageNumber=1&virtualBrand-Channel=0.

[14] Siemens, "Modernizing Infrastructures: New Life for Old Plants," http://www.siemens.com/innovation/en/publikationen/pof_fall_2009/infrastruktur/kraftwerke.htm.

[15] The Australian Coal Association, http://www.australiancoal.com.au/the-australian-coal-industry_coal-loading-ports.aspx (accessed March 1, 2010).

[16] Alan Copeland, "Abare: Australian Commodities," September 2007, http://www.abare.gov.au/publications_html/ac/ac_07/ac_sept07.pdf.

9

The Other Energy

Coal, natural gas, and oil will continue to account for most global primary energy use for decades to come. Of the remaining sources of energy, nuclear and hydroelectric are the most important and most economically viable over the next few decades.

Solar and wind power get the most attention as alternative fuels and are often pitched as a means of reducing emissions and weaning the world from dependence on fossil fuels. But alternatives have a decidedly mixed history of success and are unlikely to make a meaningful contribution to global power supplies for decades to come. Nonetheless, aggressive government policies to promote alternatives will generate significant growth in the industry.

British economist John Maynard Keynes once wrote that the long run is a misleading guide to current affairs because "in the long run, we are all dead." Energy investors would do well to remember this observation.

The world's big three energy plays are oil, coal, and natural gas. These three commodities account for more than 85 percent of all primary energy consumed in the world today. Although it's true that developed countries tend to employ a more diverse slate of energy supplies, the real difference is minimal—the same big three account for 81 percent of primary energy use in the developed world and are projected to meet 78 percent of demand in 2030.[1]

Given their dominance, it's only proper that the big three energy plays receive the most attention from investors, companies, and governments. This is certainly the case in parts of the developing world;

China and India have both taken steps to secure access to strategic commodities in recent years.

However, in the developed world—and particularly in the mass media—the big three frequently get short shrift in favor of alternative sources of energy such as wind, solar, and biofuels. Unfortunately, this has led to the widespread delusion that these alternatives are destined to replace the big three in the short to intermediate term. Politicians from all over the political spectrum feed this popular and dangerous myth by proposing naïve and simplistic silver-bullet solutions to the world's energy supply challenges. Investors largely overestimate the promise and importance of new and alternative energy technologies and underestimate the time and investment required to accomplish a meaningful shift in energy supply.

We've attempted to convey the immense complexity of global energy supply. Energy is arguably the most important industry in the world and is among the heaviest of all. Companies and governments have built immense physical infrastructure costing trillions of dollars to supply the world with the power and fuel it needs. It's completely infeasible that this can all be replaced or changed in any reasonable time frame, even assuming access to unlimited financial resources. And given the perilous state of sovereign and household finances in the Western world, neither the consumer nor the government can afford a shift from fossil fuels any time soon.

Successful investing requires forward thinking and a strategic view of the future. However, there's an equally pernicious danger in the form of trying to think too far into the future and overestimating the speed at which change can occur. This doesn't mean there aren't investment opportunities in energy sources outside coal, gas, and oil. Some technologies, such as nuclear and hydroelectric power, are already well-developed, proven, major sources of energy and will expand in coming years. And developing-world countries are major drivers of investment and demand for both. Other alternatives, including solar, wind, and biofuels, are heavily supported by government policy and will grow rapidly, albeit from a low base.

Nuclear and Hydroelectric

Outside the major fossil fuels, nuclear power and hydroelectric are the most important sources of energy worldwide, accounting for around 13 percent of primary energy consumption.[2] The only meaningful market for nuclear and hydroelectric is, of course, the generation of electricity.

Figure 9.1 illustrates that nuclear power accounts for 13 percent of global electricity generation while hydroelectric makes up a further 16 percent. Both share a few major advantages over other sources of electricity.

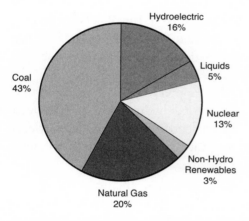

Figure 9.1   Global electricity generation by fuel, 2010.

(Source: Energy Information Administration International Energy Outlook, 2009)

First, neither requires the import of large quantities of commodities. Hydroelectric power simply uses the force of a river to turn a turbine. Meanwhile, the fuel for nuclear power is uranium, or, more particularly, uranium that's been enriched and processed into fuel rods. But uranium is widely available compared to oil, natural gas, and even coal; even for countries that import uranium, the quantities required are low. The cost of fuel just isn't a major contributor to the cost of nuclear power. In the US variable operating and maintenance expenses including fuel costs account for just 8 percent of the total cost of nuclear power, compared to 20 to 25 percent for coal and 65 percent for natural gas.[3]

The other major advantage of both nuclear and hydroelectric power is that both power sources are environmentally friendly. Neither nuclear nor hydroelectric plants release direct emissions of any pollutant including sulfur dioxide (SOX), nitrous oxide (NOX), mercury, or carbon dioxide (CO_2). Countries that garner a large portion of their power supply from one or both of these power sources often also rank among the least carbon-intensive of any countries in the world.

The largest producers of hydroelectric power in the world today are China, Canada, Brazil, the US, and Russia. Brazil gets the largest percentage of its total electricity demand from hydro—in 2008, the country had a total of 160 operating hydroelectric facilities generating nearly three-quarters of the country's total electricity supply. Thanks to its massive resource of powerful untapped rivers, it's estimated that only around 27 percent of Brazil's total hydro capacity has been explored.[4] The second-largest hydroelectric facility in the world is Itaipu Binacional, a massive 14 gigawatt (GW) facility on the Paraná River that serves both Brazil and Paraguay.[5]

The only hydroelectric plant larger than Itaipu is the Three Gorges project in China. The mile-long dam over China's Yangtze River was completed in 2008 and has a total of 26 generating turbines and a capacity of 18.2 gigawatts (GW).[6] In the future, growth in hydroelectric power capacity is likely to come from the emerging markets—extensive planning is already under way in China, India, and Brazil. While hydroelectric power is a reliable and large-scale source of power, it's limited by the availability of rivers of the size required to build a plant. Building a power plant on the scale of Itaipu or Three Gorges has major impacts on people located near the river; it's estimated that about 1.4 million people had to be moved as a result of the Three Gorges dam project.[7] Although the benefits of the dam—power generation and flood control—can certainly outweigh those costs, that further limits the potential locations where a hydroelectric facility can be sited, particularly in a developed country such as the US.

There are no pure plays on hydroelectric power for investors. France-based Alstom (France: ALO, OTC: AOMFF), a play on clean coal, also builds hydroelectric plants. In fact, the company is responsible for generator installations on 36 percent of worldwide hydroelectric facilities and has a strong position in projects under way in the emerging markets. The company is building two new power plants—the Santo Antonio and Jirau—on the Madeira River in Brazil with a combined output of 2.137 GW. Both plants are scheduled for completion in 2012, and Alstom is handling the design, assembly, and supply of much of the equipment related to both facilities. Alstom was also one of the suppliers for the Three Gorges power plant in China.

Nuclear accounts for about 13 percent of global electricity generation and close to 22 percent of generation in the developed world.[8] In the US and much of the EU, nuclear is also the most important source of emissions-free power generation. Projections for growth in nuclear power vary widely. The EIA projects total world nuclear power generation to increase by 39.2 percent by 2030, equivalent to growth of about 1.7 percent annualized.[9] Meanwhile, energy giant Exxon Mobil projects nuclear power to grow at a 2.3 percent annualized pace between 2005 and 2030, considerably faster growth than for coal, oil, or natural gas, albeit from a lower base level.[10] The wide variation has to do with assumptions about the future cost and availability of fossil fuels. The cost of nuclear power mainly stems from capital costs and ongoing fixed maintenance expenses, including the huge up-front costs of building a new nuclear facility as well as the costs associated with monitoring and maintaining the plant safely over time. But the fuel costs are extraordinarily low.

In contrast, natural gas plants are more sensitive to commodity prices because fuel is far and away the most important determinant of the cost of gas-fired power. Although coal-fired power costs are less sensitive to commodity prices than gas, the price of coal can be an extremely important cost factor in countries that must import a large percentage of their coal needs.

We expect natural gas to remain more plentiful than oil in coming years, and this will help make it a much cheaper source of energy, particularly in countries such as the US with large domestic supplies.

However, rising demand for gas will ultimately push up prices for liquefied natural gas (LNG); higher commodity prices will tend to decrease demand for fossil fuels and increase demand for nuclear.

Carbon regulation is another major issue. Although controversial, many countries around the world have imposed or are discussing the use of a so-called carbon cap-and-trade system to reduce emissions of greenhouse gases (GHG). Under a cap-and-trade system, the government sets absolute caps on the total amount of emissions and then allows emitters to trade allowances among themselves; each emissions credit would be worth 1 metric ton of carbon dioxide equivalent. If one utility emits too much carbon in a given year, it could buy emissions credits from a firm that emits less than allowed. This effectively puts a price on carbon emissions, encouraging firms that emit too much carbon to cut back and directly rewarding those companies that emit less than allowed. Over time, as the government reduces the allowed cap, emissions credits would become scarcer and more expensive.

With no cost for carbon emissions, coal is the cheapest source of power in the US, followed closely by natural gas. If CO_2 costs USD30 per ton, gas overtakes coal to become the cheapest source of power and nuclear plants become cost-competitive or potentially cheaper than coal. Finally, at USD60 per ton, nuclear becomes more cost-effective than natural gas.[11] As a carbon-free source of energy the higher the assumed cost of CO_2, the more attractive nuclear power.

One point that most forecasters do agree on is that much of the growth in nuclear will come from countries in the developing world. China, India, and Russia plan significant build-outs of nuclear capacity in coming years. As of the end of 2009, there were 435 commercial nuclear reactors operating globally with a combined capacity of 372 GW.

Table 9.1 shows 11 countries that either have major existing nuclear power programs or are planning a major expansion of the technology in coming years.

China and India currently get just 2.2 and 2 percent, respectively, of their power from nuclear but figure prominently in the outlook for future growth. And both countries have proved their stated commitments to expansion of the power source is far more than just words; China has 18 reactors in various stages of construction, India six.

Although many developed countries haven't put a new nuclear reactor into service in decades, China's industry is relatively new: China's first nuclear power plant went into operation in the early 1990s and has grown rapidly to 11 reactors in operation at the end of 2009.

TABLE 9.1 Global Planned Nuclear Energy Expansion

	Share of Electricity Supply (2008 %)	Existing Capacity (GW)	Under Construction (GW)	Planned (GW)	Proposed (GW)
China	2.2	8587	19240	37000	79000
India	2.0	3779	2976	21500	20000
Russia	16.9	21743	7130	8000	36680
USA	19.7	101119	1180	13800	25000
Canada	14.8	12652	1500	4400	3800
UK	13.5	11035	0	6600	9600
France	76.2	63236	1630	1630	1630
Germany	28.3	20339	0	0	0
Italy	0.0	0	0	0	17000
South Korea	35.6	17716	6700	8190	0
Japan	24.9	46236	2285	17915	8388

(Source: World Nuclear Association)

In recent years China has steadily boosted its target for nuclear power generation. In March 2008, the State Energy Bureau (SEB) indicated that China should target 5 percent of its electricity from nuclear power by 2020, a target that would imply the need to have 50 GW of capacity in operation by then, up from 8.6 GW at the end of 2009. Since that pronouncement there have been reports that Chinese officials are targeting even more aggressive targets for 86 GW installed by 2020.[12]

India's nuclear power industry has received a big boost from agreements on nuclear technology with the US and international organizations. The country was previously barred from participating in the international uranium markets because it hasn't signed the

Nuclear Non-Proliferation Treaty (NPT). And since its nuclear weapons test in 1974, India has had no access to US civilian nuclear technology; US technology will dramatically lower India's costs for fueling its reactors. As a result, India has been forced to rely on low-quality, high-cost domestic reserves of uranium to power its existing plants. Prior to signing the deal, the capacity factor—the percent of total nuclear capacity actually being utilized—for Indian nuclear power plants has been hovering around 50 percent due to these inefficiencies. In addition to the catalyst of a nuclear deal with the US, India faces the same basic challenges China does in terms of attempting to meet its rapid growth in demand for electricity and simultaneously diversify its power supply from coal. Nuclear will be a big winner in this effort; India already has six reactors that will nearly double the size of its nuclear capacity under construction. Planned and proposed reactors would increase the country's total capacity by a factor of 11.

Russia's motivation for rapidly expanding its nuclear program is a bit different from that of other nations. Russia's domestic natural gas consumption has ramped up significantly in recent years due to subsidized pricing and strong economic growth. In 2008 the country consumed 40.5 billion cubic feet per day (bcf/d) and produced 58.1 bcf/d. The country consumed nearly three-quarters of its massive gas production, leaving less available for export.[13] Building nuclear plants will increase the total amount of natural gas the nation has available for export to the EU and Asia, where realized prices are many times higher than domestic Russian gas. All told, Russia already derives close to 17 percent of its power from its 31 nuclear plants and has 9 new plants under construction.

Although most of the growth in nuclear capacity will be from the developing world, a nuclear Renaissance is also under way in developed countries. France generates more than three-quarters of its power from nuclear plants and has benefited enormously from its strong commitment to the technology over the years. France emits just 0.24 metric tons of CO_2 per thousand US dollars of gross domestic product (GDP) compared to 0.38 tons in Germany, 0.31 in the UK, and an average of 0.36 tons for Europe as a whole.[14] Thanks to its plentiful nuclear resources, France is Europe's largest exporter of electric power and has among the lowest electricity prices in the EU. The average French household pays EUR0.0959 per kilowatt-hour (kWh) compared to an average of EUR0.1259 for the average consumer in the euro area.[15] France has continued its commitment to nuclear, with one reactor under construction, one planned, and one proposed.

Germany derives more than one-quarter of its power from nuclear but has a mixed history of support for the technology. The Green Party in Germany is stridently antinuclear and in the late 1990s crafted a plan to phase-out all nuclear power plants in the country over time. In 2001 the industry reached a compromise with the government that would allow operating plants to continue for an average of more than 30 years before closing. The new government, elected in 2009, is committed to ditching the phase-out plan for nuclear plants altogether.[16] However, the ongoing uncertainty surrounding its nuclear power industry has prevented any meaningful plans or discussions revolving around new plant construction. And Germany would find it next to impossible to cut its CO_2 emissions meaningfully if it were to phase-out nuclear power. The latter point has prompted some historically antinuclear environmentalists to reconsider or change their position on the power source entirely.

The UK recently reaffirmed its commitment to nuclear as a means of cutting carbon intensity and making up for falling gas supplies from the North Sea. And Italy, a country that closed down all of its operating plants in the 1980s, has a long-term goal of restarting and expanding its nuclear industry.

In the US there are 104 operating plants generating about 20 percent of total electricity supply. Although no new plants have been put into service since the 1970s, one is already under construction, and another 11 are in advanced stages of planning. To aid the restart of the industry, the US Congress is weighing USD18.5 billion in loan guarantees as part of the Energy Policy Act of 2005. In early 2010, the Obama administration proposed more than tripling that amount to USD56.5 billion as part of the 2011 budget. It's likely that support for nuclear power and natural gas would have to feature prominently in any comprehensive energy bill in the US.

There are two obvious plays on the global nuclear renaissance: companies involved in the construction of nuclear plants and uranium mining firms.

US-based Shaw Group's (NSDQ: SHAW) largest source of revenue is building power plants including conventional coal and gas-fired facilities as well as next-generation nuclear plants. Shaw owns a 20 percent stake in Westinghouse Electric Company—which is majority-owned by Japan's Toshiba (Tokyo: 6502; OTC: TOSBF)—and handles design, engineering, and construction work relating to Westinghouse's AP1000 nuclear reactor. The AP1000 is one of the world's leading reactor designs and is expected to form the basis of the Chinese nuclear program in coming years.

France-based Areva's (Paris: CEI; OTC: ARVCF) European Pressurized Reactor (EPR) is the main competition for the AP1000 design. Areva's goal is to capture one-third of the market for new-build nuclear plants, and it's in good shape to meet that target thanks to existing relationships with many of the world's largest operators of nuclear power plants including French giant Electricite de France (EDF).

Another advantage for Areva is that it participates in all stages of the nuclear fuel cycle. In addition to building new reactors, Areva ranked as the world's largest uranium miner and handles the conversion and enrichment of raw uranium oxide into useable nuclear fuel. The company also handles the back-end work related to nuclear plants, including maintenance, waste handling and reprocessing, and recycling of nuclear waste into fuel. Many potential builders of nuclear plants are looking for uranium supply and processing services as well as simple reactor construction. Areva is well placed to offer a true turnkey approach.

Uranium is the key fuel for nuclear power plants and is typically mined in the form of uranium oxide. But mined supplies of uranium are insufficient to meet current demand; operators have been relying on existing inventories of uranium and other secondary sources such as reprocessed nuclear warheads to satisfy an expanding industry. Over the long term, as these secondary sources decline, utilities will need more mined supply. And steady growth in new reactor construction will push up uranium demand even further in coming years. This will be a general tailwind for uranium mining firms with access to proven, producing mines.

Cameco Corporation (Toronto: CCO, NYSE: CCJ) is the world's largest pure-play uranium producer. The company taps what are the world's richest, highest-grade uranium mines. To put this into perspective, some of Cameco's mines have ore grades over 20 percent uranium oxide; some mines being mined globally and commercially have ore grades less than 0.5 percent. This contributes to the fact that Cameco's cash costs for uranium are among the lowest in the world at under USD20 per pound. This is also why the company was among the only players to survive the long uranium bear market intact.

Leveraged play Paladin Resources' (Australia: PDN, TSX: PDN) Langer Heinrich mine in the African nation of Namibia was the first new uranium mine to come into production in decades. Maximum production from the mine is expected to be 6 million pounds of uranium per year. Paladin's Kayelekeera mine in Malawi also began producing uranium in 2009 and should attain maximum capacity of 3.3 million pounds of uranium annually.

Paladin is now moving out of the ranks of junior uranium exploration and mining firms and into the big leagues. It will soon be one of the biggest producers in the world.

Wind and Solar

The two alternative energy technologies that get the most attention are wind and solar power. Of the two, wind is far and away the more important and the more practical from a cost perspective.

Costs of wind and solar vary by country and region. Certain regions of the world experience near-constant winds and are ideal for wind-power generation. In the US the total cost of wind power per megawatt-hour (MWh) is around USD149.30 compared to USD119 for nuclear plants, USD100.4 for a conventional coal plant, and USD79.30 for an advanced combined cycle gas turbine.

Wind itself is free, so there is no fuel cost associated with generating wind power. Capital costs—building the turbines and maintaining them in good working order—make up the bulk of budgets.

Higher natural gas or coal prices would make wind look more attractive from an economic standpoint.

The intermittent nature of wind is a major disadvantage that many fail to fully appreciate. The basic problem is that power isn't stored on the electric transmission grid; supply and demand must balance at any given time. Power output from a wind turbine is related to the cube of wind speed. A doubling in wind speed produces an eightfold increase in power output; even minor changes in wind speed have major impacts on the power supplied to the grid. The generating capacity—the maximum power output—of wind turbines is rated assuming a wind speed of roughly 30 to 32 miles per hour. If the wind speed drops to 80 percent of that level, the actual output from a wind turbine will be just half its rated capacity. And anyone who lives near a wind farm will tell you that, often, many of the turbines aren't turning at all. That's because a minimum wind speed of around 10 miles per hour is required to power the plant. At that minimum wind speed the turbines' power output is just 3 percent of rated capacity.[17]

Even within regions known for their consistent wind, such as parts of Texas, there are surges and lulls in wind speed that cause the actual output from plants to fluctuate rapidly. To compensate, utilities generally install shadow capacity in the form of natural gas peaking plants that can be started quickly to feed power onto the grid when the wind speed hits a lull.

It's estimated that Germany had a total installed base of 23,907 megawatts (MW) of wind capacity at the end of 2008, up from 22,247 MW at the end of 2007. Germany was second only to the US in terms of total installed capacity; at the end of 2008, the US had 25,170 MW of capacity.[18] Wind accounted for 19 percent of Germany's total electric-generating capacity at the end of 2008, but in the same year it provided only around 6.5 percent of output. Germany's wind power plants rarely operate at anything close to their full rated capacity.[19]

E.ON Netz operates one of the largest electricity transmission networks in Germany. The largest proportion of Germany's total wind energy capacity is connected to this transmission system. Germany has been heavily subsidizing wind since the early 1990s, so E.ON Netz has arguably more experience with wind transmission than any other company. According to E.ON, to reliably balance the surges and lulls in power output produced by wind farms, operators must install shadow capacity equal to 90 percent of rated capacity. That means if an operator integrates 1,000 MW of wind energy onto the E.ON Netz network, it must also install 900 MW of traditional power plants—likely natural gas-fired—just to balance the grid and ensure the reliability of electric supply.[20] Given the difficulties E.ON has experienced integrating intermittent wind power onto the grid, the company believes that in 2020, with total German wind power capacity expected at 48,000 MW, those plants will only replace 2,000 MW of traditional power production.[21]

Some proponents of wind energy point to the success of Denmark and Spain in integrating larger percentages of wind power into their grids. These two countries generated 30 percent and 21 percent, respectively, of their total electric power generation using wind in 2008.[22] But one of the common rationales for expanding wind power is that it reduces a country's CO_2 emissions. Wind power appears to have produced mixed results in both Denmark and Spain, as both countries have a carbon intensity—in terms of metric tons per thousand dollars of GDP—that's in line with the European average. Both countries emit far more CO_2 per unit of GDP than nuclear-centric France.[23] Meanwhile, consumers in both nations spend about 30 percent more on electricity than households in France.[24]

The problems with wind are multiplied when it comes to solar power. The current cost of solar photovoltaic power in the US is five times that of a modern gas plant and more than three times that of a wind installation.

Both wind and solar will become more important parts of our energy supply mix. But neither is a panacea for the world's energy problem. The idea that these power sources can replace the big three of coal, natural gas, and oil over the next 30 years is completely asinine. Given the major cost disadvantages facing wind and solar power and the difficulties inherent in integrating these technologies with the grid, one might wonder why companies would bother to pursue wind and solar at all. The answer is simple: Heavy government subsidies and mandates drive growth in the alternative energy industry.

Mechanisms to encourage renewable energy vary widely by country. In European countries such as Germany, feed-in tariff structures are common. Under such a system, utilities are required to purchase renewable energy supply at tariffs that are higher than normal electric rates. The idea is that by paying special, higher rates companies generating renewable power are guaranteed an attractive return on their capital. Over time, these feed-in tariffs can be reduced to encourage renewable power producers to develop ways to reduce the costs of these technologies. In the US, production tax credits (PTC) are offered to incentivize renewable energy. For example, in the US companies that generate wind power get a 2.1 cent per kilowatt-hour PTC for the first ten years of a renewable energy project's existence.[25]

In addition to subsidies and tax credits, some governments use renewable fuel mandates to encourage renewable energy generation. In the US many of these mandates are set by individual states requiring a certain percentage of power to come from alternative energy by a certain future date. There have been proposals to enact a stringent federal alternative energy standard as well.

China has taken the approach of coming up with official targets for renewable energy. For example, the country recently announced it is targeting 150 GW of installed wind capacity by 2020 up from roughly 25 GW today. This is actually higher than the country's 86 GW capacity target for nuclear capacity by the same year. The key is the use of the term "capacity" rather than "generation." "Capacity" simply means that the total rated capacity of wind turbines built equals 150 GW, but these turbines are likely to generate far less than their rated capacity most of the time. Generously assuming a capacity factor of about 35 percent for wind and 90 percent for nuclear, the latter will still remain a more important source of actual power generation in 2020. Nonetheless, sixfold growth in capacity over a ten-year period still spells a big surge in orders for wind turbines and profits for companies selling alternative energy products. Because it's highly unlikely governments will discontinue their subsidies for renewable energy or abandon their targets, wind and solar will grow in coming years.

Denmark's Vestas Wind Systems (Denmark: VWS; OTC: VWSYF) is the world's largest manufacturer of wind turbines with a roughly 20 percent global market share. Vestas benefits from its broad geographic exposure. Europe remains the company's largest market, accounting for more than half of total MW delivered and two-thirds of revenue, but the company has a strong presence in the Americas and is seeing rapid growth in Asia.

India's Suzlon (India: SUEL; OTC: SZEYF), a more direct play on growth in alternative energy in the emerging markets, is the third-largest wind turbine manufacturer in the world with a 12 percent market share. Although the US and EU are Suzlon's largest markets, the company has long held a greater than 50 percent market share in India, a market that's expected to see significant growth in wind capacity in coming years.

Hexcel Corporation (NYSE: HXL) manufactures carbon-fiber composite materials. Carbon fiber is used in a wide variety of applications from automobiles to aircraft and wind turbines. One of the most important applications is a new generation of fuel-efficient, carbon-fiber aircraft—for example, The Boeing Company's 787 Dreamliner. Lighter airplanes such as the 787 are the wave of the future, and the long-delayed Dreamliner's maiden test flight was an upside catalyst for Hexcel. Hexcel also manufactures carbon fiber used in wind turbine blades. Blades made of carbon fiber are lighter and increase the conversion efficiency of turbines, generating more power than traditional turbines under the same wind conditions.

SunPower (NSDQ: SPWRA) designs and manufactures photovoltaic (PV) solar cells; PV cells simply convert solar energy into electric power. The company manufactures PV cells aimed at both the commercial and residential markets. SunPower is the technological leader in the solar market, thus typically commands a premium price.

First Solar (NSDQ: FSLR) is a leader in the so-called thin-film solar market. Thin-film solar differs from the type of solar cells used by the likes of SunPower. First, Solar's cells are less than half as efficient as SunPower's. Although that may seem a disadvantage at first glance, that's not necessarily the case. First Solar's cells don't require polysilicon and are far cheaper to produce than traditional polysilicon-based cells. It's likely this technology will achieve full grid parity—the cost of power will drop more in line with conventional energy sources—before traditional poly PV cells. First Solar also signed a deal with China to build the world's largest solar power plant, a 2 GW facility located in Inner Mongolia.

An even more interesting market than alternative energy is energy efficiency. Typically, the cheapest source of power for most companies and residential customers alike is power you're able to save. Itron (NSDQ: ITRI) is a leading play on energy efficiency and "smart grid" technologies. Itron is already a leader in automatic meters that transmit data via a radio signal directly to technicians, accelerating the meter reading process and cutting costs for utilities.

Itron has a 50 percent market share for automatic meters in the US and close to a third globally. Smart meters are the next step. These meters will not only transmit data about how much energy a residence or business uses but also valuable data about how energy is used. This information can be used to cut costs and enhance efficiency. For example, businesses could benefit from performing certain energy-intensive tasks at off-peak hours when total demand for power is low. Data from smart meters could be used to identify those potential savings or even to automatically manage power demand.

There's no single solution to the world's energy problems. The only way to meet rapidly growing demand in a cost-effective, environmentally friendly manner is to employ a range of technologies. Renewables can be part of that mix, but coal, oil, and gas, and to a lesser extent nuclear and hydroelectric, will remain the main components for decades to come.

Endnotes

[1] EIA International Energy Outlook 2009, http://www.eia.doe.gov/oiaf/ieo/.

[2] Ibid.

[3] EIA Assumptions to Annual Energy Outlook 2010, http://www.eia.doe.gov/oiaf/aeo/assumption/index.html.

[4] Dilma Rousseff, "Brazil Aims to Avoid Long-Term oil 'curse'" *Oil & Gas Journal*, November 9, 2009.

[5] Itaipu.gov, "The History of the World's Largest Hydroelectric Power Plant," http://www.itaipu.gov.br/index.php?q=en/node/356 (accessed March 2, 2010).

[6] "China Three Gorges Project," http://www.ctgpc.com/benefifs/benefifs_a_4.php (accessed March 2, 2010).

[7] Reuters, "FACTBOX: Facts about China's Three Gorges Dam," http://www.reuters.com/article/idUSPEK117552200711114.

[8] International Energy Outlook 2009.

[9] Ibid.

[10] ExxonMobil Energy Outlook: A View to 2030, http://www.exxonmobil.com/Corporate/news_publications.aspx (accessed March 3, 2010).

[11] Ibid.

[12] "Nuclear Power in China," World Nuclear Association Updated February 15, 2010, http://www.world-nuclear.org/info/inf63.html.

[13] BP Statistical Review of World Energy 2009, http://www.bp.com/productlanding.do?categoryId=6929&contentId=7044622.

[14] EIA, International Carbon Dioxide Emissions and Carbon Intensity, http://www.eia.doe.gov/emeu/international/carbondioxide.html (accessed March 3, 2010).

[15] European Commission Eurostat, http://epp.eurostat.ec.europa.eu/portal/page/portal/energy/data/main_tables (accessed March 4, 2010).

[16] World Nuclear Association, "Nuclear Power in Germany," http://www.world-nuclear.org/info/inf43.html (accessed March 3, 2010).

[17] "Windmills in Paradise," *Oil & Gas Journal*, April 7, 2008, http://www.ogj.com/index/article-display/324932/articles/oil-gas-journal/volume-106/issue-13/regular-features/journally-speaking/windmills-in-paradise.html (accessed March 2, 2010).

[18] Global Wind Energy Council, http://www.ewea.org/fileadmin/ewea_documents/documents/press_releases/2009/GWEC_Press_Release_-_tables_and_statistics_2008.pdf (accessed March 2, 2010).

[19] EIA International Energy Statistics, http://tonto.eia.doe.gov/cfapps/ipdbproject/IEDIndex3.cfm (accessed March 1, 2010).

[20] E.ON Netz Wind Power Report 2005, http://www.wind-watch.org/documents/wp-content/uploads/eonwindreport2005.pdf.

[21] Ibid.

[22] EIA International Energy Statistics (accessed March 1, 2010).

[23] Ibid.

[24] European Commission Eurostat.

[25] American Wind Energy Association, http://www.awea.org/legislative/#PTC.

10

Water Is Money

Less than 3 percent of the water on Earth is fresh. Ensuring the quality of this 3 percent is critical for everyday life. We need to drink it, we need it to farm, and we need it for industry. The problem is that people have wasted available freshwater and disrupted its renewal through inefficient use and poor agricultural and industrial practices.

Three distinct investment areas are worthy of consideration by investors: water supply, demand reduction, and management of inefficiencies. Furthermore, an important issue about water's usage in Asia and its economic importance is the regional diet. Two of the region's basic foods are rice and fish. Compared to other staples, these two products require significant amounts of freshwater resources, even when grown or bred in highly efficient settings.

In light of these facts and rising meat consumption in the region, it's easy to see how Asia's dietary changes will have a staggering affect on water use.

Economic growth has always been damaging to the water cycle and therefore to water's availability for consumption. Throughout history developing economies, which have a combination of large agriculture sectors and immense industrial production, have disrupted the water cycle the most. Population growth puts another strain on freshwater supplies. As populations grow, so does their overall use of freshwater. At a basic level more people means more water being consumed. As standards of living increase, people tend to eat more meat, which requires a lot of water to grow the grain that feeds the livestock. As illustrated in Table 10.1, meat requires anywhere from 100 to 1,000 times as much water as crops alone.[1]

TABLE 10.1   Water Intensity for Agriculture Products

Product	Average Water Required per Cubic Meter or Ton
Rice (paddy)	2,291
Wheat	1,334
Maize	909
Soybeans	1,789
Sugar cane	175
Barley	1,338
Sorghum	2,853
Coconuts	2,545
Millet	4,596
Beef	15,497
Pork	4,856
Goat meat	4,043
Sheep meat	6,143
Chicken meat	3,918
Eggs	3,340
Milk	990
Cheese	4,914

(Source: Hoekstra and Chapagain)

China illustrates the current situation. Only about 5 percent of Chinese are considered middle class, but this share is forecast to grow to 56 percent by 2030.[2] Chinese eat two times as much meat as Indians and 40 percent more than they consumed in 1990.[3] A similar expansion of the middle class in the rest of Asia and other developing regions would place even more strain on freshwater supplies.

Developing economies' freshwater needs change dramatically over time. Ensuring that supply meets growing demand is critical for governments. The question isn't whether but how demand will be met.

A Closer Look at Asia

Asia's water use is already at alarmingly high levels. Four hundred of China's 600 cities currently suffer from water shortages.[4] And 32 percent of Asia's population sources its drinking water from groundwater, which can be difficult to both measure and replenish.[5] Although per-capita water consumption is relatively low in Asia (see Table 10.2), a number of factors have led to water shortages and the need for massive water infrastructure projects.

TABLE 10.2   Per-Capita Water Consumption in Asia

Country	Total Water Footprint (Gm3/yr)	Per Capita Water Footprint(m3/cap/yr)
Bangladesh	116.49	896
China	883.39	702
India	987.38	980
Indonesia	269.96	1,317
Pakistan	166.22	1,218
Thailand	134.46	2,223
Global	7452	1,243

(Source: Hoekstra and Chapagain, 2005)

Even with a relatively low per-capita rate, because of its large population Asia registers enormous overall freshwater usage.[6] India (13 percent) and China (12 percent) make up 25 percent of the global total. Other Asian countries also use significant amounts, Indonesia, 4 percent, Pakistan and Thailand, 2 percent. The reasons for these high values, as well as the disparity between the low per-capita rate and high total usage, are numerous. The important point is that the supply situation is becoming more difficult, and this creates worldwide incentives to shore up Asia's water-usage profile.

The "at-the-ready" supply of water is rapidly decreasing in Asia. Eighty percent of China's major river areas are too polluted to sustain fish (and human) life.[7] Shanghai spent USD300 million to move its

water intake systems farther out to sea because of coastal-area pollution.[8] And leading up to the 2008 Beijing Olympics tens of thousands
of Chinese were used to clear algae blooms from waterways used for
various events, such as rowing and sailing. These examples illustrate
that once freshwater reserves are polluted, they must be treated—
usually at great cost—to be used again. In addition to cleaning damaged freshwater reserves, water may need to be moved from one
place to another because of changes in demand. China has three-
quarters of its water in the south, but three-quarters of its farming
and industry is in the north and northeast.[9]

Asia's governments have undertaken some of the most expensive
and incredible water-related infrastructure projects to address the
water issue. China has built more than half of the world's large dams
since 1950,[10] while the even more ambitious South-to-North Water
Transfer Project will move 45 billion cubic meters of water to the
north once completed. China is also the fastest-growing market for
desalination equipment.[11]

The region as a whole has done a good job of providing basic
water services, evidenced by reductions in the number of people who
lack access to potable water and sanitation facilities. Between 1990
and 2006 the percentage of the population with access to drinking
water (of some amount) increased from 68 to 88 percent. Nevertheless, 44 percent of those classified as poor live in South Asia, and the
vast majority still lack adequate access to water facilities. Twenty-five
million people per year die because of bad water, and half of the
world's diseases are transmitted via water.[12]

Water-related infrastructure investment will only increase, particularly given the expected supply-and-demand gap that will be
exposed over the next 10 to 20 years (see Figure 10.1).

The availability and quality of water are critical factors to consider
when evaluating the health of Asian industry. Corporations from all
sectors are participating in efforts to secure water sources and reduce
inefficiencies, which reflects water's important role in all types of economic activity. One major reason for companies' concern is water's
role as an important ingredient in various products. In China, for

example, industrial water use is dominated by key sectors such as textiles, steel, and paper-product manufacture.[13] Without continuously flowing water these industries and the economies of which they are a part would suffer tremendously.

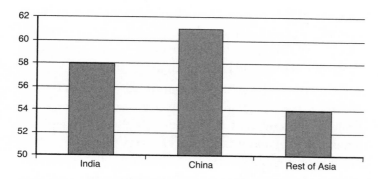

Figure 10.1   Expected amount of change in water demand (2030), percent change from 2005.

(Source: 2030 Water Resources Group)

The Water Investment Theme Is Under Way

Three distinct investment areas are worthy of consideration by investors: water supply, demand reduction, and management of inefficiencies.

Managing the water supply is the best way to increase volume and guarantee continuous flow, the main issues for governments and consumers alike. Finding new water reserves is the easiest way to address these. Unfortunately, however, the discovery of new water reserves is neither easy nor common.

Because of centuries-long abuse, finding new underground water sources now requires expertise and equipment of similar complexity to that demanded by oil exploration and other mining efforts. More to the point, because of the improbability of finding new reserves, investing in "water exploration" venues isn't a good idea. Some companies are buying existing, mostly untapped water reserves, with plans to sell later at a price that reflects their new, higher value. Investors should avoid these companies because water is still viewed by most people as a right. Not only will governments make it readily available to people but they'll also do so at affordable prices. The last thing an investor wants to be faced with is a backlash against a company seen to be attempting to profit from the scarcity of one of man's fundamental needs by boosting prices during times of stress. In countries such as India and China, such a public outcry could snowball at a rate and to a degree that would crush such a company.

Political instability will be a big problem if water access doesn't continue to improve. Popular demand for water services is generally expressed through peaceful and legal channels, but violence isn't unusual. Militias have regularly fought over water resources in the Shenxian and Linzhou regions in China.[14] The rivalry has its roots in the 1970s but grew quickly in the 1990s. But governments—particularly those in charge of the fastest-growing economies in the world—can't afford to allow general anarchy to break out because of water, or for any reason, for that matter. And it is by now an axiom of public policy that investing in water infrastructure boosts economic progress dramatically. Credible studies have shown that for every USD1 invested in water services there's a return of USD4 to USD12.[15] Methods that treat existing water supplies will likely be in high demand by Asian governments and offer the best opportunities for investors.

Desalination is the process of purifying salty water, usually for drinking or irrigation purposes. It's believed that seawater was first distilled by alembic in the Spanish presidios in North Africa in the 16th century, making desalination probably the oldest water purification process available.[16] Although there are now a number of processes to cleanse salty water, every method separates salt and other impurities to produce clean water. Regardless of the method used, the process is energy-intensive; the Gulf Cooperation Council States and Saudi Arabia, blessed with vast energy resources, favor desalination. But the process leaves behind highly salinated water that must be carefully released back into natural bodies to prevent problems downstream.

There are a few dominant desalination methods currently in use, but there are many new methods emerging that could reduce energy requirements and increase output while lowering overall costs. As Figure 10.2 illustrates, new desalination capacity exploded during the preceding decade. New plants regularly produce water at about USD0.50 per cubic meter, which begins to approach the amount most industrial customers in developed countries pay for water.[17]

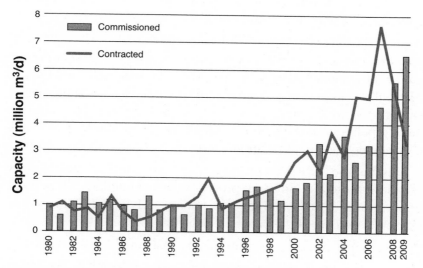

Figure 10.2   New desalination capacity 1980-2009.

(Source: Global Water Intelligence)

Most desalination plants use a method called reverse osmosis (RO), which employs high pressure and filters to force water to the next stage and keep particles like salt behind. The method has a long history but has been used commercially for desalination purposes since the 1970s. Because RO doesn't use heat it's less energy-intensive and therefore less expensive. The lower energy costs associated with RO make it the preferred desalination process, although experimental methods, like the use of nanotechnology, and continued research will certainly lead to additional competitive methods.

Freshwater supply can also be created by treating wastewater. Developed parts of the world have already invested in wastewater treatment facilities that allow for tremendous freshwater savings by cleansing and making use of wastewater. Developing areas, however, lag behind. This is quickly changing in Asia, as countries realize that up-front investments in the facilities lead to medium- and long-term payoffs. Even with the increased investment and rapid expansion of wastewater treatment facilities, though, there remains a tremendous amount of room for improvement. China treated about 45 percent of its wastewater in 2004 and is expected to increase that to 60 percent in 2010.[18] although this change is significant, it leaves a lot of potentially reusable wastewater untreated.

Singapore-based Hyflux Ltd (Singapore: 600, OTC: HYFXY) operates and develops membrane technology in four divisions: water, industrial manufacturing processes, specialty materials, and energy. The bulk of its revenue is generated in China, where Hyflux has a strong presence in municipal water-treatment systems. The company has a pipeline of more than 30 projects in China, the bulk of which also include maintenance agreements.

Hyflux also has a good presence in the Middle East; the company recycles oil used in industrial processes and in engines, filtering out impurities with its membrane technology. Hyflux technology can extract 80 percent of the base oil from waste.

Municipal projects generate almost half of the company's revenue, with projects ranging from water and wastewater treatment and recycling to desalination. The bulk of its China-based projects are in high-growth coastal areas, where urbanization will continue to drive demand for expansion.

Japan-based Kurita Water Industries (Japan: 6370, OTC: KTWIY) sells water and wastewater treatment-related equipment and chemicals. It also operates a division that specializes in water and soil remediation. In addition to selling the equipment, Kurita also offers operation-management and maintenance services through the use of ten-year contracts.

Ashland (NYSE: ASH) is a global specialty chemicals company that operates through five segments. About one-third of revenue is generated outside the US, and 20 percent of sales are related to the water industry. Foreign sales should continue to grow as Ashland manufactures a wide variety of chemical components critical to manufacturing and water-infrastructure development. The company is investing heavily in the development of distribution channels in Brazil, Russia, India, and China.

Energy Recovery (NASDAQ: ERII) is a leading manufacturer of energy recovery devices, which, by significantly reducing energy consumption, help make desalination affordable and enable the rapid expansion of desalination plants worldwide.

Energy Recovery's PX Pressure Exchanger technology is a rotary-positive displacement pump that recovers energy from the high-pressure waste stream of SWRO systems at up to 98 percent efficiency, with no downtime or scheduled maintenance, and reduces energy consumption by as much 60 percent.

Energy Recovery's technology was selected for use in the world's first osmotic power plant, which uses the osmotic potential difference between saltwater and freshwater to pressurize a fluid stream that drives energy-producing turbines. Although the process is still being refined, it has the potential to generate cheap, truly renewable energy. This, coupled with the necessity of using the desalination process to ensure the supply of available drinking water, puts Energy Recovery's technology at the forefront of future global development.

China-based Dongfang Electric Corporation (Hong Kong: 1072, Germany: DEUF) manufactures equipment for large thermal-power, hydropower, and nuclear-power stations. It's one of three major power-generation equipment makers in China. The company has production capacity of 30 gigawatts per year and controls 30 percent of the domestic market for large-scale steam/hydro equipment. The company is a direct play on water infrastructure.

Finally, IVRCL (India: IVRN) is an India-based engineering and construction company operating projects that span four key infrastructure segments: water, transportation, buildings, and power. Most of its revenue comes from government spending. The company has also benefited from the fact that most of its construction contracts include service agreements to maintain or operate newly built infrastructure facilities. The company operates across the water spectrum.

Demand Reduction

The easiest way to reduce water demand is to increase the price people pay for it. Traditionally, though, governments around the world have heavily subsidized water. This is one of the main reasons why, despite the enormous costs of water-related infrastructure projects, water costs to consumers remain relatively low. "Water-as-a-right" thinking also explains why it wasn't until the 1980s that water began being metered, which allowed companies to more effectively collect payments in New York City.[19] Water was essentially being given away in one of the world's capitalist centers; imagine how it was being treated elsewhere.

Governments do try to increase prices, though. Both India and China have done this regularly since the 1990s with little opposition because prices, even with regular increases, are held below painful thresholds. Between 1998 and 2007 water-supply charges in China increased by more than 50 percent, and most cities began charging for wastewater.[20] Nowhere do the fees come close to the actual cost involved in supplying and treating water, but they do introduce a new revenue stream.

In addition to encouraging conservation, higher prices provide capital for governments and companies to improve services and availability. Water utilities and companies tightly associated with them in developing countries are likely to experience a double capital injection: government investment and consumer-sourced revenues. Where water utilities are either private or the result of a joint venture of some sort there's likely to be a profitable investment during the next few years, especially as the market opens and companies expand their presences.

Beijing Enterprises Water Group (Hong Kong: 037) will benefit from this trend. It has two water-treatment plants and 24 sewage-treatment plants in Guangdong, Zhejiang, Shandong, Hunan, Sichuan, Guangxi, and Guizhou in China. Beijing Enterprises boasts water-processing capacity of 1,885,000 tons per day, while sewage processing capacity is 1,735,000 tons per day and water-supply volume is 150,000 tons per day. Its subsidiaries are engaged in the construction of sewage- and water-treatment plants, sewage treatment, water treatment and distribution, the provision of technical services, and licensing of technical know-how related to sewage treatment in Mainland China.

Agriculture is one of the main reasons people fight among themselves over water. Agriculture consumes 70 percent of the world's water supply, a ratio reflected in Asia as well.[21] In countries throughout the region, but especially in India, large population booms were fed through similar booms in agriculture productivity. This productivity increase, which started in the 1960s and has been dubbed the "Green Revolution," was possible because of the rapid expansion of efforts that led to a tripling of India's irrigated farmland between 1970 and 1999.[22] Water usage increased dramatically, as did the exploitation of available land.

After more than 40 years of such agricultural use, depleted water reserves and decreased land productivity, often the result of increased salinity due to rudimentary water irrigation methods, have created problems for rural societies. In 1995 China and India had 15 percent and 17 percent, respectively, of their irrigated lands negatively affected by saline levels.[23] Pakistan's numbers were even worse at 26 percent. These figures have only grown during the 15 years since such estimates were first made.

On top of bad water management, a reduction in the actual amount of arable land has also become a problem around the world. Many reasons explain this, but perhaps the most worrying is desertification. Desertification typically occurs when land is overgrazed and/or overfarmed, and local water supplies are overexploited. The result is the creation and expansion of desert or desertlike landscapes that make use of the land difficult at best and future use questionable. At present there's no definitive way to rescue desertified areas.

Africa is the continent most threatened by desertification, but Asia also faces serious problems. Twenty-seven percent of China's territory is already desertified, and this total is increasing by 7,500 square kilometers per year. Already USD7 billion in economic losses have been incurred in China because of desertification.[24] Vietnam suffers similar conditions, with 28 percent of its land desertified.

Whether farmland has been hurt through increased salination or desertification the result is loss of productivity. Targeting changes in agriculture is an excellent way for a country to reduce water usage. Much of the water efficiencies found over time throughout the world have been a result of better farming practices. Asia's governments see this and have been actively working to improve agriculture's water efficiency.

One way to more efficiently use water is to avoid raising water-intensive crops. Governments can facilitate this switch in a number of ways, including increasing the cost of water to farmers, as India has done to a mild degree, changing subsidy structures, and reducing tariffs on imported crops. An extreme but useful example of this crop-switch method is Saudi Arabia's 2008 decision to abandon its long-standing policy of wheat self-sufficiency. The policy was driven by significant price guarantees and meant many farmers used large amounts of water to grow the crop in the desert. The new policy is that the country will import all its wheat by 2016, allowing other crops, industry, and people to use the water. The increased profits due to the shift from water-hungry crops also provide a buffer of sorts in the event that external sources of food suffer their own water difficulties and are forced to raise prices to make changes needed to continue farming.

Many developing countries have traditionally used flood irrigation systems, which simply flood a given farm area with water. Whatever water the plants need, they take. Whatever water the soil retains for later use, it does. And whatever water remains runs off into surrounding waterways. This method is commonly used because it's cheap to implement. But it also means using water inefficiently and stripping nutrients from the dirt. Use of this method is a significant reason why developing areas with high economic and population growth suffer from water availability issues.

One of the most appealing alternative irrigation methods is drip irrigation. This method uses underground pipes and metering pipes to drip only the amount of water a given plant needs. Results include less water use, a reduction in the amount of nutrients and particulates washed away, and increased crop production. These benefits more than make up for the costs associated with installing such systems. It's this cost calculus that's led to 15 percent annual growth in India for these types of alternative irrigation methods during the past decade.[25]

Another way to reduce run-off and wastewater is what's called "leveling" farmland. This method, pioneered by Israeli farmers who have strict water-usage limitations, reduces the amount of run-off water, often by using lasers to improve accuracy. Less run-off water means less water and fewer particulates that are needed to grow food but may contaminate water resources. As with drip-irrigation methods, better leveling farmland requires an investment in equipment, know-how, and usually brings better irrigation methods with it.

Whether it's from evolving toward more efficient crops, leveling crop areas, or introducing newer irrigation technologies, agriculture represents a major avenue for conserving freshwater supplies. Most of these efforts require infrastructure changes that benefit companies that have either the expertise or supply equipment for such improvements. Of those companies, the ones best suited to succeed are the companies that already have relationships with Asia's governments and know the local marketplace.

Jain Irrigation (India: JAINIRRIG) is the largest firm in India's micro-irrigation systems business, which includes drip and sprinkler irrigation systems. The company is also involved in the agro-processing and onion dehydration business, as well as the plastics business. As farmers' incomes improve, better irrigation systems will be put in place. In addition, state and central governments have been subsidizing as much as 50 to 70 percent of the total cost to install micro-irrigation systems.

Improvement in the farming process and use of better seeds will also help the water issue and are therefore integral parts of the investment theme. Seed companies and agricultural machinery companies will benefit.

Japan-based Kubota (Tokyo: 6326, NYSE: KUB) produces and exports manufactured farm equipment as well as pipes, principally ductile iron pipes, and related equipment for water supply and other utilities. The company's products include tractors, combine harvesters, rice transplanters, power tillers, and reaper binders.

Switzerland-based Syngenta AG (SWISS: SYNN, NYSE: SYT) is an agribusiness company engaged in the crop-protection and seeds businesses. Crop-protection chemicals include herbicides, insecticides, and fungicides that control weeds, insects, and diseases. The seeds business operates in two commercial sectors, seeds for field crops including corn, oilseeds, cereals, and sugar beets, and vegetable and flower seeds.

Improve Efficiencies

The final major way to address Asia's increasing water difficulties is to improve efficiencies. Fixing inefficient points in the supply chain could lead to significant amounts of newly available water. Most often such improvements are found via new metering technology, but replacing and/or installing new piping and pumping equipment also work.

Meters, pipes, and pumps may sound like trivial solutions to such a complex problem as water scarcity, but nearly every solution outlined previously relies to some degree upon these pieces of equipment. This includes the basic need to transport water from water-rich areas to water-poor areas, an increasingly common and lengthy ordeal. Most existing water infrastructure around the world has aged to the point of needing either repair or replacement. Introducing water meters to areas without them is expected to eliminate waste by as much as 15 percent.[26] This sometimes overlooked sector is forecast to grow by 32 percent from 2008 to 2012 according to water consulting firm McIlvaine Company; Asia will lead the way. About 70 percent of future investment in water supply and drainage networks will involve upgrading and expanding pipe networks and pumping stations.[27]

The anticipated savings from replacing existing pipes or using new technology could be huge. China, for example, has more than double the amount of water lost per kilometer compared to Brazil and Russia and ten times that of the United Kingdom.[28] Upgrading to new pipes and other equipment could have a quick and significant impact on Asia's water difficulties.

Even in established cities in developed economies, large amounts of water are being lost during transport from pumping stations to homes because of old pipe technology or aging equipment. Smart meters, known more technically as advanced metering infrastructure (AMI) systems, are a big component in the improved efficiency theme. AMI systems enable companies to monitor energy flows throughout their systems from a central location.

The industry leader in AMI is Itron (NSDQ: ITRI), which focuses on the global energy and water industries. Itron operates under two names: Itron in North America, Actaris outside of North America. The company has a global customer base of close to 8,000 individual utilities, giving it one of the largest blue-chip revenue streams of any company in the world.

Another emerging subsector in the water business is the rehabilitation of water and sewer lines. Insituform Technologies (NSDQ: INSU) is one of the companies best positioned to benefit. The company's most innovative product is its fast-growing "trenchless" repair service for aging and cracked pipes. Rather than dig up and replace actual pipes, the process involves injecting a compound into the pipe itself that seals any breaches. The result is a lower-cost, far less intrusive repair.

Flowserve (NYSE: FLS) is a manufacturer and after-market service provider of comprehensive flow control systems. The company develops and manufactures precision-engineered flow control equipment such as pumps, valves, and seals for critical service applications. Flowserve's products are used by a variety of industries such as oil and gas and chemical processing. Two key industries served are water supply and distribution utilities and the nuclear power industry, for which Flowserve is one of the largest suppliers.

Japan-based Ebara Corporation (Tokyo: 6361, OTC: EBCOY) manufactures transfer machinery for fluids for a range of industrial processes, including for use in waterworks and sewage systems. The company derives 53 percent of its sales from water activities.

India's Jindal Saw (India: SAWN, OTC: JNDLY) is a pipe manufacturing company. Its product portfolio is diversified across end-user segments such as energy transportation, industrial application, and water and sewerage transportation. Forty percent of its sales come from water-related projects.

Pentair (NYSE: PNR) is a diversified industrial manufacturing company that consists of two business segments, water and technical products. The company's Water Group (mainly pumps and filtration products) provides products and systems used worldwide in the movement, storage, treatment, and enjoyment of water. Seventy percent of sales are water-related.

Fishing Profits

Another important issue about water's usage in Asia and its economic importance is the regional diet. Two of the region's basic foods are rice and fish. Compared to other staples, these two products require significant amounts of freshwater resources, even when grown or bred in highly efficient settings. In light of these facts and rising meat consumption in the region, it's easy to see how Asia's dietary changes will have a staggering effect on water use.

Fish is of particular interest here because it's a big source of proteins for an increasing number of people in Asia. Fisheries and related companies will be profitable investments because they're critical to Asia's culture and its economies, as is demonstrated in Table 10.3. Fish consumption has been on the rise around the world, making the Asian fisheries' story a global investment theme with multiyear growth prospects.

TABLE 10.3   Contribution of Fisheries to Economies

Economy	Agricultural Exports (%)	Avg Animal Protein Intake (%)	Economically Active Pop. Involved (%)
Bangladesh	76	51	1.9
China	not identified	19	not identified
India	22	13	1.4
Malaysia	3	37	1.1
Pakistan	12	3	0.5
Philippines	23	41	3.2
Thailand	38	40	1.0
Viet Nam	40	34	2.5
Averages	31	30	1.6

(Source: Thorpe, Reid, van Anrooy, and Brugere, When Fisheries Influence National Policymaking, The World Food and Agriculture Organization's The State of World Fisheries and Aquaculture)

Asia is critical to worldwide aquaculture, a broad term used to describe water-based food production and capture. Eighty-nine percent of aquaculture production (in terms of quantity) and 77 percent of its global value comes from Asia.[29] China is the major player, with 67 percent of the world's production and 49 percent of its value. New areas of the aquaculture industry, such as aquatic plant life harvesting, are also centered on Asia; 72 percent of this work is done in China. Eighty-six percent of the world's fishers and fish farmers live in Asia, mainly in China, India, Indonesia, the Philippines, and Vietnam.

Aquaculture also plays an important role in Asia's employment situation; see Table 10.4. Not only do fishers and fish farms contribute to direct employment. They also create a strong secondary employment group. It's estimated that for every person employed in the primary aquaculture sector up to four more are employed in the secondary market.[30]

TABLE 10.4   Top Aquaculture Producers

Country	World Ranking	2004 Production (tons)	2006 Production (tons)	Annual Growth (%)
China	1	30614968	34429122	6.05
India	2	2794636	3123135	5.71
Vietnam	3	11986617	1657727	17.6
Indonesia	4	1259983	1385801	4.87
Bangladesh	5	914752	892049	-1.25
Philippines	10	512220	623369	10.32

(*Source:* The World Food and Agriculture Organization's The State of World Fisheries and Aquaculture)

Besides ocean- and sea-sourced fish, so-called internal waterways-sourced fish is also an important part of the business. This is a growing component of Asia's aquaculture economy, as almost two-thirds of the world's inland catches are in Asia. In addition to being an important source for fish, these inland waterways are also used to transport goods—fish and nonaquaculture material—across the region. Water levels and quality play an important role in continued economic growth and stability.

China Fishery Group (Singapore: B0Z) operates through two business segments: fishing, which comprises fishing, the sale of fish and marine catches, and the rental of unutilized fishing quota, and fishmeal and fish oil production. Trawling and fishmeal processing account for 74.6 percent and 25.4 percent of total revenue, respectively.

The company also has a Peruvian fleet of 39 purse-seine fishing vessels and eight fishmeal processing plants. The company is organized on a worldwide basis into four major fishing and production locations: the Pacific Ocean (excluding Peruvian Waters), Peruvian Waters, the Atlantic Ocean, and the Indian Ocean. It recently launched trial operations in the South Pacific.

Unlike many of its European counterparts, China Fishery utilizes trawling operations—essentially going to the fish—rather than farming and keeps its vessels at sea approximately seven months of the year, one of the longest average voyages in the industry. It also keeps a tight rein on costs by using the global logistics and distribution network of its parent, Pacific Andes Group.

Pacific Andes International Holdings (Hong Kong: 1174) is broken into four revenue producing units. Frozen fish supply chain management generates around 42 percent of revenues and handles the sales of fish and seafood products, primarily to distributors. The processing and distribution division generates around 37 percent of revenue and is the value-add segment of the business. It processes the catch into a variety of products, from simply headed and gutted fish to breaded, preportioned products. It owns many subsidiaries throughout the world and three processing plants in China, which are ISO22000 certified in international food safety standards, allowing foods processed in the facilities to be shipped internationally.

The industrial fishing division generates around 21 percent of revenue and handles all harvesting operations as well as the production and sale of fishmeal and oil, which has proven to be a particularly successful endeavor. Andes maintains about one-fifth of the Chinese fish market share.

Norway-based Cermaq ASA (Oslo: CEQ, OTC: CRMQF) operates three businesses. Mainstream is engaged in fish farming. EWOS is Cermaq's fish-feed business, while EWOS Innovation comprises the company's research and development operations. Feed is by far the company's largest revenue generator, accounting for

62 percent of income, while farming operations account for 23 percent. The remainder comes from R&D and miscellaneous operations. Norway accounts for more than half of revenue, Chile generates about one-third, and most of the rest comes from Canada and the UK.

Grieg Seafood ASA (Oslo: GSF), also based in Norway, engages in deepwater fish farming at depths of up to 40 meters, which helps maintain proper aquaculture temperature and allows the company to farm year round, whereas many other operations are seasonal. It also propelled the company from 20th to 6th among the world's largest salmon producers in 2006, with production of about 80,000 tons of gutted fish annually. The company has excellent access to export markets; its base of operations in Norway affords it the shortest export route to Russia, while its Canada operations have easy access to Asia and the US, and its Scotland operations are a short jump from continental Europe. Proximity to market allows the company to offer some of the quickest shipment times in the business.

Finally, Netherlands-based Nutreco (Amsterdam: NUO) primarily produces feed for a variety of livestock and fish. It has a diversified production base and operates on every continent except Africa. It's the world's third-largest animal nutrition operation based on revenue. The company's Sada division is also the largest chicken producer and processor in Spain. It also produces eggs for the pharmaceutical industry in Canada. The company has sales in more than 80 countries. Nutreco has enjoyed robust growth of about 2 percent annually amid rising global incomes and populations; these trends will drive demand for products that support meat-based diets.

Fish farming has also been a growing business as more than 45 percent of fish consumed globally are farmed rather than caught in the wild, which drives feed demand. Because the fish feed market is highly fragmented, Nutreco has been able to pursue an aggressive acquisition strategy to grow market share. Almost 70 percent of revenue is generated in Europe, about one-quarter in North America, the remainder in South America and Asia.

Endnotes

1 William Houston and Robin Griffiths, *Water: The Final Resource* (Hampshire, Great Britain: Harriman House, 2008), 135.

2 2030 Water Resources Group, "Charting Our Water Future" (McKinsey & Company, 2009), 58.

3 Jenny Wiggins, "Developing Tastes," *Financial Times*, January 26, 2008.

4 Houston and Griffiths, *Water: The Final Resource*, 112.

5 B. L. Morris et al., "Groundwater and Its Susceptibility to Degradation: A Global Assessment of the Problem and Options for Management, *Early Warning and Assessment Report Series*, RS. 03-3, 3.

6 A. Y. Hoekstra and A. K. Chapagain, "Water Footprints of Nations: Water Use by People as a Function of Their Consumption Pattern," *Water Resources Management*, 2007.

7 Marq De Villiers, *Water: The Fate of Our Most Precious Resource* (New York: Mariner Books, 2000), 89.

8 Ibid., 90.

9 Ibid., 267-68.

10 Peter H. Gleick, *The World's Water 2008–2009* (Washington, DC: Island Press, 2008), 91.

11 Shirley Knott, "Water Scarcity: The Defining Crisis of the 21st Century?," UBS AG, October 10, 2006, 26.

12 Morris et al., "Groundwater and Its Susceptibility to Degradation," 7.

13 2030 Water Resources Group, "Charting Our Water Future" (McKinsey & Company, 2009), 18.

14 Peter Gleick, *The World's Water*, 90. For additional commentary about water-related violence in China, see "The Gloom, Boom & Doom Report" (June 2005), 19. India has similar types of violence over water; see Shirley Knott, "Water Scarcity: The Defining Crisis of the 21st Century?," 8.

15 World Water Assessment Programme. *The United Nations World Water Development Report 3: Water in a Changing World* (Paris, France: Earthscan, 2009), 88.

16 Fernand Braudel, *Civilization and Capitalism Volume I* (New York: Harper & Row, 1981), 227.

17 For pricing information, see "Water and Farms Towards Sustainable Use," *OECD Observer*, March 2006.

18 Greg J. Browder et al., *Stepping Up: Improving the Performance of China's Urban Water Utilities* (The World Bank, 2007), 14.

19 Michael Specter, "The Last Drop," *New Yorker*, October 23, 2006, 63.

20 Browder et al. *Stepping Up*, xx.

[21] 2030 Water Resources Group, "Charting Our Water Future" (McKinsey & Company, 2009), 18.

[22] David Biello, "Is Northwestern India's Breadbasket Running Out of Water?," *Scientific American*, August 12, 2009.

[23] Morris et al., "Groundwater and Its Susceptibility to Degradation," 87.

[24] United Nations Convention to Combat Desertification, "Fact Sheet 12," http://www.unccd.int/publicinfo/factsheets/showFS.php?number=12 (accessed on December 3, 2009).

[25] Browder et al., *Stepping Up*, 106.

[26] Shirley Knott, "Water Scarcity: The Defining Crisis of the 21st Century?," 33.

[27] Browder et al., *Stepping Up*, xxxii.

[28] Ibid., 17.

[29] Food and Agriculture Organization of the United Nations "The State of the World Fisheries and Aquaculture 2008" (FAO, 2009).

[30] Ibid., 26.

11

Back to the Future

Trains are important to business and commuters. They are also the preferred method of transportation for an increasing number of people around the world. Trains are not only viewed as convenient and fast, but also as more environmentally friendly. This attribute is a significant factor in both China's and India's decision-making processes as their governments seek ways to improve their environmental record without hurting economic growth. The investment cycle in the sector has just started.

In 1980 India and China were each the recipient of 0.1 percent of global foreign direct investment (FDI). By 2008 India had welcomed 2.4 percent of overall FDI, China 6.4 percent.

The United Nations estimates that the top five FDI destinations for the 2009 to 2011 period will be China, the US, India, Brazil, and Russia.

China and India figure prominently in everyone's list of top FDI destinations, as detailed in Table 11.1. But India's FDI inflows are growing from a low base relative to China—there's greater upside potential on the Subcontinent. Much of that foreign cash will go to fund India's efforts to improve its infrastructure.

Governments around the world have come to appreciate the way infrastructure improvements can help domestic economies grow to their potential. Officials are working the globe to arrange financing for such projects. The 2007–09 financial crisis forced many to cut back or cancel planned projects, but the major emerging economies, moving toward an eventual decoupling from the developed ones, are acting on the view that infrastructure improvement is the most important component of their economic growth and consequent poverty alleviation. More than 60 percent of the funds included in the various stimulus packages introduced by emerging economies during 2008 were committed to infrastructure-related spending in 2009; China and India led the way, with 88 percent and 83 percent, respectively. In the next ten years emerging economies will spend between USD15 trillion and USD20 trillion on infrastructure projects. Asia will account for about 67 percent of this spending. China and India, whose economic growth and expanding urban populations leave them no choice, will spend the most.

TABLE 11.1   Top 6 FDI Destinations, by Home Region

Home Region	Most Favored Destinations
North America	China, UK, Russia, Germany, Brazil, US
Europe	United States, China, India, Brazil, Russian, UK
Japan	China, India, US, Brazil, Vietnam, Germany
Developing Asia	China, US, Indonesia, Australia, India, Vietnam

(Source: United Nations Conference on Trade and Development)

Infrastructure-related investment has become a popular theme in the 21st century. Although some well-known sectors will produce solid returns, investors have to look harder to identify "the next big thing." Here's a little help: Our view is that railway-related investments will produce the biggest returns for investors over the long term, particularly those made in fast-growing countries with continentlike characteristics. Improving train operations while expanding and upgrading networks is becoming synonymous with economic growth in these areas.

China Shortens the Distance

It is 30 kilometers (19 miles) between the Shanghai International Airport and the city's financial district. The easiest way to span the distance is to ride the Maglev, the world's fastest commercial train.

The result of collaboration between Germany's Siemens and ThyssenKrupp, the train reaches maximum speed of 430 kilometers per hour (267 miles per hour). It'll get you from the airport to Shanghai in about eight minutes. Maglev—short for "magnetic levitation"—employs a sophisticated electromagnetic system to suspend rail carriages a centimeter above a single track to create a fully frictionless and wheelless rail system. The first commercial ride took place in October 2003, and since then the Maglev has become a tourist attraction, even for out-of-town Chinese. Maglev travels at top speed for only about 52 seconds—it takes four minutes to accelerate to this level. After it peaks it begins to decelerate, three minutes out from the Shanghai station.

Japan has also invested in the technology and now controls some of the most advanced Maglev ideas in the world; Japanese engineers were able to test their Maglev at a speed of 581 kilometers per hour (361 miles per hour) in 2003. Japan is home to the famous bullet trains, the world's first modern high-speed services, since 1964. Bullet trains have continued to evolve at an astonishing pace, but domestic observers have pointed out that by 2025 "bullet" technology will be 60 years old. This is why Japan is trying to take the Maglev to the next level—longer distances at higher speeds.

China's rail-infrastructure spending started to pick up in 2008, when the government spent USD50 billion to extend total track length in operation to 80,000 kilometers. In the first half of 2009 railway investment in China increased by 127 percent, driven by the government's stimulus package as well as private-sector loans. The Ministry of Railways' (MoR) long-term network plan (see Table 11.2) calls for total track length of 120,000 kilometers by 2020. Independent studies suggest total track length in China could actually surpass 180,000 by the end of the current decade. As for the short term, the MoR's plan calls for USD100 billion for basic rail investment in 2010 and another USD110 billion in 2011.

One of the most important challenges China faces is the modernization and expansion of its high-speed passenger lines, which totaled only about 1,200 kilometers in total rail length in 2008. According to the MoR total high-speed passenger lines will reach 15,000 kilometers by 2012. These lines will run parallel to existing ones and will be used exclusively for passenger trains. According to a summer 2009 Morgan Stanley report, these lines will cover 80 percent of China's population, 83 percent of China's urban population, and 87 percent of total China GDP.[1]

TABLE 11.2   China's Mid- to Long-Term Railway Plan (Km)

	2008	2010E	2012E	2020E
Railway operation length—total	8000	92000	110000	120000
Electrified track	28000	41400	55000	72000
Electrified rate	35%	45%	50%	60%
Double track	29000	41400	55000	60000
Double rate	36%	45%	50%	50%
New line construction	12000	17000	16000	41000
High-speed passenger line construction		7000	13000	16000%

(Source: MoR)

The highly anticipated Beijing-Shanghai high-speed line should be ready sometime between 2012 and 2015. The new railway will feature trains traveling at 300 kilometers per hour and will reduce travel time between Beijing and Shanghai from 14 hours to 5. An estimated 220,000 passengers per day will use the system.

Financing is a potential problem, however, because the MoR won't be able to cover the total costs for all these projects. As recently as 2005 the MoR was the dominant financier of all of China's rail projects. But things have changed; 74 percent of the funding for the Beijing-Shanghai high-speed train will come from non-MoR sources. The project is expected to cost around USD12 billion, and the MoR has indicated that it won't be the main financier. Instead, local governments will contribute 11 percent and insurance companies 7 percent; bank loans and the issuance of rail bonds will contribute 51 percent.

The National Social Security Fund (NSSF), an indirect SWF established in August 2000, will finance 5 percent of the project. The NSSF is administered by the National Council for Social Security Fund (SSF), a government agency. This reserve is funded mainly by capital and equity assets derived from reduction of state-owned shares, fiscal allocation of the central government, and other investment proceeds. It invests mainly in China, though officials have proposed an allocation for overseas investing through external money managers.[2]

The NSSF's involvement is a sign that Chinese officials attach some urgency to the issue of upgrading the country's railway system.

Although it's long been an important aspect of China's economy—around 47 percent of the freight and 36 percent of the passenger transport market is conveyed by rail—Chinese had been relatively slow to reform operations. To a certain degree the train business is today one of the most centralized in China, while the structure of the organization that oversees operations is complex and fragmented. It's a vestige of a long-gone era.

Four entities oversee China's railways; in addition to the MoR, they are the National Development and Reform Commission (NDRC), the Ministry of Finance (MoF), and the State Council. The MoR is the primary regulatory body. The NDRC is responsible for the approval of new railway projects that are less than 300 kilometers long. The MoF owns the state railway assets, on behalf of the central government, and is also responsible for collecting funds for railway construction that are later allocated by the MoR. The State Council is responsible for the ultimate approval of railway construction projects more than 300 kilometers in length and must approve any proposed railway tariff hike.

Growth in Chinese railway construction is a relatively well-known investment theme by now. The next opportunity lies in investments related to railway vehicle procurement and railway operators. Between 2009 and 2010 the MoR will disperse more than USD70 billion for railway vehicle acquisitions. And because railway equipment investment follows rail infrastructure construction, companies that manufacture railway equipment should see strong growth in 2010 and beyond.

Electrical multiple unit (EMU) trains and high-power electric locomotives loom as the next big investment themes in Chinese infrastructure. Urbanization requires more high-speed passenger lines, which, in turn, will create strong demand for EMU. China will experience an influx of EMU trains in the next three to four years, with around 800 sets expected to be in operation by 2012, up from 176 in 2008. Demand for high-power electric locomotives will accelerate as China increases the electrification of its tracks. In 2008 China's 80,000 kilometer network had a rail electrification rate of 35 percent; the MoR expects to reach a 50 percent by 2012. If these plans become reality, the railway system will be in great need of electric

locomotives. At the end of 2008 the total number of electric locomotives was 6,300, and high-power electric locomotives in particular
totaled a meager 744 units. Their number is expected to increase to
around 7,900 units by 2012.

Urban subways will also be a source of long-term growth. At the
end of 2008 only 10 cities had 29 subway and light-rail networks, with
a total length of about 820 kilometers. By 2015 22 cities will spend
USD130 billion to build 79 new subways, boosting total subway track
length by 2,260 kilometers.

Look first to Chinese names, particularly the railway equipment
companies and operators, to get exposure to China's rail expansion.

Zhuzhou CSR Times Electric (Hong Kong: 3898, OTC: ZHUZF)
manufactures train-borne electrical systems and electrical components. Most important, the company manufactures and sells electrical
systems and components related to locomotive and rolling stock,
which accounts for 78 percent of revenue. It supplies a range of on-
board electrical systems, including train power converters, auxiliary
power supply equipment, and control systems, train operation safety
equipment, and electrical control systems for large railway maintenance vehicles.

Daqin Railway (Shanghai: 601006) is the top choice for investors
among China's railway operators. The company transports coal products from the inland to southeast coastal areas, north China, and
northeast China. It principally transports steam coal, which is used in
electric-power generation and steel smelting.

Daqin is also involved in railway passenger transportation services, which will allow it to participate in future growth. Daqin should
also benefit from the MoR's capital-raising sale of operating assets to
rail companies.

Although China is making progress developing its own technology for this new era of train travel, much will need to be imported
from abroad. Local companies, however, benefit from the use of
locally produced components, which allow for higher profit margins.
For some types of locomotives up to 70 percent of production takes
place in China. The most important foreign players operating in
China that boast cutting-edge technology are Japan's Kawasaki Heavy
Industries, France's Alstom, Canada's Bombardier, Germany's

Siemens, and America's General Electric. GE is the main player in heavy-hauling diesel locomotives.

Kawasaki Heavy Industries (Tokyo: 7012; OTC: KWHIY) is one of the most respected names in the industry. A major player in China, the company secured a contract for USD6.7 billion from China in October 2009 to produce 140 new E2 Series Shinkansen bullet trains. The trains will be used on the Beijing-Shanghai and Beijing-Guangzhou rail lines beginning in the first half of 2010 and will operate at a maximum speed of 350 kilometers per hour. Kawasaki Heavy is also developing the new, 350 kilometer per hour Environmentally Friendly Super Express Train (EFSET), which is expected to be the go-to unit around the world for railways making upgrades.

Alstom (Paris: ALO, OTC: AOMFF), a pure infrastructure company, is one of the biggest beneficiaries of the global urbanization trend. The company focuses on two major types of projects: railroads (33 percent of sales) and power plants (67 percent of sales). It's a leader in urban transport and high-speed passenger-train markets as well as in signaling, related infrastructure equipment, and all associated services. In China Alstom controls 21 percent of the high-speed train market and 50 percent of the electric freight locomotive market.

Alstom is also a big player in Russia, where it has formed a strategic partnership with Transmashholding (TMH), Russia's major supplier to the Russian rail transport operator RZD.

The purpose of the joint venture (JV) is to manufacture 1,210 double-deck passenger cars. The new JV is only a first step in cooperation between both groups, as Alstom also plans to jointly manufacture freight and passenger locomotives. Russia is, according to Alstom's statements, a market with the potential for around 1,000 locomotives annually between now and 2030.

Plane and train manufacturer Bombardier (Toronto: BBD/B, OTC: BDRBF) is also involved in China. In September 2009 it secured a contract for 80 ZEFIRO very-high-speed trains (380 kilometers per hour) for USD4 billion. The first train is scheduled for delivery in 2012, while final deliveries are expected in 2014. Through its JV Bombardier Sifang (Qingdao) Transportation in China the company is building the world's fastest sleeper trains—capable of speeds of up to 250 kilometers per hour—for the MoR.

Finally, NWS Holdings Ltd. (Hong Kong: 0659) is a leading infrastructure company in China. Its infrastructure division is involved in road, energy, water, and port projects. The company is developing 18 rail container terminals across China.

Faster, Longer, Heavier

India's 150-year railway history is closely associated with the country's development, is viewed as a uniquely Indian experience, and is credited with "spanning the vast open spaces of central India."

Indian Railways (IR) is a ministry within the federal government that employs 1.4 million and has 1.1 million pensioners. Its network of routes extends to more than 63,000 kilometers (40,000 miles), making it one of the world's largest. The IR runs approximately 13,000 trains each day. It carries more than 2 million tons of freight and around 17 million passengers between 7,000 railway stations each day. The company has a fleet of 200,000 wagons, 40,000 coaches, and 8,000 locomotives. It's been calculated that Indian trains travel each day four times the distance from the earth to moon and back.[3] To build such a network now would cost about USD1 trillion.

IR's history can be divided into three phases: the building era of the mid-19th century, the nationalization and modernization period after 1947, and the operational crisis of the 1980s. This latter period led to the crisis of 2001, during which IR reached the point where expenses were growing by 13 percent a year while revenue was lagging operating costs by 8 percent. At that time railway experts submitted a comprehensive, three-volume report to the Government of India that painted a very dark future for the entity.[4] The report warned, "bluntly," that

> ...the "business as usual low growth" will rapidly drive IR to fatal bankruptcy, and in fifteen years, Government of India will be saddled with an additional financial liability of over INR61,000 crore (USD14.2 billion)....on a pure operating level IR is a terminal debt trap and can only be presented by continuing and ever increasing subsidies, year-on-year, from the central government. As is well known such subsidies are not available.[5]

India, adhering to its reputation for adding a little color to every-thing it does, needed a populist politician from the poorest state in the country (Bihar) to turn around the massive IR system. Lalu Prasad Yadav, briefly imprisoned in 1990 on allegations of corruption stemming from a fodder subsidy scandal, was named, for reasons of political balance, Minister of Railways in 2004 during the first Man-mohan Singh government. At the time, the decision of choosing Lalu was ridiculed by almost everyone. And yet over the four years IR was turned around through the use of simple entrepreneurial practices, which have stoked the admiration of internationally renowned institutions and companies alike.[6]

In his opening remarks in his February 2008 IR budget speech then Minister of Railways Lalu Prasad noted

Each year we have progressively raised the bar based on our own successes. The cash surplus of the Railways rose steadily from Rs 9,000 crore in 2005 to Rs 14,000 crore in 2006 to Rs 20,000 crore in 2007...in 2007-08, we will create history once again by turning in a cash surplus before Dividend of Rs.25,000 crore (USD6 billion). Our operating ratio[7] has also improved to 76 percent. Indian Railways is a Government Department. However, we take pride in the fact that our achievement, on the benchmark of net surplus before Dividend, makes us bet-ter than most of the Fortune 500 companies in the world.[8]

Under the guidance of Lalu Prasad, who proved to be as deter-mined as ever to demonstrate that his administrative skills and "rus-tic" common sense could make a difference, IR embarked on a trip of total transformation. The outcome proved that a government entity can indeed improve and become profitable while not losing any of its social characteristics. From the small things to the big, almost all the changes introduced during these four years added something impor-tant, tangible or intangible, to the process. The minister's actions sometimes didn't make sense to technocrats. Being a politician, Lalu understood that there's a balance between society and business that must be maintained. In light of IR's iconic status this reality was para-mount. Among the "small" things he did was ban the use of plastic cups on railway stations and trains, replacing them with kulhads (clay pots) made by rural artisans. In similar fashion, he replaced all synthetic upholstery and linen used throughout the organization with locally produced, hand-spun and hand-woven cotton cloth.

He surprised observers again in 2006 when he persuaded the Railway Board to reduce by one rupee (USD0.025) the cost of a second-class ticket. The prevailing view was that the reduction would cost IR around USD58 million and that passengers wouldn't notice because a single rupee has almost no value. The minister responded as follows: "A milk vendor from Hathua sells her milk not in Delhi, but in Siwan. And the train fare from Hathua to Siwan is just seven rupees. It seems that those who reside in air-conditioned offices do not realize what a rupee means to a poor milkmaid."[9] At the end of the meeting the reduction was approved.

On the business side of things, the new strategy called for faster, longer, and heavier trains. "Faster" referred to the reduction in the time elapsed between two successive loadings. "Longer" referred to simply adding more coaches to the popular routes, thus eliminating waiting times and getting passengers where they want to go on time. "Heavier" meant that more tonnage was to be added on each wagon—this drew the most criticism, on safety grounds. In the fall of 2004 IR leadership "officially" learned that most of its trains run massively overloaded, based on the weight allowed at the time, but the IR wasn't getting paid for it. Based on this observation and the fact that IR had spent USD6 billion in the 1990s to upgrade and strengthen its tracks, which were now capable of supporting bigger loads up to 23 tons axle load and up to 25 tons axle load with some improvements, increasing the loads was the next logical step.[10]

These, then, were the main pillars of IR's transformation, which, coupled with market-driven initiatives, resulted in a renaissance for the most traditional, most important of India's transportation complex. In a September 2006 speech at Ludhiana in north India Prime Minister Dr. Manmohan Singh discussed the importance to the regional economy of IR's transformation; the prime minister's words could easily describe almost any other part of the country, which underlies just how important trains are on the Subcontinent. Prime Minister Singh noted

> This project will change the face of Punjab and of all regions through which it passes. It will bring top class transport links

to Punjab. The products of Punjab will find easy access to our ports and to export markets. Coal will now come easily to the state, removing the power shortage and giving a spur to the establishment of more thermal power plants. It will also bring steel from steel plants in the east. And all this will be done at a cheaper cost. I am confident that this project will usher in a new era of industrial growth and prosperity in Punjab.[11]

A Race Against Time

The Dedicated Rail Freight Corridor (DRFC), a USD6 billion project, was conceived in 2005 after the prime ministers of India and Japan made a joint declaration calling for studies of the feasibility and possible funding of the project. According to the plan, two new freight-dedicated corridors, the Western DFC and the Eastern DFC, spanning a total length of about 3,000 kilometers (1864 miles), will be built.

As illustrated in Figure 11.1, the Eastern DFC, starting from Ludhiana in Punjab, will pass through the states of Haryana and Uttar Pradesh and terminate at Son Nagar in Bihar. The Western DFC will traverse the distance from Dadri to Mumbai, passing through the states of Delhi, Haryana, Rajasthan, Gujarat, and Maharashtra.[12]

The DRFC feasibility study, which Japan's International Cooperation Agency submitted to India's Ministry of Railways in 2007, noted that the proposed line will pass though a total of ten states that are home to a total population of 620 million people. India's west coast region, centered on the city of Mumbai and encompassing the states of Maharashtra and Gujarat, is served by several deep sea ports and is a thriving center of industry and commerce. The region centered on the capital city of Delhi is densely populated and is a developing center of industry, commerce, and agriculture. The northern region includes the state of Punjab, blessed with fertile soils and known as the "bread basket" of India, and the district of Ludhiana, a rapidly industrializing hub of manufacturing and information technology. The east coast region (West Bengal State), centered on the city of

Kolkata, has achieved remarkable economic growth over recent years. Adjoining West Bengal on its inland border is the state of Jharkhand, which is developing as a center for heavy industries such as steel mills, which rely on the state's rich coal and iron ore resources.[13]

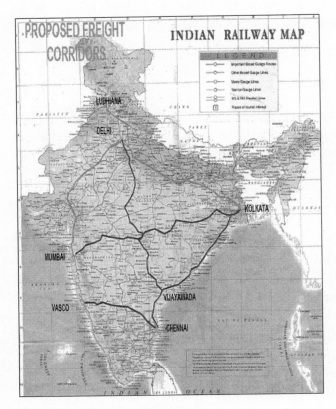

Figure 11.1   Indian railway map.

(Source: Government of India Secretariat for Infrastructure, Planning Commission)

Upon completion, Indian freight cargos will be able to run more efficiently because freight trains will no longer share tracks with passenger trains. The project will allow India to increase its line electrification percentage from its current 25 percent. It will enable better planning by companies and government agencies because travel times will be more predictable. The Indian economy will be one step closer to realizing its growth potential. This potential is comparable to China's but has been stunted by India's poor infrastructure.

Japanese assistance will play a significant role in the development of the project. Japan has been similarly involved in projects all over Asia through its Official Development Assistance (ODA) program. Although not as generous as it was in the mid-1990s, the program remains an important contributor to the region's economic growth. The ODA offers either assistance or favorable loans to governments in Asia and around the world. The purpose of the program is to assist developing nations but also to secure contracts for Japanese companies overseas. India as a whole doesn't figure prominently in Japan's long-term planning. But Japan will benefit, too, from improvements to regional commercial infrastructure as India and China will be two of Japan's biggest markets for the foreseeable future.

Japanese companies invested around USD6 billion in India in 2008. Because of extensive Japanese involvement at the highest levels of government, there's unlikely to be any pushback against its participation the project. Companies such as Nippon Koei (Tokyo: 1954), Japan's largest construction consultant, which has advised the Japanese government with regard to Vietnam's rail construction program, will also play a big role in India.

According to the Department of Industrial Policy and Promotion (DIPP) of India's Ministry of Commerce and Industry, FDI flow into railway-related components was USD76.7 million from April 2000 to August 2009, a meager 0.08 percent of the total. This ranked the sector 47th among all the sectors that received FDI during the same period. The potential for a serious jump of such a low base as rail-related infrastructure plans come together to make this one of the most compelling global investment stories. Many Indian companies will experience direct or indirect benefits from these projects and the revival of IR generally.

Bharat Heavy Electricals (India: BHEL)[14] is India's largest engineering and manufacturing enterprise in the energy-related infrastructure sector. Most trains used by Indian Railways are equipped with Bharat Heavy's traction propulsion systems and controls; the company is also building coaches for IR.

Companies offering better connections between ports and markets and among Indian cities are good candidates for investors' dollars. Container Corporation of India (India: CONCOR) is the largest container railroad player in India. Concor operates on export-import (EXIM) and domestic routes, handling around 30 percent of India's EXIM container traffic through its 59 terminals.

Gateway Distriparks (India: GDL) is the second-largest container operator in India. It holds the biggest share of the market, 2 percent, at Jawaharlal Nehru Port Trust (JNPT), India's largest container port. The company has expanded its CFS (container freight station) capacity and has established new ICDs (inland container depots) at key locations to benefit from the high growth in container traffic to and from India.

Because of IR's turnaround and the continuing urbanization of India, rail-related investment should pick up dramatically in the future. This will include both IR-related investment as well as in local metro projects, which will gradually become Indians' preferred medium of urban travel. If you've never been to Mumbai, a visit to the Mumbai Metropolitan Region Development Authority's (MMRDA) Web site offers a quick look at current traffic in one of the most populous cities in the world. The situation is already dire for urban and suburban transportation. Given India's demographic reality—it's a nation of young people—solutions are needed now.[15]

A million people travel daily in Mumbai by public transport, 48 percent of them by rail. Suburban rail traffic has increased by six times, while capacity increased by only 2.3 times. Four-thousand five-hundred passengers travel per train, against the carrying capacity of 1,750, resulting in unbearable overcrowding. The number of vehicles on Mumbai's streets increased from 61,000 to more than 1.02 million over the last four decades. The first phase of the city's 146.5 kilometer (91 miles) metro project is expected to be completed by 2012. A China-based company has received orders from MMRDA to provide 16 trains.

China South Locomotive & Rolling Stock Corporation (Hong Kong: 1766, OTC: CSRGY) will deliver by April 2010 64 new coaches that will be used at the Mumbai metro. The company's major products include locomotives, passenger coaches, freight wagons, and multiple-unit and rapid-transit vehicles. It also provides these products) in China, making it a double-play and a great buy for investors able to access the Shanghai market.

Beyond Rail

Forty-six percent of FDI flow into India has been captured by five sectors: services, computer software and hardware, telecommunications, and construction, in this order. Power-related projects account for 4 percent, while port-related projects, another area were India needs a lot of improvement, ranked 18th with 1.5 percent of total FDI.[16]

These statistics indicate that, in addition to rail transport, ports and power will experience significant growth in the future. Ports, in particular, on which little money has been spent, present the biggest upside potential. India has 12 major and 187 minor ports. According to the Indian Ports Association, these major ports together handled a total of 519.2 million tons (MT) of cargo in 2007-08, an increase of 11.9 percent over the 463.8 MT handled in 2006-07. In 2008-09 cargo traffic at major ports increased to 530.4 MT. The Indian government set up the National Maritime Development Plan (NMDP) to improve facilities at India's 12 major ports, and it plans to invest USD 12.4 billion in its efforts. Plans to spend another USD11 on shipping- and inland waterways-related projects are also in the works.

Larsen & Toubro (India: LT, OTC: LTOUF) is the largest player in India's domestic infrastructure market, with 70 percent of its revenue coming from engineering and construction. The company is also involved in port-related projects such as building shipyards and port facilities. The unique combination of scale, diversity, and growth puts L&T's core business in a league of its own in the Indian construction sector. L&T remains the best, lowest-risk way to play India's long-term growth story. The company has expanded into the Middle East, where infrastructure construction remains strong.

Tata Steel (India: TATASTEEL) also benefits from India's infrastructure boom. One of the top ten steel producers in the world, Tata boasts existing annual crude steel production capacity of 30 MT.

An indirect way to participate in India's infrastructure development is through IDFC, Infrastructure Development Finance Corporation (India: IDFC). Key sectors to which IDFC lends include energy, telecom, transportation, and commercial and industrial infrastructure. IDFC's management team is highly respected and it maintains a solid balance sheet.

The power sector has attracted a great deal of interest from foreign and domestic investors alike, as the Ministry of Power initiative "Mission 2012: Power for All" has made it one of the most important infrastructure segments in the country. The Central Electricity Authority estimates total additions will be 78,577 megawatts (MW) under the eleventh five-year plan (covering fiscal years 2008 through 2012), augmenting total installed capacity of 132,330 MW as of the end of fiscal 2007.

There are two companies investors should look to for long-term exposure to India's power sector. GVK Power and Infrastructure Group (India: GVKPIL) is a diversified conglomerate with a substantial presence in the infrastructure sector. Its infrastructure division focuses on power-generation assets, roads, airports, coal mines, and oil and gas assets.

BGR Energy Systems (India: BGRENERGY) is a midsized engineering and construction company. It provides turnkey balance-of-plant services mainly for large power plants. It also supplies all the equipment required to build power plants except for boilers, turbines, and generators. BGR also provides engineering, procurement, and construction services for smaller power plants.

Endnotes

[1] Kate Zhu and Bin Wang, "China Construction & Infrastructure," Morgan Stanley, July 28, 2009.

[2] National Social Security Fund, SWF Institute, http://www.swfinstitute.org/fund/nssf.php.

[3] Sudhir Kumar and Shagun Mehrotra, *Bankruptcy to Billions* (New Delhi: Oxford University Press, 2009), 30.

[4] The Expert Group on Railways was constituted under the chairmanship of Rakesh Mohan, the then Director General of the National Council of Applied Economic Research (NCAER).

[5] Kumar and Mehrotra. *Bankruptcy to Billions*, 3-4.

[6] Ankit Gupta and Vidya Bhat, "Indian Railways Growth, Sustenance and the Leap Forward—A Case Study," Delhi: Indian Institute of Technology, May 1, 2007 1.

[7] Operating ratio is a company's operating expenses divided by its operating revenues. The operating expenses include all expenses except dividends paid to the government of India. Operating revenues are gross traffic receipts. The lower the operating ratio, the more efficient the enterprise. In 2001 the operating ratio for the IR was 98.3 percent.

[8] Budget speech, Minister of Railways, February 26, 2008, www.hindu.com/nic/railbudget2008-09.pdf.

[9] Kumar and Mehrotra, *Bankruptcy to Billions*, 2.

[10] The axle load is the maximum weight of an axle permitted on a given track.

[11] PM Manmohan Singh Inaugurates Chandigarh–Morinda New Railway Line Ludhiana, September 27, 2006, http://pmindia.nic.in/speeches.htm.

[12] Dedicated Freight Corridor Corporation of India (DFCCIL), http://dfccil.org/wps/portal/DFCCPortal (accessed November 2009).

[13] Japan International Cooperation Agency, "The Feasibility Study on the Development of Dedicated Multimodal High Axle Load Freight Corridor with Computerized Control for Delhi-Mumbai and Delhi-Howrah in India," September 2007, http://www.jica.go.jp/english/operations/social_environmental/archive/reviews/pro_asia/pdf/india04_04.pdf.

[14] All ticker symbols refer to India's National Stock Exchange, http://www.nse-india.com/.

[15] Mumbai Metropolitan Region Development Authority, http://www.mmrdamumbai.org/projects_metro_rail.htm (accessed October 2009).

[16] Department of Industrial Policy & Promotion, Ministry of Commerce and Industry – India, http://dipp.nic.in/.

12

Age, Youth, and Upward Mobility

Two major demographic forces will prove critical to investors in the coming decade: Aging and the needs of the youth in developing economies, especially Asia.

These are not new developments and have impacted previous economic cycles. The difference today is that these economies are richer—and therefore more money will be spent to stay healthier longer as well as on the upbringing of children.

Increases in societal wealth will be felt at the government as well as the individual level; this will have profound impact on the amount of spending on health-care and education-related services.

At the end of 2006, India-based pharmaceutical company Dr. Reddy's Laboratories announced the formation of an alliance with New Zealand's University of Auckland to work toward a revolutionary pill that would "provide a vastly simpler and more effective treatment for heart disease."

The so-called polypill should launch in India sometime in 2010 upon approval by the Drug Controller General of India. Polypill is a combination of four drugs—aspirin, a statin, a beta blocker, and an ACE inhibitor—for patients who have suffered heart attacks; the medication is designed to prevent another attack. The new pill, code named "Red Heart" by Dr. Reddy's, will make it easier for patients to follow their doctor's orders in one step, and the cost for patients will reportedly be USD1 per month. India, site of the initial launch, and China together are home to more people affected by cardiovascular disease than all the developed economies combined.

Similar research efforts have taken place in Spain and in England, where scientists at the Wolfson Institute of Preventative Medicine are working toward a five-in-one pill that will contain a statin, three blood-pressure-lowering drugs, and folic acid. The goal is to launch by 2012. Backers hope to make the pill available to everyone in the UK over age 55 for less than USD2 a day.[1]

Such pills will be very useful to companies that are trying to reach rural populations in emerging markets. Although large in total number, these potential customers are usually unable to follow multi-course drug treatments because they're too expensive. The social implications of the polypill are therefore important as well; rural populations are huge in India and China and are critical to economic development in both countries. India's government still distributes iron pills to the poor. Women, in particular, are susceptible to anemia because of malnutrition.

Economists have traditionally referred to health care as a "luxury good" because richer people (and nations) buy it in greater proportions. As you would expect, the United States has a high level of per capita health care spending compared to countries with a lower per capita GDP, although US health care spending is still 60 percent higher than its GDP would predict.[2] More important, the world's most advanced economies also pay more for their citizens' health care needs. As wealth increases, so does not only the tendency to spend more—and more readily—on health care, but governments also typically boost their contributions as living standards among their citizens rise.

Even in the US, where many citizens are under the impression that the government hasn't been involved much in the industry, 45 percent of health care costs are paid by the government. Out-of-pocket health care expenditures have fallen in the US by 40 percent since 1970, and households are now paying 2.8 percent of final consumption funds as out-of-pocket expenses, below the OECD average (see Figure 12.1).[3]

On the basis of combined private insurance and out-of-pocket payments, Americans and their employers pay around 55 percent of health care costs, while Chinese and Indians pay 61 and 81 percent, respectively (see Figure 12.2).

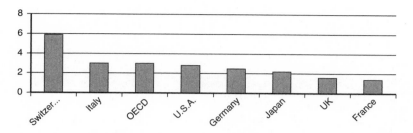

Figure 12.1   OECD out of pocket health care expenditure as a share of final household consumption, 2007.

(Source: Organization for Economic Cooperation and Development Health Data 2009)

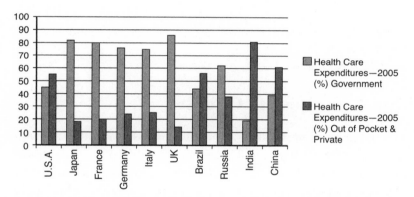

Figure 12.2   Share of health care expenditures covered by government versus share covered by individuals out of pocket and with private insurance.

(Source: World Health Organization, World Bank)

Analysis of the pharmaceutical profit cycle reveals that profits increase steadily as the government and employers increase subsidies. It's reasonable, therefore, to assume that as emerging economies move to more universal health care systems—at the same time experiencing solid economic growth—the propensity to consume pharmaceutical products will rise. Figure 12.3 illustrates the long-term impact the pharmaceutical industry is forecast to have over the next decade.

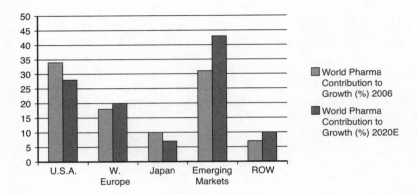

Figure 12.3   Contribution of the pharmaceutical industry to global economic growth.

(Source: IMS Health, International Monetary Fund, UBS)

China Changes Its Course

China fully commercialized its health care system in 1987. Hospitals turned into independent companies, although the largest remained under state ownership. Having health care insurance was not the norm; patients were forced to pay most of their health care expenditures out of their pockets. Chinese were paying full price for all their health care needs, from pills to surgery. Out of a pool of 191 countries, China was ranked 188th in 2000 on fairness in health care financial contribution. India was ranked 43rd, Germany 6th, the US 54th.[4]

China's privatization efforts have been a tremendous financial burden on its people. Chinese accumulated savings at extremely high rates because they had to prepare for unforeseen sickness. Providing for health care is one of the main reasons the savings rate in China reached 33 percent of disposable income in 2006. None of the OECD countries had savings rates remotely near that number, even traditionally prudent Germany, where the rate was 15 percent of disposable income.

Other side effects of the commercialization of China's health care system include reluctance among Chinese to visit the hospital, and, according to reports, deaths during emergencies because of lack of patient funding. The government soon embarked on a new course of health care reforms, the first step of which was to offer basic medical insurance to all urban residents, including children and the unemployed. In January 2009 the Chinese government announced it would spend USD123 billion to establish a form of universal health care for its citizens. The first step is to introduce medical insurance of some sort for most Chinese by 2011.

According to a report published by a panel of Chinese experts in 2008, China's plan is to become a "welfare state" by 2049, in three stages. The first stage, already under way, involves creating a safety net that will include minimum living allowances, medical insurance, and pensions for all urban and rural residents by approximately 2012. The second, from 2013 to 2020, will focus on implementing policies such as free primary education in rural areas, where 737 million Chinese still live, and other measures designed to make the social security network stable and sustainable. The final stage, from 2021 to 2049, will include anything else required to "build a socialist welfare society with Chinese characteristics."[5]

Pharma's Opportunity

Because of changes in health care delivery in developing economies and a global aging process that will include more people this time around, pharmaceutical sales will grow steadily during the next decade; even moderate growth would still take total revenue above USD1 trillion from USD733 billion in 2008.

This will be a gradual process. Pharmaceutical companies must learn to adapt to the realities of new markets. Countries such as China and India have, for instance, price limits on many medicines; even prices for those without limits are lower than in developed economies. Volume and margins will be the main metrics for companies operating in these developing economies. Margins will prove very important for companies and their stocks, as sales growth should be a multiyear phenomenon in emerging economies. This will help account for the impact of lower prices. Setting up research laboratories and production facilities in local markets will prove cost-effective while boosting profit margins on a global scale. A new vaccine developed in a multinational company's facilities in India can still be sold for higher prices in Western markets.

Pharmaceutical companies must adapt to Chinese and Indian norms at the same time drug pricing is changing in markets that have traditionally been more favorable to them. In the US drug prices are often as much as 50 percent higher than in other countries, including almost all its developed counterparts. Health care reform will remain at the forefront of the US political debate so long as 16 percent of the population remains uninsured. Among the potential outcomes are measures aimed at curbing pharmaceutical companies' profits. Such changes would make serious exposure to emerging economies even more important. Companies will attempt to balance their eventual profit losses in the US with new cash flow from other markets.

Japan provides another interesting case study. The island nation is going through a massive aging process and has only recently opened its market to big non-Japanese pharmaceutical companies. At the same time, Japan's generic drug usage is extremely low, which makes it an outlier among developed economies. Forty-two percent of the Japanese market is controlled by medicines with expired brands, compared to 22 percent of Europe's five leading markets and 9 percent for the US.[6]

That being said, emerging economies are quite fragmented from the perspective of the major multinational pharmaceuticals. In the US, for instance, the world's 20 biggest pharmaceutical companies control around 73 percent of the market. The same companies control about 16 percent of the Chinese market. The main reason for this fragmentation is income discrepancy. As even after years of solid economic growth, which for China and India is a secular trend, emerging economies still have many people in need of lower-priced medicines. And this will be the case for years to come. Generics, therefore, will be an important force in the global pharmaceutical market.

In developed economies, too, an aging population—with diminishing incomes, living in economies with enough long-term problems to last a generation—makes cheaper alternatives a necessity rather than a simple choice at the pharmacist's counter. Generics will remain at the forefront of the pharmaceutical business, as both the developed and developing economies are getting more accustomed to them. By 2012, eight of the biggest small-molecule drugs in terms of sales will have become generic.[7]

Indian consumers have the choice of selecting the same medicine sometimes offered by two or three different local pharmaceutical companies; the best-known company's version is typically more expensive. Different companies often simply cater to different segments of the population. Some simply charge more, taking advantage of people's vanity by giving them the opportunity to express their ability to afford the most recognized brand-name medicine.

Nevertheless, market fragmentation has made multinationals eager to partner with local companies to get easier, and a lot of times better, access to a local market. The obvious benefits of such moves are better distribution channels and favorable treatment from governments, especially on the provincial level. Lower penetration levels offer greater upside potential for gaining market share, as companies make developing economies their main growth priority. At the same time good generic companies remain a force on their own.

The solid growth of generic pharmaceutical sales in the past ten years has also dramatically changed the "business as usual" attitude for the more established pharmaceutical companies. Highly innovative and complicated drugs will be sought by the big pharmaceutical companies as a way to protect new sales. As in every industry, not all companies are prepared for this transformation, and the ones slow to adapt will eventually pay the price.

The generic pharmaceutical company every investor should own is India's Dr. Reddy's Laboratories (NYSE: RDY). An inexpensive workforce operating 16 Indian production facilities provides a significant cost advantage. Geographic convenience plays a similarly beneficial role, as Dr. Reddy's is in the middle of rapid growth in Asian markets. The company's generic drug segment (70 percent of sales) sells off-patent drugs primarily in North America, India, Europe, and Russia, operations that have generated a compound annual growth rate (CAGR) of approximately 25 percent over the past decade.

Dr. Reddy's also develops and manufactures pharmaceutical active ingredients used in the manufacture of other drugs as well as proprietary branded products.

A similar but more unique company is Tianjin Tasly Pharmaceutical (Shanghai: 600535), which offers a broad range of products encompassing both traditional Chinese medicines (TCM) consisting of teas and dietary supplements, cosmetics, and what Westerners would consider modern drugs. Its products, currently available in more than 34 countries around the world, generated almost USD32 million in global sales in 2006.

The company operates a large chain of agricultural plantations that produce the bulk of the organics that go into the production of its products. Relatively few ingredients used in TCM operations are sourced through outside vendors.

Big Pharma Still Strong

Big pharmaceutical companies have been accused in recent years of being slow to adapt to change. There's a lot of truth in this accusation. But drastic shifts in the global economy and the reemergence of epidemic diseases should be instrumental in driving them to their former prominence. The former will push them to become more innovative in all aspects of their business, while the latter will create an important revenue stream.

Infectious diseases have for centuries been a drawback to economic development and have devastated periodically big parts of the world. As recently as 1735 chemical treatises suggesting that "spirits of wine rightly used is a short of panacea" were widely accepted, while brandy was for ages the most-used medicine against plague, gout, and loss of voice, among other maladies.[8] Eventually vaccines came along and allowed the world to bypass a number of health obstacles, contributing to economic growth and advancement.

In January 2003 the SARS epidemic broke out in China. The world, it seems, has entered a new era of infectious diseases. Even though the majority of them may never amount to anything close to the legendary Spanish Flu pandemic of 1918–19 that killed between 20 million and 40 million people globally, the thought that such an outcome is still possible terrifies people.

Consumers and governments, rather than pushing for cheap prices, now clamor for newer, more effective treatments. Vaccines are now viewed not only as a social benefit. It's conventional wisdom that the necessary funds to support the extended research and development process required for their development should be forthcoming. One of the main profit centers for pharmaceutical companies going forward will be vaccines.

Governments in emerging markets are striving to offer a higher standard of living to their citizens; this trend should not only remain intact but also strengthen in importance as more and more countries expand health care access as their wealth increases. China, for example, increased the number of vaccines included in its national immunization program from 5 to 15 in 2008 and boosted its budget for research and development from USD75 million to USD400 million.[9]

Vaccines are on the verge of a multiyear golden age in terms of importance for consumers and companies, to be ushered in as the urbanization theme unfolds in the major emerging economies. Global vaccines sales surpassed USD20 billion in 2008, but keep in mind that vaccines are the one segment of the pharmaceutical chain where generics aren't generally an option. At any rate, preventing a disease outbreak—not controlling costs—is the major theme of this story.

Five pharmaceutical companies control 85 percent of the vaccines market. Barriers to entry are very high; it takes a long time to set up first-rate R&D operations and even more time—as many as ten years—to bring a new vaccine to market. The incumbents—GlaxoSmithKline, Sanofi-Aventis, Merck & Co, Novartis, and Pfizer-Wyeth—will control the market for at least for the next decade. Switzerland-based Novartis (NYSE: NVS), which operates in 140 companies, is best-positioned among the majors to capitalize on the new realities. The company is a leader in all critical aspects of the business: brand medicines, generics, consumer health care, vaccines, and diagnostics.

UK-based GlaxoSmithKline (NYSE: GSK) has a significant presence in emerging markets, particularly India. Glaxo also occupies a leading spot in the over-the-counter (OTC) consumer business. The OTC business is becoming a big component of future growth for many companies, as rising incomes and increasing health awareness around the world allow more people to make use of nonprescription medication and other "well being" OTC services.

The company has also used its ample resources to create the next generation of pharmaceuticals and develop what is arguably one of the best pipelines in the business. Glaxo has more than 100 new products or existing products in some phase of trials for new uses. More than 20 drugs were in Phase III trials in 2009.

The vaccines segment represents its best growth opportunity because many of its competitors have dropped out of the market, increasing Glaxo's pricing power for new vaccines.

Glaxo is experiencing strong growth in its emerging markets operations; sales in 85 nations classified as emerging generated approximately 13 percent of revenue, the fastest growth coming from Eastern and Central Europe and the Asia-Pacific region. Annual pharmaceutical sales in emerging markets are expected to reach USD400 billion by 2020, equivalent to current sales in the US and the major European markets combined.

Denmark-based Novo Nordisk (NYSE: NVO) is the most important player in the fast-growing global diabetes market, controlling anywhere between 40 and 60 percent in any given market. It has a 52 percent share of the worldwide insulin market and is the No. 1 provider of modern insulin products such as long-lasting Levemir and quick-acting NovoRapid. The company has a presence in all major markets of the world, particularly in emerging economies, where obesity and diabetes are growing fast. As a chronic disease, diabetes often requires lifelong treatment. Global diabetes care costs are expected to increase from an estimated USD376 billion in 2010 to USD480 billion by 2030, which is forecast to account for almost 12 percent of global health care costs. Diabetes treatment is an attractive niche for a pharmaceutical company.

Medical Products and Services

One of the fastest-growing segments of the health care industry is equipment-making. Rising demand from emerging economies is driving growth here, too. A fragmented industry will eventually entice the biggest players toward consolidations and takeovers, which will push stock prices to higher levels long term.

Hong-Kong based Mingyuan Medicare Development (Hong Kong: 0233) is principally engaged in the design and manufacture of protein chips and related equipment and genetic testing equipment used in disease detection and diagnosis. A full 95 percent of revenues are generated within China, and the company has benefited from the growing wealth of Chinese consumers and their concomitant desire to seek Western-style medical care.

The company's diagnostic testing operation has been licensed by Chinese health authorities to develop kits to detect the presence of Influenza A (which includes the H1N1 variant of the virus) in human samples.

Shandong Weigao Medical Supplies (Hong Kong: 8199, OTC: SHWGF) manufactures and markets disposable medical products including syringes, blood bags, and infusion sets, as well as dental, anesthetic, and blood sampling products. Minneapolis-based Medtronic (NYSE: MDT) holds a 15 percent equity interest in Weigao and two places on the board of directors, providing the Chinese company with valuable technological know-how and financial backing.

China-based Mindray Medical International (NYSE: MR) develops, manufactures, and markets a wide array of products in three primary segments: patient monitoring and life support products, in-vitro diagnostic products, and medical-imaging systems. The company sells to more than 40,000 health care facilities in China and exports devices to 190 countries. Approximately 10 percent of annual revenue is devoted to research and development. Its primary R&D center is in China, though it did open facilities in Seattle in 2006.

China Medical Technologies (NSDQ: CMED) develops, manufactures, and markets enhanced chemiluminescence immunoassay (ECLIA) diagnostic systems, which have long been in use in the US and Western Europe but are relatively new to China. It's one of the lowest-cost producers in the country and is rapidly gaining market share. China Medical, however, is up against more established US and European players such as General Electric and Phillips Electronics, which have established footprints in the country.

US-based Thermo Fisher Scientific (NYSE: TMO) is the undisputed leader in laboratory supply operations, offering testing equipment, laboratory consumables, analytical software, and services. Consumables such as reactive reagents used in testing account for 49 percent of sales, of which equipment generates 30 percent. Software and service sales to the life sciences, health care, and environmental industries make up the remainder, a large percentage of which is based on sales of environmental monitoring equipment to China and India, the company's two most rapidly growing markets.

Singapore-based Biosensors International (Singapore: B20) develops and markets critical-care catheter systems and related devices used during heart surgery and intensive care treatment. It entered the interventional cardiology market in 2000 with its proprietary coronary stent and accompanying stent-delivery system. Biosensors was the first company to develop a proprietary drug—Biolimus A9—specifically for coronary stent use. The drug reduces the effects of inflammation and helps maintain blood flow through the stent site. US-based Sequenom (NSDQ: SQNM) develops technology, products, and diagnostic tests that target and serve discovery and clinical research and molecular diagnostics markets.

The company also has a noninvasive test for Down syndrome that was developed in cooperation with the Chinese University of Hong Kong. The test is considerably more accurate than others on the market, with a specificity of 99.9 percent versus the average 70 percent to 90 percent.

In addition to test kits the company also develops and markets genetic analysis equipment such as its MassARRAY systems. Enabling researchers and diagnosticians to rapidly profile tumor initiation and progression, the system is enjoying a growing acceptance among cancer researchers.

Parkway Holdings (Singapore: P27, OTC: PKWHF) operates a comprehensive health care network throughout Asia consisting of

16 hospitals (3 in Singapore, 11 in Malaysia, 1 in Brunei, and 1 in India), 49 clinics (including 6 in Shanghai), 9 radiology clinics, 4 laboratories, and 48 patient-assistance centers spread across Asia, Russia, and the Middle East. About 60 percent of patients are Singaporean, with the remainder primarily of other Asian nationalities. While Parkway has focused on developing its in-patient services and caring for acute cases, it's also exploring outpatient services, which are in rapidly growing demand. Although in-patient care typically results in higher margins, outpatient care generates hefty volumes.

India's Apollo Hospitals (Mumbai: 508869) is an integrated health care company that controls the largest hospital network in Asia. The group and its subsidiaries own 26 hospitals, 20 of which it operates. These hospitals comprise more than 8,000 operational beds. Apollo has a network of more than 2,000 doctors, approximately 2,000 nurses, and around 1,000 paramedical personnel on its payroll. It also operates a network of primary-care clinics, a medical back-office operation, a health insurance company, and a health care staffing company that provides nurses to the UK, the US, and other countries. Its retail pharmacy business is one of the largest in India, with a network of 873 outlets.

Fortis Healthcare (Mumbai: 532843), another Indian hospital company, was incorporated in 1996. Fortis is now one of the largest hospital chains in India, with a network of 37 hospitals and more than 3,000 beds under management.

China Nepstar Chain Drugstore (NYSE: NPD) is China's largest retail drugstore chain based on number of locations. It's grown from a single location in 1995 to 2,337 stores in 2009; its directly operated outlets cover 67 cities in China. Direct operation, rather than franchising, ensures consistent service and quality standards, though it does increase operating costs. Nepstar operates with almost no debt and in fact has USD290 million of cash and equivalents on its balance sheet. This means it can finance growth internally.

The company operates in a unique environment in which hospital pharmacies still dominate the market and the pharmaceutical retailing industry is crowded and highly fragmented. This makes for many attractive acquisition opportunities that ultimately will allow Nepstar to access new markets on the cheap. Nepstar is also moving to build better diversity into its product mix by offering more health-related nonpharmaceutical products in its stores as it evolves from primarily a dispensary into a more Western-style retailer.

The Time for Education

Four hundred and fifty million people of India's population are between the ages of 5 and 24. As a result, and because of the country's economic developmental trajectory, demand for more and better education remains a constant of Indian society. Education-related expenses are among the last households are willing to cut when times are tough, and they're the first to increase when things are good.

Education is becoming a pressing problem for India, extending far beyond any individual's social or employment needs and ambitions. India hasn't been very successful in battling illiteracy—around 270 million people above the age of 15 are classified as illiterate. In terms of sheer size this is the most of any other county. India's illiteracy ratio climbed to 34.6 percent in mid-2000s from 31.2 percent in 1990.[10] India is part of a greater problem that's seen 16 percent of the world's adult population characterized as illiterate by the United Nations Educational, Scientific and Cultural Organization (UNESCO) and other multilateral agencies. Although the world is expected to achieve a literacy rate of 87 percent by 2015, the situation is still dire in a lot of places around the world.[11] It's alarming as well that some OECD countries continue to have pockets of illiteracy. According to the United Nations "one million native Dutch speakers in the Netherlands are classified as functionally illiterate, while in metropolitan France, some 10 percent of the population aged 18 to 65—more than 3 million people—lacks basic reading, writing, arithmetic and other fundamental skills despite having attended French schools."[12]

Traditionally, Indians as a whole have an extreme affection to schooling, which is viewed as the main avenue to social and professional success. More often than not education is the only way for people from the lower strata of the society to "do well in life." This aspiration is reflected in the fact that the extracurricular activity most mentioned by people in India is "academic coaching." In some of the more affluent sections of the society parents try to improve their children's basic academic skills from an early age. Courses like mental mathematics and memory and speed reading for children in grades one to eight are growing more popular.

Indian households spend around 15 percent of their disposable income on children's education, third in priority after paying the rent or the mortgage and buying groceries. Education expenses are one of the main reasons Indian families save money, and Indian children for the most part recognize the real sacrifice being made—usually by the whole family—for them to receive their schooling. As a result they are determined and hard-working. Letting one's family down is not an option.

This last observation is not figurative; in India dramatic terms that people in the developed economies often use lightly still convey their real meaning. Words like "hunger," "sacrifice," "poor," and the like express vivid, real situations that would shock ordinary Westerners. Indian families will continue to spend as much as they can for their children's education. Because of the incessant problems plaguing the Indian public education system the private sector's presence will continue to grow.

India's economic growth has brought more prosperity. Consequently, public spending on education has dramatically increased. In 1992 central and local governments spent around 0.3 percent of gross domestic product (GDP) on education. By 2009 this figure had risen to close to 4 percent of GDP, which is still low compared the like the UK and the US, which spend 5.4 percent and 5.6 percent, respectively. The issue in India, though, is that 97 percent of government funds devoted to schooling go to salaries. Add to this the great segmentation in India's education system between the haves and have nots and the outcome is a dual one: a percentage of students that graduate with the best skills that can be found anywhere in the world and a set that either lacks basic literacy and arithmetic skills or doesn't attend school at all. There's an expectation among observers of the Indian economy, which we share, that the private sector may be able to change this. Not only can private actors offer the affluent more and sometimes better education, but they also should eventually be able to pick up expenses the government currently incurs. The government will therefore be able to plow money more effectively.

The Indian government plans to increase education-related out-
lays at the federal level, but the big bet for India will be the contribution of the state governments in these efforts. State officials are
influential in setting educational guidelines, but some are open and
proactive on behalf of their constituencies' educational needs, while
others are not. Some state governments now allow the establishment
of private universities, with the hope of increasing access to higher
education, while also bringing higher education closer to rural areas
through the creation of satellite campuses. Many states are in the
process of creating the framework for private education.[13]

Career-wise four main avenues are generally viewed as "a must"
by parents and, to a certain degree, children, too: engineering, medicine, civil services, and business. Every year a great number of students sit for entrance examinations for India's two most prestigious
institutions of higher learning, the Indian Institute of Technology and
the Indian Institute of Management. Both schools have campuses in
multiple cities.[14]

Nearly two-thirds of medical and engineering colleges in India
are run by the private sector. Under current regulations only not-for-
profit trusts and societies registered under the Societies Registration
Act can operate private schools. There are around 3,000 private institutions where students can receive a four-year engineering education, a five-year medical education, or try for a two-year MBA
program.

The Indian government has been instrumental, though indirectly,
in opening the way for more private participation in the complemen-
tary educational business such as preschools, tutoring, multimedia
content, IT training, and e-learning. E-learning was boosted by government initiatives to provide information and communications technology (ICT) in schools. The program initially called for outsourcing
the supply, installation, and maintenance of IT hardware and software, as well as teacher training and IT education, in government or
government-aided schools. The government has also allowed more
industrial training institutes (ITI), which are typically run by corporations. Some have been awarded the distinction of the "deemed university," which conveys autonomy on teaching methods and materials.
And the diploma conferred by such institutions is widely recognized
and respected.

The best opportunities for the private sector, in the early stages of this transformation cycle, will be found in the preschool, test preparation, and vocational training sectors of the industry.

The hospitality, health care, airline, hotels, retail, and information technology sectors will be the sectors with the most demand for new nondegree hires over the next decade. Because many companies will need well-trained, gray-collar employees, vocational certifications will become even more popular and structured as young people try to make themselves more marketable.[15] This latter segment of the market will prove to be very lucrative as the Indian economy moves steadily toward a more services-oriented future where companies require more certificates of specific knowledge than just a degree or a diploma.

Aptech (Mumbai: 532475) is a Mumbai-based for-profit educational company offering training in IT, multimedia and animation, hardware and networking, aviation, hospitality, and travel and tourism. It also offers corporate training, assessment solutions for corporations and academic institutions, and custom content development for overseas and domestic customers. Through local campuses and online programs, it currently has a presence in 36 countries on five continents, including Africa.

In India, its primary market, Aptech enjoys the benefits of government spending of about USD30 billion and private spending of USD40 billion annually on education. The government has placed a major emphasis on technology and IT training, fueling a USD225 million market for such courses. Aptech Computer Education (ACE), which offers educational programs in technology fields for which students can receive government funding, has been a major beneficiary of this effort.

Educomp (Mumbai: 5326966), the largest education company in India, is connected to more than 25,000 schools and 14 million students around the world from its home offices and satellites in Canada and the US. Unlike other educational companies that tend to focus exclusively on higher education, Educomp focuses on K through 12 curriculum design and teacher education. Examples of its offerings include the Smart Class teacher-led content delivery system, "Roots to Wings" preschool programs, and e-tutoring services. The company's focus on K through 12 gives it a wide economic buffer because of the often compulsory nature of primary education.

In addition to its online operations, the company also currently operates 20 brick-and-mortar high schools in India with more than 16,000 students. Educomp expects to add 23 more facilities by July 2010. It's also one of the largest preschool operators in India, with more than 400 Eurokids locations.

NIIT (Mumbai: 500304) focuses on manpower training; its major focus is training for corporate clients. Its program offerings in IT, business process outsourcing, banking, finance and insurance, executive management education, and communication and professional life skills enroll about 5 million students a year. NIIT also offers school-focused solutions that help integrate IT-assisted learning to more than 9,500 government and private schools in the K through 12 segment, primarily in India.

As of 2009 the company had 500 learning centers in India, 192 in China, and 158 more around the world. With global presence, including in many of the most popular offshoring destinations, NIIT is executing on its mission of facilitating the ongoing trend toward globalization. It's helping students develop the skill sets needed in more services-based economies. As such, through its various programs NIIT touches learners at all stages of the educational process.

The Chinese Opportunity

China is among the five most illiterate countries in the world. But it's the only one of those five that's been able to improve its status in the last 20 years. In 1990 20.8 percent of Chinese above the age of 15 were classified as illiterate by UNESCO. By the mid-2000s the rate had dropped to 11.3 percent. The Ministry of Education is responsible for the education system in China, which offers 12 years of free schooling, 9 of which are compulsory.

As is the case with India the population numbers are vast in China—450 million between the ages of 5 and 29 years. Only around 6 percent of the total Chinese population has a college degree, while 3 million students were enrolled full-time in university, indicating a potential upside for the sector.

China's educational system was seriously damaged during the Cultural Revolution. It therefore didn't have enough talent to respond to the economic and technological challenges of the 1980s. Things gradually changed, and China was able to produce 47,000 MBAs in 2004. Chinese are beginning to understand as well that higher education rewards people financially; workers who have a college degree are paid 60 to 70 percent more than people with associate's degrees or lower.

The private sector is rapidly establishing a vocational training component to China's educational system, a viable alternative for young people who come to big cities from rural areas with minimal education. Attending such training can increase wages by 60 to 70 percent, but a typical Chinese will have to work a lower-paying job first to be able to pay for it—annual tuition fees range from RMB10,000 to RMB15,000 (USD1,400–USD2,220).

Education in China has always been viewed as a way to better provide for the family, and people have traditionally spent as much as they could possibly afford. But steady growth in the economy has made for more to be desired. As Chinese gradually satisfy their more basic needs, and the state continues to allocate more money into the education system (it spent USD630 billion in 2008), families pay even more money for education, especially for tutorial lessons, music, computers, English, and the like. The "one child" policy has led parents in urban areas to spend freely for their children's education. Affordability is up, as are expectations.

Founded in 1993, New Oriental (NYSE: EDU) is now the largest provider of private educational services in China. It offers foreign-language training, primary and secondary education, and test-preparation services primarily to Chinese students preparing to enter overseas universities, both online and offline. The company currently operates a network of 48 schools, 287 learning centers, 25 Oriental-branded bookstores, and an affiliate network of more than 5,000 third-party bookstores. New Oriental's online program also has more than 5 million registered users.

In 2009 New Oriental became the first and only language school in China authorized to administer the Cambridge Young Learners English exam, the English for Speakers of Other Languages program through the University of Cambridge. The program is aimed at students between the ages of seven and 12 and is geared toward easing the path to international study.

China Education Alliance (AMEX: CEU) provides online-exam-oriented tutoring services, offering downloadable sample tests and study materials. It also operates a large tutoring facility in Harbin that can accommodate 3,200 students as well as a twice-weekly newspaper and vocational and English-language training.

Educational advancement is extremely competitive in China, with state examinations for entry both to high school and university. Exam-preparation services are in high demand among Chinese parents seeking to ensure the best possible placement for their children.

Wide achievement gaps among school districts in developed and developing regions of China help create a huge demand for such services, particularly as only 13 percent of 18- to 22-year olds typically enroll in higher education.

China Education Alliance generates the bulk of its revenue (67 percent) from its online programs and materials, with 12 percent coming from its onsite tutoring program, 10 percent from vocational education, and 11 percent from advertising sales both on its Web sites and its newspaper.

Other Asian Educators

Raffles Education Corp (Singapore: E6D) is a for-profit educator. It opened its first college in 1990 in Singapore and has since grown to three universities and 24 colleges spread throughout Singapore, China, India, Indonesia, Vietnam, Malaysia, Thailand, Mongolia, Australia, and New Zealand. It's the largest private education group in the Asia-Pacific Region, offering a variety of programs, from Fashion and Graphics Design to Accounting and Psychology.

Benesse Corporation (Tokyo: 9783) is a Japan-based education service provider that operates in six segments. The Education Business Group provides home-study courses, home English teaching materials, and practice tests for university entrance exams and English proficiency exams.

Megastudy (Seoul: 072870) offers both online and offline courses for K through 12 students, test-preparation services for students about to take university entrance exams and those preparing for civil-service testing, and seven offline high schools based in northern Seoul. About 19 percent of revenue is generated by purely online students, 55 percent of sales are generated by primarily online students who take advantage of some offline components, and 26 percent of sales are generated by purely offline students.

Offering a high degree of convenience for students, offline students typically take only one subject at time over a two-month term, meeting for classes two to three times per week. Online students similarly take only one course at a time over a term of 90 days.

In the coming years Megastudy intends to deemphasize its offline schools in favor of its higher-margin online model, which carries lower capital costs and augments its efforts to expand into Vietnam and China.

Endnotes

1 Pharmaceutical Executive, "Are you Ready for the Revolution," volume 29, number 10, October 2009.

2 C. L. Peterson and R. Burton, "U.S. Health Care Spending: Comparison with Other OECD Countries," (RL34175) [Electronic copy] (Washington, DC: Congressional Research Service), 33.

3 Health at a Glance 2009: OECD Indicators, December 8, 2009, http://www.oecd.org/document/14/0,3343,en_2649_33929_16502667_1_1_1_37407,00.html.

4 The World Health report 2000, The World Health Organization, http://www.who.int/whr/2000/en/whr00_en.pdf.

5 "Report: China to Become Welfare State by 2049," Window of China, http://news.xinhuanet.com/english/2008-11/02/content_10295173.htm (accessed November 2009).

6 Pharmaceutical Executive, "Are you Ready for the Revolution," volume 29, number 10, October 2009.

7 The majority of the wide circulation drugs are considered "small-molecule" meaning that they have structures composed of relatively few atoms, such that their structures can generally be portrayed by diagrams showing linkages of specific atoms.

8 Fernand Braudel, *Civilization & Capitalism 15th-18th Century—Volume I: The Structures of Everyday Life* (New York: Harper & Row, 1981), 242.

9 Amy Zou and Janet Sun, "2009 Outlook: Investment Opportunities from Medical Reform," UBS AG, January 9, 2009.

10 "Education for All: Literacy for Life," UNESCO, Paris, 2005.

11 *Overcoming Inequality: Why Governance Matters*, UNESCO, (Paris: Oxford University Press, 2008).

12 "Education for All: Literacy for Life," UNESCO, Paris, 2005.

13 Some of the states that have followed this route are Chattisgarh, Gujarat, Rajasthan, Maharashtra, Uttranchal, Andhra Pradesh, and Karnataka.

14 In 2007 around 400,000 students took the entrance examination for the four-year engineering studies offered at IIT and around 230,000 took the test for the two-year MBA program offered by the IIM. More than 1 million students took examinations for regional engineering colleges.

15 "Indian Education: A Leap Forward." Edelweiss Securities, October 7, 2009.

13 ——————————

The Asian Frontiers: Mongolia, Cambodia, Vietnam

Frontier markets are by nature much riskier than developed and emerging ones. They're generally overlooked by the majority of investors, which makes their assets relatively inexpensive. Initially they are the playground of private equity firms willing not only to wait but also to increase their investments when actual risks reduce to perceived ones. When this transition occurs there's no better time to invest in a frontier market.[1]

The main characteristics of a frontier market are a relatively youthful population, relatively open economic policies, and increasing urbanization. The latter is also the foundation of the investment case for Asia.

The urbanization process holds great promise for Asia.

Socialist economic policies of the past emphasized a nonurban model of economic development. Governments in countries such as China, Cambodia, and Vietnam made it extremely difficult for people to migrate to cities. This artificial development path proved disastrous, but at the same time created a force that's proven extremely powerful now that it's been allowed to develop. The result is an unprecedented multiyear urbanization cycle (see Figure 13.1).

Urbanization can generally be divided into three stages. The first is when big numbers of usually low-cost laborers start to migrate into cities in search of work. This has been true in Asia, where urban penetration is around 30 percent, the level we're seeing in Cambodia and Vietnam. India is ready to surpass this stage; the United Nations expects it to reach urban penetration above 30 percent by 2011 and

32 percent by 2015. Thailand is in the same category, as the urbanization level is forecast to hit 36 percent by 2015.

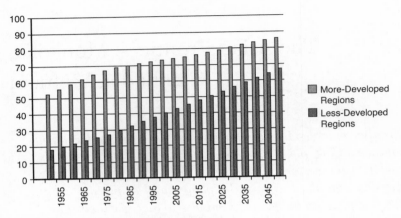

Figure 13.1   Levels of urbanization.

(Source: UN World Urbanization Prospects: The 2007 Revision Population Database)

The second stage is when a country's population starts to become wealthier, and workers start spending more on goods and services. Vietnam, Cambodia, India, and Thailand should be in this sweet spot for the next 10 years. India is the prime market to focus on because the second stage is well under way, and its enormity alone makes it a formidable market. China, Indonesia, and The Philippines will hit the third stage in the next 5 to 20 years, during which time urbanization levels will surpass 60 percent (see Table 13.1).

TABLE 13.1   Proportion of Population in Urban Areas

Country	1960	2005	2015	2050
Cambodia	10.30%	19.70%	26.10%	53.20%
Indonesia	14.6	48.1	58.5	79.4
Vietnam	14.7	26.4	31.6	57
China	16.7	40.4	49.2	72.9
India	17.9	28.7	31.9	55.2
Thailand	19.7	32.3	36.2	60
Malaysia	26.6	67.6	75.7	87.9
S. Korea	27.7	80.8	83.1	89.8

TABLE 13.1   Proportion of Population in Urban Areas

Country	1960	2005	2015	2050
Mongolia	35.7%	56.7%	58.8%	74.8%
Philippines	30.3	62.7	69.6	83.9

(Source: UN World Urbanization Prospects: The 2007 Revision Population Database)

In the third stage, the economic development model usually transforms from manufacturing to services and domestic demand. China has proactively developed big cities close to agricultural areas, the idea being that urbanization can be brought to the agricultural regions, as opposed to a phenomenon of endless migration. This way the dynamics of the local economy can also play a role in the growth process—manufacturing and other activities associated with an urban setting aren't affected solely by economic conditions in other regions of the world.

Mongolia

Mongolia is a unique story in Asia. The country is expected to surpass the 60 percent urbanization rate by 2020. Because of its 2009 decision to systematically develop its rich mineral resources, its proximity to China, and its small population, Mongolia is on track to become an urbanized and affluent society relatively fast.

Mongolia is a tiny economy; GDP was USD4.1 billion in 2009. Its main activities include mining, agriculture, and herding. The country's main trading partners are Russia and China, the latter accounting for about 75 percent of Mongolia's exports,[2] the main one of which is copper.

There are approximately 2.7 million people living in Mongolia, and 50 percent of them are under the age of 25. Half of the population lives in Ulaanbaatar, while the country's literacy rate is relatively high at around 97.3 percent.[3]

The Mongolian economy is resource-oriented and is therefore very cyclical. It generally does well during times of global economic expansion and suffers during contractions. Mongolia's proximity to China and the latter's structural need for resources should prove a sustainable long-term positive for the country's economic growth (see Table 13.2). The downside is the potential of a collapse in China's demand for natural resources, which would jeopardize Mongolia's growth prospects, especially if it comes early in the investment cycle.

TABLE 13.2   Mongolian Exports (% of Total)

Type	Share of Total
Copper	26.4%
Gold	18.4
Coal	15.4
Zinc	6.4
Petroleum (unprocessed)	6.0
Iron ore	4.0
Cashmere	3.7
Fluorspar ore	2.5
Other	16.0%

(Source: National Statistics Office of Mongolia)

Our view is that China's economic development will remain on track a lot longer than most observers expect. Although China's economic progress shouldn't be carelessly extrapolated into the future, the transformation is real and will endure. Mongolia is the closest source of substantial commodities reserves and should remain one of the biggest beneficiaries of China's economic growth for the foreseeable future.

On October 6, 2009, during an official ceremony at the State Palace of Mongolia, the government signed the much-awaited Oyu Tolgoi copper and gold exploration agreement with mining giant Rio Tinto Plc and Canada-based Ivanhoe Mines. Oyu Tolgoi is the largest undeveloped copper deposit in the world. The mine should reach full production of about 450,000 tons of copper per year and 330,000 ounces of gold per year by 2015. The project is expected to operate for about 30 years and generate USD30 billion to USD50 billion in revenue; the government will receive a prepayment of USD500 million and own 34 percent of the newly formed company that will hold the license for the project. Oyu Tolgoi alone has the potential of lifting the country's GDP per capita by around 25 to 30 percent to USD2,000.

The Oyu Tolgoi agreement came to fruition after several years of hard negotiations. The main obstacle was the 68 percent windfall tax Mongolia introduced in 2006 for all gold and copper projects. This harsh measure was the result of an extreme reaction by a country whose people went from communism to capitalism overnight, the majority perceiving that a lot of the country's assets were distributed to few Mongolians. Mongolia dealt with the same issues that confronted Russia during the 1990s, when its natural resources were given away while the country and its people were ridiculed around the world. This all changed with the ascendency of Vladimir Putin to Russia's presidency.

During Mongolia's privatization process in the early 1990s, relatively few wealthy individuals were able to buy big shares in privatized companies. These few amassed controlling stakes in Mongolia's assets. Many of these companies were run as private fiefdoms—corporate governance was weak, and political connections counted much more than management skills. Although such practices are far from rare in a developing economy, especially in one as small as Mongolia's, they represent a particular threat at this stage. The country has an opportunity to establish sustainable growth and to earn inclusion in the global economy. Mongolia has recognized, as did Russia before it, that privatization can't be done in a rush. A coalition government that came to power in 2009 has managed the process in a pragmatic and businesslike way, opening the door for what could prove to be the most dramatic economic and social transformation of a nation since the Emirates of Arabia discovered what was sitting under the sand in their deserts.

Mongolian officials, after realizing that a well-functioning capital market is essential to economic progress, have worked toward offering global investors access to government-controlled business entities through initial public offerings (IPO) in foreign exchanges. The plan calls for the creation of entities that will represent the Mongolia's stake in companies that aren't publicly traded but operate in the country's natural resources, infrastructure, and power sectors. Stakes in companies such as Erdenet Mining Corporation will eventually be available through this scheme. Erdenet is one of the biggest copper and molybdenum concentrate mining and processing companies in Asia. Established in 1978, the company is owned by Mongolia (51 percent) and Russia (49 percent).

That being said, the government expects the Oyu Tolgoi project to succeed, opening the way for further exploration of Mongolia's massive resources. Coal is one of these resources. Mongolia's potential reserves are around 100 billion tons. One of its biggest deposits, the Tavan Tolgoi, is being pursued by Anglo-Australian giant BHP Billiton, Brazil-based Vale, Japan's Mitsui & Company, and China Shenhua Energy Company.

Uranium is another notable resource. Mongolia has at least 62,000 tons of proven uranium reserves, which will take more time to develop than the coal reserves. The Mongolian parliament passed in 2009 the so-called Nuclear Energy Law, which will allow the state to own at least 51 percent of all uranium deposits if exploration is funded by the state, 34 percent if exploration is funded privately. At the same time all mining and exploration licenses were reviewed and new ones were issued, effectively placing the uranium sector next on the waiting list of resource issues to be tackled.

Given the high political stakes, domestic and international, attached to the development of uranium, the decision should come as no surprise. Not only must Mongolian political forces come to an agreement about the most beneficial way to develop the country's uranium resources, but Mongolia must also establish a close working relationship with the International Energy Agency (IEA) so it doesn't run into surprises on the global stage.

"The gratification of wealth," Miguel de Cervantes wrote, "is not found in mere possession or in lavish expenditure, but in its wise application." The Spanish author had seen his country's inability to properly utilize the gold that its ships were bringing home from Latin America. In Mongolia's case the so-called Dutch Disease is the obvious danger.

In the 1960s the Netherlands experienced a vast increase in wealth after discovering large natural gas deposits in the North Sea. Unexpectedly, this ostensibly positive development had serious repercussions on important segments of the country's economy, as the Dutch guilder became stronger, making Dutch non-oil exports less competitive. Although the disease is generally associated with a natural resource discovery, it can occur in the wake of any development that results in a large inflow of foreign currency, including a sharp surge in natural resource prices, foreign assistance, and foreign direct investment.[4]

A large inflow of FDI is an obvious danger for Mongolia; already SWF capital and direct investment have been pouring in, as Figure 13.2 details. China, in particular, has been active in Mongolia's resource and infrastructure sectors. In 2009 the China Investment Corporation (CIC) reached a deal to invest up to USD700 million in Mongolia-focused Iron Mining International Ltd., which owns a majority stake in the Eruu Gol iron ore project. This investment followed a USD300 million investment in the same project by Singapore's Temasek Holdings and private equity firm Hopu Investment Management. Iron Mining is planning an IPO in Hong Kong. Once this happens the company will offer one more alternative for investors looking for exposure to Mongolia's resource industry.

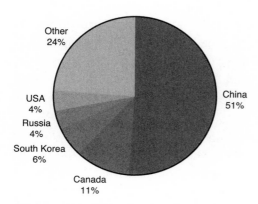

Figure 13.2   FDI by countries.

(Source: Mongolian Foreign Investment & Foreign Trade Agency)

The CIC has also invested in Canada-based SouthGobi Energy Resources (Toronto: SGQ), which is majority owned by Ivanhoe Mines and will also make an IPO in Hong Kong in 2010. The company has received USD500 million in financing from the CIC, which will also participate in the IPO. SouthGobi is a coal development company with the majority of its operations in Mongolia, though it also operates in Indonesia.

China is also investing USD385 million in the construction of a railway connecting the Middle Kingdom to the Tavan Tolgoi's coal mines—infrastructure is one of Mongolia's main challenges. The country's road network is around 11,000 kilometers (km), only 1,300 km of it only paved, while its railway network is 1,815 km, most of it the one that connects China to Russia and runs through Mongolia. Energy supply is also a problem; a big part of the population has no electricity. And the water system basically consists of deep wells, which constrains long-term planning. The government expects mining development to be the catalyst for better infrastructure. The companies involved will work with national and supranational agencies, such as the World Bank, to make sure the streams of commerce are adequate to support their operations, which will further economic development for the country at large.

All the companies discussed above offer direct exposure to the Mongolian story. The following three offer more leveraged exposure.

Mongolia Energy Corporation (Hong Kong: 276, MEC), a mining and energy developer that also gathers energy and resource concessions, operates in Mongolia and Xinjiang in northwestern China. Since 2007 MEC has acquired 330,000 hectares of concession areas for coal, ferrous, and nonferrous metal resources. The company has discovered vast amounts of coking coal that's characterized as high-value, high-quality, low-ash, and low-sulphur, with high a caking index. MEC also owns 20 percent of two oil and gas projects in western and southern Mongolia.

MEC's strategy is to become the leading coking coal supplier for steel producers in Xinjiang, China, which is emerging as the future economic highland of China's western region. Demand for coking coal for the Xinjiang steel producers is projected to grow strongly, and the company is upgrading and expanding a 340 km road, the "Khushuut Road," from its Mongolian coal mines to Xinjiang.[5]

UK-based Petro Matad Ltd. (London: MATD), an oil explorer, is the first substantially Mongolian owned company to list on an international stock exchange. The group's principal asset is the production sharing contract (PSC) for Matad Block XX, a petroleum block with an area of 14,250 km^2 in the far eastern part of Mongolia, near the Chinese border. Recently the company signed two more Production Sharing Contracts on Bogd Block IV and Ongi Block V, a total of approximately 71,000 km^2 in central Mongolia.[6]

Finally, Canada-based Entrée Gold (AMEX: EGI) is a leveraged way to play Mongolia's resource exploration sector. Ivanhoe Mines and Rio Tinto hold approximately 15 percent and 16 percent, respectively, of the company. Entrée's main property is a big copper-gold deposit near the border with China in the south Gobi Desert.

Thirty Years After

Cambodia is coming back from the dead, again.

A little over a decade ago Cambodia was battling through a bloody political crisis reminiscent of the days after Phnom Penh fell to the Khmer Rouge in 1975. Since then, however, the country has achieved relative political stability compared to its past and has pursued pro-development policies as it integrates into the global economy.

Cambodia, being a true emerging market, still faces challenges when it comes to corruption and a weak legal system.[7] Although corruption is easily accounted for in the investment decision-making process, absence of respect for the rule of law is a serious obstacle. Nevertheless, Cambodia has one of the most open economies for international investors: Foreigners are allowed to hold 100 percent stakes in businesses so long as the assets aren't land. Investors face no meaningful restrictions on moving money in and out of the country, a contrast with Vietnam, for instance.

Quite a few Asian governments have been investing and loaning money to Cambodia based on rising appreciation for the country's economic potential. Local sources have reported that China has pledged over USD500 million in loans to finance the construction of roads, dams and bridges, ports, irrigation systems, and rural electrification projects in Cambodia, this on top of USD260 million in 2009 (see Figure 13.3). Meanwhile, visiting Korean President Lee-Myung Hak topped up Korea's loan commitment to Cambodia from USD120 million to USD200 million through 2012.[8]

Cambodia is still largely a dollarized, cash-based economy. Local currency in circulation represents about 6 percent of GDP; the Cambodian riel is mainly used in the interior of the country and only for small transactions.[9] The country's economy is small, with a GDP of

USD8 billion and a population of 14.4 million. But 60 percent of Cambodians are under the age of 25. Cambodia's is primarily an agricultural society, with 80 percent of the population living in rural areas. Just 13 percent of the workforce is engaged in industrial activity beyond garment manufacturing. The economy is not well diversified; the garment industry, tourism, and agriculture are the major sectors. The country's five main products account for more than 60 percent of total exports, among the highest rates in the region (see Figure 13.4). The US absorbs 50 percent of the country's exports, mainly garments, leaving Cambodia vulnerable to gyrations in the American economy.

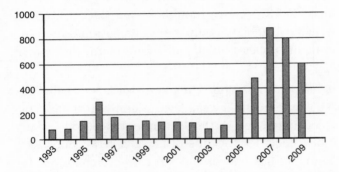

Figure 13.3   Foreign direct investment in Cambodia (USD) million.

(Source: World Bank; 2008, 2009 are estimates)

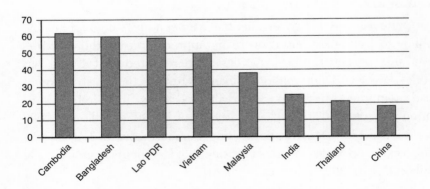

Figure 13.4   Share of five main products in exports (percent).

(Source: World Bank)

Fifty-nine percent of the country's labor force is involved in agriculture (including fishing and logging/timbering). The country's main agricultural products are rice, logs, fish, maize, and rubber, which is the biggest. Cambodia's arable soil is considered very fertile and relatively unspoiled, as pesticides and fertilizers are used more rarely and in smaller quantities than in other agriculture-focused countries. The lack of fertilizer usage has hampered Cambodian production yields. In 2008 its rice yield (measured in tons per hectare) was 2.6 percent, while Vietnam yielded 4.9 percent and China surpassed 6 percent. Cambodia doesn't even have enough rice mills to process its rice-paddy production, much of which is therefore exported for processing in Thailand and Vietnam—Cambodia forfeits large sums of income because of this. According to researchers similar issues afflict other parts of the agricultural sector such as soybeans, maize, palm oil, and rubber. Cambodian farmers also face substantial irrigation issues because only 7 percent of cropland is irrigated; agricultural production is dependent on the rains.

As World Bank analysts noted in early 2009

> Rural infrastructure in Cambodia is characterized by inadequate rural roads and poor road maintenance; one of the lowest electrification rate outside of sub-Saharan Africa (hence reliance on generators and high energy costs); and still low penetration of telecommunication services (and also high telecoms charges). The cost of poor infrastructure is compounded by informal charges paid during transportation.[10]

From an investment perspective, this situation could prove extremely profitable when Cambodia eventually addresses issues of irrigation, agricultural mechanization, and the like. With the right policy choices Cambodia could transform into an important source of food for Asia.

The most direct way to invest in the Cambodia's agricultural sector—and for that matter in the Cambodian story—is through private equity funds run by professionals with experience in Asia's emerging markets. One such company investors should be aware of is Leopard Capital (www.Leopardasia.com). The company was founded in 2007 by Douglas Clayton as a partnership of experienced Asian investment professionals with backgrounds in fund management, investment banking, business consulting, and operations management. The group leverages its partners' multidisciplinary insights with local expertise to source unique deal-flow.

Tourism, which at the end of 2008 accounted for USD1.6 billion in revenue, is Cambodia's fastest-growing industry, with arrivals recording consistent double-digit growth—except, of course, during the Great Recession of 2008-09. South Korea, Vietnam, Japan, the US, and China are the countries where the majority of tourists arrive from, collectively accounting for 43 percent of the total.[11] The prime attraction is the temples at Angkor, one of the biggest religious complexes in the world. The temples cover some 40 miles around the village of Siem Reap, about 192 miles from the Cambodian capital, Phnom Penh. They were built between the 8th and 13th centuries and range from single towers made of bricks to vast stone temple complexes. The government has also encouraged the creation of holiday resorts in an effort to capitalize on the country's unspoiled beaches.

The only direct play on Cambodia that trades on a public exchange is Naga Corp (Hong Kong: 3918, OTC: NGCRF), a Hong Kong-listed tourism company that operates a casino and hotel in Cambodia's capital. It holds a license to operate casinos in Cambodia until 2065, exclusive within a 200-km radius of Phnom Penh until 2035. The company's primary target is foreign visitors, and its business model is to attract regional midsize players to its relatively low table limits. Its 14-story hotel wing boasts 508 rooms, restaurants, and entertainment venues.

The country's banking system is small but not insanely so given the size of the economy. At the end of 2007, there were 17 commercial banks, of which 11 were either branches of foreign banks or majority foreign-owned. ATM machines were introduced in 2005 in Cambodia, and the majority of bank assets are held in US dollars. In terms of loan levels, Cambodia's economy is now where India was 30 years ago. Loans totaled USD1.6 billion at the end of 2007, and at 19 percent of GDP, or USD114 per person, they are by far the lowest in the region. There's huge upside potential here.

The indirect way to gain exposure to the sector is by investing in a foreign bank doing business in Cambodia. The Australia and New

Zealand Banking Group (Australia: ANZ, OTC: ANZBY) has partnered with a domestic conglomerate, the Royal Group of Cambodia, to create ANZ Royal Bank, which has 19 branches in the country. Australia and New Zealand holds 55 percent of the company.

Malaysia's Public Bank (Malaysia: PBKF) is one of the largest and best-run domestic banks in Malaysia. Public Bank is very active in Cambodia, with 14 branches. It also has operations in Hong Kong, China, Vietnam, Laos, and Sri Lanka.

There are also early indications that Cambodia may have oil and gas exploration potential, but no commercially viable discovery has yet been made. A consortium of companies led by US-based Chevron announced that it had struck oil in 2005, but as of early 2010 there's been no official confirmation. Cambodia may in the future have more luck with natural gas, as there are offshore areas in the Gulf of Thailand that are potentially rich in this commodity. The issue here is that these are overlapping claims areas (OCA), and Cambodia is locked in an ongoing dispute with Thailand over these OCAs, which has prohibited exploration for both.

Mining, which accounts for less than 1 percent of GDP, has grown rapidly in recent years but from a very low base; the sector remains mainly artisanal.[12] The country lacks the technology and expertise required for more systematic exploration. The Cambodian legislature passed a law on mining and minerals in 2001 that opened the way for foreign companies to participate in exploration efforts. Cambodia has 19 known gold deposits, and gold mining is becoming an increasingly important occupation. Conservative estimates place sector employment between 5,000 and 6,000 miners during the peak season. Processes remain largely primitive, though observers expect more to be done in the sector.[13] In October 2006 Mitsubishi Corporation (Tokyo: 8058, OTC: MSBHY) signed a mineral exploration agreement with the Cambodian government and BHP Billiton to explore for Bauxite and to evaluate the potential for an alumina refinery.

According to estimates by private equity fund Leopard Capital, Cambodia's mobile market has grown at double-digit rates since the late 1990s and should continue to deliver robust results. Penetration remains low at around 29 percent, and consolidation is on the way because the country now has nine mobile operators.[14]

In addition to investing through a private equity fund, investors can also gain indirect exposure by buying the shares of foreign companies that participate in the Cambodian telecom market. Telekom Malaysia (Kuala Lumpur: T, OTC: MYTEF) operates in Cambodia through its subsidiary Telekom Malaysia International Cambodia (TMIC) under the "Hello" brand. The company has a 15 percent market share and is working aggressively to grow it.

Sweden's TeliaSonera (Stockholm: TLSN, OTC: TLSNY) is also a player in Cambodia, operating under the Star-Cell brand name. In 2008 Star-Cell hired network equipment supplier Ericsson to install a GSM base station combined with satellite transmission in a solar-powered site, enabling Star-Cell to expand its network coverage to remote rural areas, where the majority of Cambodians live. Ericsson was also selected by TMIC to deploy its network in 20006.

Finally, as economies grow eating habits change. In addition to an increase in protein consumption, many emerging markets have shown affection for US-style fast food. One company that's successfully exploited this trend is Kentucky-based Yum! Brands (NYSE: YUM), the owner of KFC, Pizza Hut, and Taco Bell. Yum! opened its first KFC restaurant in Cambodia in March 2008.

Cambodia is in the early stages of meaningful economic development and could become one of the fastest-growing economies in the world on a broader and sustainable basis. Anticipating this development could prove very lucrative for patient investors. Early movers will be rewarded even more when big money eventually flows once Cambodia enters the mainstream of the global economy.

Rebuilding the country's professional class is Cambodia's main challenge. The process will be slow because the country's professional class was wiped out by the Khmer Rouge more than 30 years ago. As Karl D. Jackson of Johns Hopkins University noted

> When the Khmer Rouge seized power in April 1975, they did so with the intention of obliterating its hierarchical political culture in order to reconstruct Cambodian society from ground zero as the world's most egalitarian, and therefore revolutionary social order.[15]

Vietnam's Doi Moi

Walking through the slick Ho Chi Minh City airport, the casual traveler can't fail to notice that Vietnam has come a long way from the times of endless war and distraction.

The government of Vietnam initiated major economic reforms ("doi moi" literally translated means "renovation") in 1986, and the country has gradually transformed into a globally integrated, market-oriented economy while maintaining some of its socialist characteristics.[16] As a result, and because of its size, Vietnam is one of the most widely followed frontier economies, receiving increasingly higher amounts of foreign direct investment (FDI) from around the world.[17] Vietnam experienced rapid economic growth between 1996 and 2006 and is now a USD65 billion economy. Exports have increased from below 5 percent of GDP in 1980 to 65 percent in 2009, while imports surpassed 73 percent of GDP. Industrial activity, the most important component of the economy, now represents 32 percent of GDP, up from 18 percent when economic reform started in 1986.

Agriculture remains a very important part of the Vietnamese economy, accounting for around 20 percent of GDP. Vietnam is now a net exporter of food, which accounts for 17 percent of total exports. More important, 57 percent of the labor force is still employed in the agricultural sector. The government has aided the sector through subsidies and rural credit. The country's main agricultural exports are rice (it's the world's second-biggest exporter), coffee, rubber (it's the world's fourth-biggest exporter), cashew nuts, and pepper. Major imports include soya beans, cotton, wheat, and palm oil.

Vietnam is one Asian country the long-term economic potential of which is boosted by demographics. The median age of the population is around 25 years and is expected to reach 29 by 2015. Adult literacy is more than 90 percent, suggesting the presence of a reliable workforce.

The country has a 2,140 mile coastline; upgrading existing ports and building new ones, particularly deepwater ports, is now a significant priority for the government. Early in 2010 the prime minister said that around USD20 billion will be required for port construction until 2020.

Estimates put Vietnam's total infrastructure needs at around USD200 billion for the same period, but some critics have noted the absence of a coherent strategy to deploy the funds. One report published in 2008 asked

The argument for building an oil refinery is reduced dependence on refined oil imports, but does Vietnam need three oil refineries? What is the economic rationale for building deepwater sea ports all over the country when a few strategically located ports would suffice? Does Vietnam really needs a high speed rail network which offers no cost advantage over air travel and defeats the purpose of establishing a cheap rail and road network for transporting cargo?[18]

Even if these concerns are indeed legitimate, the way the author frames them implicitly concedes that the Vietnamese economy is on a rigorous growth path that will reward long-term investors.

Vietnam is relatively well endowed with natural resources. The country has the world's third-largest bauxite ore reserves (5.4 billion tons), significant deposits of iron ore, and substantial quantities of rare-earth metals used for high-tech products such as plasma screens. Although the government has worked to develop its resource sector, there remains much to be done; slow implementation coupled with numerous tariffs has held up a lot of projects. It took two and a half years for India's Tata Steel to get the necessary permissions to build a USD5 billion, 4.5 million tons per year steel plant for which the it had signed a memorandum of understanding with Vietnam Steel Corporation (VSC) in 2007.[19] Slow process aside, companies such as Tata Steel and others that have moved early into Vietnam will benefit from the country's industrialization going forward and will also be able to use the country as a springboard to access other markets in Indochina and Southeast Asia.

Vietnam's oil and gas sector attracts a lot of interest from foreign investors. Although Vietnam's oil production and exports should be relatively marginal in the global picture, they will be important to the domestic economy. Relatively small energy companies rather than the majors are better for exposure to this market.

Canada's Talisman Energy (Toronto: TLM, NYSE: TLM) is an upstream oil and gas company with 95 percent of its production in three core areas: North America, the North Sea, and Southeast Asia. In Vietnam the company mainly contacts offshore explorations.

UK-based SOCO International (London: SIA, OTC: SOCLF) operates 100 percent offshore in southern Vietnam. The company also operates in Africa (Congo and Angola) as well as Thailand.

Another UK company, Salamander Energy (London: SMDR), has its main operations in Thailand and Indonesia. The company started operating in Vietnam in the Mekong River Basin, which is geologically and structurally similar to the nearby Cuu Long Basin. The latter includes one of Vietnam's larger fields, the estimated 1 billion to 2 billion barrel Bach Ho field. Salamander has also been active in Laos, where the potential for positive surprises exists.

Investors who prefer the majors should look at British Petroleum Plc (NSYE: BP) and France's Total (NYSE: TOT); both have significant presences in Vietnam, in both the upstream and downstream markets.

Based in the UK but managed from Australia, Archipelago Resources (London: AR, OTC: AXRSF) has two gold projects in Vietnam. The company has a 65 percent stake in the Pac Lang project north of Hanoi, an area that was exploited by the French early in the last century and became the site of a major gold rush in 1990–91 following the discovery of a large quartz vein containing high-grade gold mineralization.[20] Management is in the early stages of securing exploration permissions for its second project. Once it receives these permissions Archipelago will form a joint venture with the Vietnam National Minerals Corporation (VIMICO), which controls all stated-owned nonferrous minerals mining and processing companies.

Foreign individual investors can't invest directly in the Vietnamese stock market, which, when it commenced operations in 2000, created a lot of excitement in the local population. The stock craze turned into "stock market gambling," forcing the government to restrain extremely active trading, which led to a two-and-a-half-year bear market in Vietnam. In early 2004 the bottom was reached, the market took off, and it hasn't yet looked back.[21] The easiest way for a foreign investor to participate in the Vietnamese market is through an exchange-traded fund (ETF). Market Vectors ETF Trust Vietnam (NYSE: VNM) is the preferred vehicle.

There are also funds that have been investing successfully in the Vietnamese markets for a long time. Established in 1994, Dragon Capital is the only Vietnam-focused fund manager that survived the Asian financial crisis of late 1990s. Formed with an initial capital base of USD16 million and an eight-person staff in Ho Chi Minh City, Dragon Capital now has more than USD1.5 billion in assets under management, 100 employees, and offices in Vietnam and the UK.

Vietnam Enterprise Investments Limited Fund (SEDOL: 0933010, CUSIP: G9361H109) uses a long-term capital growth approach to investing in listed and listable Vietnamese corporations. The portfolio tends to be heavily tilted toward the financial sector, as banks account for about a quarter of the fund's portfolio, with a further quarter devoted to real estate corporations and mineral and resource outfits. The remainder is spread across food and beverage names, transports, energy, and utilities, among other sectors.

Vietnam Growth Fund Limited (SEDOL: B01H2V4, CUSIP: G9361F103) uses a similar strategy, though it's geared much more toward the Vietnamese consumer and the domestic economy. Food and beverage names make up about 25 percent of the portfolio, with another quarter devoted to materials and resources.

Vietnam Property Fund (London: VPF, SEDOL: B2NHWF0, CUSIP: G9362H108) invests in Vietnam's real estate sector through direct investment in real estate projects and indirect investment in the securities of real estate companies. Its portfolio includes stocks, bonds, and direct interests through joint ventures.

Founded in 2003, VinaCapital Group is a leading asset management, investment banking, and real estate consulting firm in Vietnam. Through its VinaCapital Investment Management Ltd. operation it offers three closed-end Vietnam-focused funds.

Vietnam Opportunity Fund (London: VOF) is a closed-end fund traded on the London Stock Exchange's Alternative Investment Market (AIM), meaning its shares are readily available to western investors. Launched in 2003, Vietnam Opportunity is one of the largest Vietnam funds, with more than USD489 million in assets under management, and one of the most successful. The fund managers focus on key growth sectors of the domestic economy.

Launched March 2006, VinaLand Ltd (London: VNL) focuses on Vietnam's emerging real estate market, including residential, office, retail, hospitality, and township (large-scale) projects. The fund currently has USD694 million in assets under management.

Vietnam Infrastructure Ltd. (London: VNI), launched in July 2007, focuses on infrastructure and infrastructure-related assets in Vietnam such as energy, transport, telecommunications, industrial parks, and water/environmental utilities. The fund currently has USD267 million in assets under management.

Endnotes

[1] The Russian market has been the quintessential example of such a situation, where the majority of managers disregarded the transformation that commenced in the early 2000s in the process failing to capitalize on one of the biggest bull markets ever.

[2] In 2009 Mongolia's exports totaled USD1.77billion.

[3] Millennium Development Goals Database - United Nations Statistics Division, http://mdgs.un.org/unsd/mdg/.

[4] Christine Ebrahim-Zadeh, "Back to Basics," *Finance & Development-IMF*, March 2003, Volume 40, Number 1.

[5] Kenny Lau, "Mining Plans on Track," *Credit Suisse*, March 26, 2009.

[6] Petro Matad, www.petromatad.com.

[7] A strong commercial court for the enforcement of contracts has been one of the main requests by foreign investors.

[8] Leopard Cambodia Fund, Monthly Newsletter October 2009, issue 18.

[9] Stéphane Guimbert et al., "Sustaining Rapid Growth in a Challenging Environment," The World Bank, February 2009, 13, http://web.worldbank.org/WBSITE/EXTERNAL/COUNTRIES/EASTASIAPACIFICEXT/CAMBODIAEXTN/0,,print:Y~isCURL:Y~contentMDK:22045032~pagePK:1497618~piPK:217854~theSitePK:293856,00.html.

[10] Ibid., 72.

[11] Kingdom of Cambodia, Ministry of Tourism, "Tourism Statistical Report 2008," http://www.mot.gov.kh/img_files/Executive%20Summary%20Report%20in%202008.pdf.

[12] According to the World Bank, the country's geology is favorable to the same types of deposits that exist in Thailand, Lao, and Vietnam: gold, porphyry copper-gold, polymetallics, and bauxite.

[13] Guimbert et al., 56.

[14] Douglas Clayton and Sarah Maghfur, "Mobile Carriers," Leopard Cambodia, July 2009, http://www.leopardasia.com.

[15] Karl D. Jackson, editor. *Cambodia 1975-1978: Rendezvous with Death*. (Princeton, New Jersey: Princeton University Press, 1989), 7.

[16] The US lifted its trade embargo, which had been in place since 1964, in 1994 while opening an embassy in Vietnam in 1995.

[17] According to the General Statistics office of Vietnam, in 2008 the top five foreign investors were, in descending order, Malaysia, Taiwan, Japan, Singapore, and Brunei.

[18] "Vietnam—Growing Pains," CLSA April 16, 2008.

[19] "New Shores: Indian Investors Set Their Sights on Vietnam," Knowledge @ Wharton, November 19, 2009, http://knowledge.wharton.upenn.edu/india/article.cfm?articleid=4427.

[20] Archipelago Resources PLC, http://www.archipelagoresources.co.uk/.

[21] On the stock market front, the Vietnamese government has been reluctant to list a decent number of state-owned enterprises (SOEs), and when they did so the IPOs were priced at extremely high levels. But unjustified high IPO prices usually work against developing governments as institutional investors refuse to put enough money into the market, thus restricting the increase in liquidity that these markets are in need of.

INDEX

A

Abu Dhabi, 35, 49
  Vision 2030 strategy, 51
Abu Dhabi Investment Authority
  (ADIA), 39, 48, 50-53
Abu Dhabi Investment Council
  (ADIC), 50
Acergy, 131
acid rain, 149
Addax Petroleum, 120
advanced metering infrastructure
  (AMI) systems, 212
Afghanistan, war in, 16
Africa, 67-68
  China investments in, 72-75, 79
  India as a trade partner, 78-81
  uranium mines, 191
  West Africa, 119-121
Africa Infrastructure Country
  Diagnostic (AICD), 73
agriculture
  consumption of water, 209
  water intensity for, 200
agro-processing, 211
air conditioners, 138
Ajman, 49
Al Kudsi, Nazem Fawwaz, 51
Al Maktoum, Sheikh Mohammed bin
  Rashid, 33
Al Sa'ad, Bader M., 36
al-Nahyan, Ahmed bin Zayed, 52
al-Qaida, 32
al-Saad, Bader Mohammed, 53
al-Shehhi, Marwan, 32
al-Suwaidi, Hamad al Hurr, 54
Alaska, Prudhoe Bay, 118
Alstom, 173, 227

alternative energy, 181-182. *See also*
  energy
  in comparison to natural gas, 149
  hydroelectric, 183-184, 186-191
  nuclear, 183-191
  solar, 191-196
  wind, 191-196
Alternative Investment Market
  (AIM), 278
aluminum, 78
American Electric Power, 58
Anadarko, 119, 130
analysis of pharmaceutical profit
  cycles, 241
Angola, 79, 119
ANZ Royal Bank, 273
Aptech Computer Education
  (ACE), 255
aquaculture, 215
Areva, 190
Ashland, 206
Asia, 40, 132-133
  consumption of water, 201-203
  demographics, 239-241
  financial crisis (1997-98), 2
  fishing profits, 214-217
  frontier markets, 261-263
    Cambodia, 269-274
    Mongolia, 263-269
    Vietnam, 275-279
  improvement of efficiencies, 212-213
  medical equipment, 249-251
  pharmaceutical companies, 243-248
  sovereign wealth funds (SWFs), 4, 47
    definition of, 55-61
    Kuwait Investment Board, 49-54
assets held by governments, 49
Associated Press (AP), 32

at-the-ready supply of water, 201
Athabasca Oil Sands Corporation, 124
Atlantis oil field, 118
Australia and New Zealand Banking
Group, 273
automobiles
China as a market for, 93
development of, 86. *See also* oil
availability of natural gas, 142

B

Bahrain, 49
Baker Hughes, 158
Balin, Bryan J., 28
Banque Paribas, 52
Barclay's, 114
Beaumont, Texas, 111
Beijing Enterprises Water Group, 208
Beijing Olympics (2008), 202
Belize, 119
Benesse Corporation, 258
Benguela, 119
BG Group, 117, 154
BGR Energy Systems, 236
Bharat Heavy Electricals, 168, 233
Bharti Airtel, 78
BHP Billiton, 177, 266
Bilkey, Edward, 33
billion cubic feet (bcf), 144
biodiesel, 121
biofuels, 121, 182
Biosensors International, 250
birth defects, 149
bitumen from debris, removing, 122
Blackstone IPO, 59
blood-pressure-lowering drugs, 240
Boeing Company, 195
Bombardier, 227
boom, shale, 154, 157-158
bottlenecks, 141
BP (British Petroleum), 112, 153
Iraq oil contracts, 129
*BP Statistical Review of World
Energy*, 115
Brazil, 112
hydroelectric power production, 184
as an oil producer, 115-117
BRIC countries (Brazil, Russia, India,
China), 13
British Petroleum. *See* BP
British thermal units (Btu), 136
Bucyrus, 177

Bush, George H. W., 12, 22
Bush, George W., 76
Business Week, 52

C

Cambodia, 269-274
Cambridge Young Learners English
exams, 257
Cameco Corporation, 191
Cameron, 131
camphen, 84
Campos Basin, 115
Canada
hydroelectric power production, 184
natural gas, 140
oil sands, 121
Canadian Pension Plan Investment
Board (CPPIB), 39, 52
Cantarell oil field, 98-99, 102
capacity, oil, 103
capitalism, state, 12, 14
*Capitalism, Socialism and
Democracy*, 6
Carabobo block, 125
carbon
capture and sequestration (CCS), 172
dioxide, 170, 184
emissions, 149, 186
Carioca, 116
Central Asia
borders, 17
gas, 18
political reform, 14
Central Banking Journal, 27
Central Electric Authority (CEA), 166
Central Huijin Investment
Company, 56
Cermaq ASA, 216
CFS (container freight station), 234
Chairman of the Standing Committee
of the National People's Congress, 12
Charles W. Eliot University
Professor, 35
Chart Industries, 154
Chavez, Hugo, 115, 125
cheap credit, 2
Chesapeake Energy, 158
Chevron, 113, 118, 120
China, 1, 48
borders, 17
coal, 163, 166
education for-profit, 258-259
FDI destinations, 221-228

foreign policy, 73
Great Leap Forward, 12
gross domestic product (GDP), 92
health care systems, 242-243
hydroelectric power production, 184
imports, 76
interest in Brazil's deepwater oil
   finds, 117
investments in Africa, 72-79
long-term economic development, 59
markets, 61-63
medical equipment, 249-251
natural gas consumption, 152
New Oil Age, 91-94
nuclear energy, 190
pharmaceutical companies, 243-248
polycentrism, 20
Shanghai Cooperation
   Organization's (SCO), 15
state capitalism, 12
The Great Game, 14
as undisputed power in Asia, 24
China Daily, 60
China Development, 117
China Education Alliance, 258
China Fishery Group, 215
China Investment Corporation (CIC),
   5, 40, 48, 55, 124, 267
China Medical Technologies, 249
China National Building Material
   Company, 71
China National Offshore Oil
   Company, 120, 125, 153
China National Petroleum
   Corporation, 129, 159
China Shenhua Energy Company, 266
China South Locomotive & Rolling
   Stock Corporation, 234
China-Africa Development Fund, 71
Chrysler, 39
Civil War, 86
Clean Energy Fuels, 145
CNOOC Ltd., 75
coal, 58, 60, 90, 163
   environmental issues, 169, 172-173
   oil, 85
   steam, 164-168
   supply and demand, 174, 177-178
Commercial Bank of China, 71
Committee on Foreign Investment in
   the United States (CFIUS), 31
communism, 11

competition, The Great Game, 14-19
compressed natural gas (CNG), 143
Confederation of Indian Industry
   (CII), 166
ConocoPhillips, 112, 153
consequences of globalization, 4
constraints, oil supply, 94-96, 98
consumer prices of oil, 94
consumption
   of coal in China, 166
   of electricity, 138
   of fish, 214
   of oil
      China, 91-94
      India, 91-94
      United States, 88-91
   of water, 199
      Asia, 201-203
      demand, 207-211
      fishing profits, 214-217
      *improvement of efficiencies,
         212-213*
      investments, 203-207
Container Corporation of India, 233
Continental, 31
Coppabella mine, 177
copper, 58
cosmetics, 246
costs
   of coal, 163-168
   of coal plants, 170
   of deepwater exploration, 114
   of environmental issues, 169-173
   of natural gas, 142
   of oil sands operations, 123
   of solar photovoltaic power, 193
   of United States power plants, 145
   of wind and solar energy, 191
Cote D'Ivoire, 120
Council of Economic Advisors, 35
credit, 2
crisis, financial system (2008-09), 2
crude oil, 86. *See also* oil
cryogenic equipment and engineered
   parts, 154

D

Dalrymple Bay, 174
dams, China, 202. *See also*
   hydroelectric energy
Daqin Railway, 226

decline of oil production, 101-107
Dedicated Rail Freight Corridor
  (DRFC), 231-234
Deepwater Block, 14, 119
deepwater
  exploration, 112
  fish farming, 217
Deepwater Golden Triangle, 111-117
Deepwater Tano, 121
demand
  Asia, 132-133
  China, oil in, 92
  coal, 174, 177-178
  consumption of water, 207-211
  natural gas, 140-149
  oil, 130-132
democracies
  India, 69
  Russia, 69
Democratic Republic of the Congo, 78
demographics, 239-241
Denmark, coal in, 163
Department of Commerce, 31
Department of Defense, 31
Department of Homeland Security, 31
Department of Industrial Policy and
  Promotion (DIPP), 233
Department of State, 31
depleted water reserves, 209
desalination equipment, 202-204
Desert Kingdom, 102
desertification, 209
development of deepwater oil
  exploration, 112
diesel
  fuel, 144
  locomotives, 227
dietary supplements, 246
diversification, 53
Dongfang Electric Corporation, 207
Dorado oil field, 118
Douglas-Westwood, 114
Dover oil sands projects, 124
Dr. Reddy's Laboratories, 245
Dragon Capital, 278
Drake, Edwin Laurentine, 83-85
Dresser-Rand, 154
Dril-Quip, 131
drilling for oil in the North Sea, 97
drip irrigation systems, 211
Drug Controller General of India, 239
Dubai, 49
Dubai International Capital (DIC), 62

Dubai Ports World, 30, 33
Dubai World, 33
Dushanbe, Tajikistan, 15
Dutch East India Company, 10

E

E.ON Netz, 192
Eagle Ford Shale of southern
  Texas, 157
East India Company, 10
Eastern European capitalist states, 13
Eastern Siberian oil fields, 127
economic objectives of SWFs, 49
education
  China, 256-258
  for-profit, 258-259
  India, 252-256
Educomp, 255
efficiencies, water, 210
Egypt, 79
El-Erian, Mohamed, 70
electric submersible pumps (ESP), 97
electrical multiple unit (EMU), 225
Electricite de France (EDF), 190
electricity
  generation of with natural gas, 145
  hydroelectric energy, 183-191
  natural gas, 136-140
Eller & Company, 30-31
Emanuel, Rahm, 32
embargos, OPEC (1973), 88
emerging markets, acceleration of oil
  consumption, 91
emissions
  of coal plants, 170
  greenhouse gases (GHG), 186
energy
  China's interest in Africa, 74. See
    also Africa
  coal, 163. See also coal
  consumption in Japan, 90
  for illumination, 86. See also oil
  natural gas, 136
  per capita consumption, 87
Energy Information Administration
  (EIA), 121, 163
Energy Policy Act of 2005, 189
Energy Recovery, 207
enhanced chemiluminescence
  immunoassay (ECLIA) diagnostic
  systems, 249
Eni, 119

Enlai, Zhou, 12
Enterprise Products Partners LP, 142
environmental issues of coal, 169,
    172-173
Environmental Protection Agency
    (EPA), 144
Environmentally Friendly Super
    Express Train (EFSET), 227
Eruu Gol iron ore project, 267
ethane, 142
ethanol, 121
ethylene, 142
European Pressurized Reactor
    (EPR), 190
exchange-traded funds (ETFs), 277
Executive Director of the Institute for
    the Analysis of Global Security, 41
exploration and production (E&P)
    firms, 130, 154
exploration wells, 97
exports
    coal, 174
    from Mongolia, 264
    natural gas, 151
extra-heavy crude oil, 121
Exxon Mobil, 118, 153
    natural gas projects, 159
    nuclear power projections, 185

F

Fahrenheit, 136
failure of regulation, 3
Fayetteville Shale of Arkansas, 157
Federal Highway Administration, 87
Federal Reserve, 13
Felix takeover, 176
filtering water, 206
financial objectives of SWFs, 49
financial sectors, effect of peace and
    prosperity, 10, 12
financial system crisis (2008-09), 2
Financial Times, 35, 56, 72
First Solar, 195
fishing profits, 214-217
Flowserve, 213
flue gas desulfurization (FGD) units,
    164, 169
FMC Technologies, 131
Forbes, 52
foreign currency reserves, China, 55

foreign direct investment (FDI),
    74, 221
    beyond rail, 235-236
    China, 222-228
    India, 228-230
foreign policies, China, 73
former Soviet Union (FSU), 94. *See
    also* Russia; Soviet Union
Fortescue Metals Group, 60
Fortis Healthcare, 251
fossil fuels, 163
France, nuclear energy in, 188
free markets
    effect of peace and prosperity, 10-12
    government interference, 10
freshwater, 200. *See also* water
frontier markets, Asia, 261-263
    Cambodia, 269-274
    Mongolia, 263-269
    Vietnam, 275-279
Fujairah, 49
futures, Ice, 140

G

GAIL, 80
GALP Energia, 117-119
Gamsakhurdia, Zviad, 23
gas
    Central Asia, 18
    natural. *See* natural gas
    oil. *See* oil
    wet, 142
Gateway Distriparks, 234
Gazprom, 80, 158-159
GCC states, 49
General Electric (GE), 51, 227
Generally Accepted Principles and
    Practices (GAPP), 48
geopolitical considerations, sovereign
    wealth funds (SWFs), 4
geopolitics, 10
Georgia, Russian conflict with, 23
Germany
    coal, 163
    wind energy, 192
Ghana, 78, 120
Ghawar oil field, 103
gigawatts (GW), 172
Gladstone Bay, 174
GlaxoSmithKline, 247
global consumption of electricity, 140

global oil. *See also* oil
    production, 94, 107
    oil supply
        Asia, 132-133
        Brazil, 115-117
        demand, 130-132
        Gulf of Mexico, 118-119
        Iran, 126-129
        Iraq, 126-129
        Russia, 126-129
        *unconventional liquids, 121,
            124-126*
        West Africa, 119-121
global war on terror, 20
globalization, consequences of, 4
governments
    intervention in financial sectors, 10
    peace and prosperity, 10-12
    Venezuela, 125
Great Game, The, 14-19
Great Leap Forward, 12. *See also*
    Zedong, Mao
Great Powers, 11
Great Recession of 2008-09, 27-28, 272
Greater Nile Petroleum Corporation
    (GNPC), 68
Green Party (Germany), 189
greenhouse gases (GHG), 170, 186
Grieg Seafood ASA, 217
gross domestic product (GDP)
    China, 92
    education costs, 253
    France, 188
    health care costs, 240
    Japan, 91
Guangdong, 208
Guangxi, 208
Guara, 116
Guizhou, 208
Gulf Cooperation Council (GCC), 39,
    47, 204
Gulf of Mexico, 112, 117
    global oil supply and, 118-119
    offshore oil exploration, 116
gushers, 96
GVK Power and Infrastructure
    Group, 236

H

H1N1 influenza, 249
Hak, Lee-Myung, 269
Handelsblatt, 52

Harvard Management Company, 70
Harvard University, 35
Haynesville Shale of Louisiana, 157
health care, 240
    China, 242-243
        medical equipment, 249-251
        pharmaceutical companies, 243-248
Hedge Funds, 37
Hedrick-Wong, Yuwa, 91
Hersh, Seymour M., 17
Hexcel Corporation, 195
Higgins, Pattillo, 111
Ho Chi Minh City, 278
Ho Chi Minh City airport, 275
Ho, Cheng, 1
Holbrooke, Richard, 16
Holding Report (2010), 57
Hopu Investment Management, 267
horsehead type pumps, 97
hospitals, 251
House Committee on Foreign, 41
Hubbert's Curve, 95
Hubbert's Peak, 95
Hubbert, Marion King, 95
Hunan, 208
hydraulic fracturing, 155
hydrocarbon production, 115
hydroelectric energy, 183-191
Hyflux Ltd, 206

I

Iara, 116
ICE futures, 140
Ikenberry, G. John, 21
Illinois Basin, 164
Imperial China, 1
imports
    China, 76
    natural gas, 151
    United States oil, 88
    Vietnam, 275
improvement of efficiencies, 212-213
impurities in steam coal, 164
in-situ production, 122
India, 15, 68
    Africa as a trade partner of, 78-81
    coal consumption, 167
    Dedicated Rail Freight Corridor
        (DRFC), 231-234
    democracy in, 69
    education, 252-259
    FDI destinations, 221, 228-230
    implementation of 10th plan, 168

medical equipment, 249-251
natural gas consumption, 152
New Oil Age, 91-94
nuclear energy, 188
pharmaceutical companies, 243-248
polycentrism, 20
India's Jindal Saw, 213
Indian Railways (IR), 228
Indonesia, 58, 69
industrial training institutes (ITI), 254
industrial use of natural gas, 136-140
  demand for, 140-149
  liquefied natural gas (LNG), 150-154
  Russia, 158-159
  shale boom, 154-158
Influenza A, 249
information and communications
  technology (ICT), 254
infrastructure in Africa, Chinese
  financed, 76
Infrastructure Development Finance
  Corporation, 235
initial public offering (IPO), 58
Insituform Technologies, 213
institutional model of order
  building, 21
interdependence of states, 15
International Cooperation Agency
  (Japan), 231
International Energy
  Outlook (1999), 94
International Monetary Fund
  (IMF), 47
International Working Group of
  Sovereign Wealth Funds (IWG), 38,
  48, 54
intervention, government
  involvement in financial sectors, 10
investments
  China in Africa, 72-79
  consumption of water, 203, 206-207
  foreign direct investment (FDI), 221
    China, 222-228
    India, 228-230
    beyond rail, 235-236
Iran, 15
Iron Lady, 10
Iron Mining International Ltd.,
  60, 267
irrigation systems, 211
Islam, 16
Islamic Revolution (1979), 129
Ismay, Lord Hastings Lionel, 11

Itaipu Binacional, 184
Itron, 196, 213
Ivanhoe Mines, 264
IVRCL, 207

J

Jack oil field, 118
Jain Irrigation, 211
Japan
  Dedicated Rail Freight Corridor
    (DRFC), 231-234
  gross domestic product (GDP), 91
  Lost Decade, 91
  natural gas imports, 152
Jawaharlal Nehru Port Trust
  (JNPT), 234
Jha, L. K., 69
jihadism, 16, 24
Jiwei, Lou, 59
joint ventures (JV), 125, 227
JV Bombardier Sifang (Qingdao)
  Transportation, China, 227

K

Kaskida, 112
Kawasaki Heavy Industries, 227
Kayelekeera mine, 191
Kazakhstan, 17, 58-60
  Shanghai Cooperation
    Organization's (SCO), 15
Kazantzakis, Nikos, 1
Keathley Canyon Block 102, 112
Keio University, 21
Kennedy, Paul, 11
kerosene, 84-85
Keynes, John Maynard, 2, 181
Khan, A. Q., 20
Khmer Rouge, 269
kilometers (km), 268
kilowatt-hours (kWh), 139, 189
King South oil field, 118
King, Peter, 32
Kolkata, 232
Koski, Chris, 52
Ku-Maloob-Zaap (KMZ), 99, 101
Kubota, 211
kulhads (clay pots), 229
Kurita Water Industries, 206
Kuwait, 50
Kuwait Investment Authority (KIA),
  10, 36
Kuwait Investment Board, 28, 49-55

Kuwait Investment Office, 49
Kyrgyzstan, 17
   Shanghai Cooperation
      Organization's (SCO), 15

L

Langer Heinrich mine, 191
Larsen & Toubro, 235
Leopard Capital, 271-273
Liberia, 120
liquefied natural gas (LNG), 117,
   150-154
   effect of nuclear power on, 186
liquids, unconventional, 121, 124-126
Lobito, 119
locomotives, 227
London Gateway, 33
Long-Term Capital Management
   (LTCM), 13
long-term trends, 53
Lost Decade (Japan), 91
low-cost laborers, 261
Lower Tertiary Gulf, 113
Lucas, Anthony, 111
Ludhiana, 231
Luft, Gal, 41
Lukoil, 127
Luxembourg Foreign Trade
   Conference, 36

M

Macarthur Coal, 176
Mackay River, 124
Maglev, 222
maintenance, offshore oil, 114
management of water supplies, 203
Marathon Oil, 120
Marcellus Shale, 157
Market Vectors ETF Trust
   Vietnam, 277
markets
   affect of peace and prosperity, 10-12
   China, 61-63
   frontier, 261-263
      Cambodia, 269-274
      Mongolia, 263-269
      Vietnam, 275-279
   government interference, 10
   natural gas, 135-136
Marubeni, 153
MassARRAY systems, 250
McIlvaine Company, 212

McNeill, William H., 25
meat imports, Africa, 78
medical equipment, 249-251
Medtronic, 249
Medvedev, Dmitry, 23, 79
Megastudy, 259
megawatt-hour (MWh), 191
megawatts (MWs), 68, 167, 192, 236
Merck & Co, 247
mercury, 184
   emissions, 149
metallurgical coal, 58
meters, water, 212
Mexico
   Cantarell oil field, 98-99, 102
   decline of oil production, 102
micro-irrigation systems business, 211
Middle East, 24
   China's view of oil assets in, 62
   natural gas demand, 142
   oil fields, 99
Middle Kingdom, 12, 55-61
   natural gas demand, 159
   oil ambitions in Africa, 75
Middlemount Mine Project, 177
Miller, Alexey, 80
Mindray Medical International, 249
Minister of Railways, India, 229
Ministry of Finance (MoF), 56, 225
Ministry of Railways (MoR), 223
Mississippi Canyon, 118
Mitsubishi Corporation, 273
Mitsui & Company, 153, 266
modern scrubbers, 164
Mongolia, 15, 58, 263-269
Mongolia Energy Corporation, 268
Monitor-FEEM database, 37, 39
Moorvale mine, 177
Morgan Stanley, 58
Mozambique, 78
MTN, 78
Mubadala Development Company, 51
Muldoon, Joseph A., III, 31
Muldoon, Joseph A., Jr., 30
Mumbai Metropolitan Region
   Development Authority's
   (MMRDA), 234

N

Nabors Industries, 158
Nabucco gas pipeline, 18
Namibia, 79
nanotechnology, 205

naphtha equipment, modifying, 142
National Development and Reform
  Commission (NDRC), 225
National Maritime Development Plan
  (NMDP), 235
national oil company (NOC), 115, 153
National Social Security Fund
  (NSSF), 224
National-Oilwell Varco, 131
natural gas, 90, 135
  Cambodia, 273
  demand for, 140-149
  electricity and industrial, 136-140
  liquefied natural gas (LNG), 150-154
  re-injecting, 97
  Russia, 80, 158-159
  shale boom, 154, 157-158
  Thunder Horse, 118
  vehicles, 145
natural gas liquids (NGLs), 142
natural resources in Africa, 67
Nayar, Baldev Raj, 11
Negroponte, John, 32
Nehru, Jawaharlal, 69
Nepstar Chain Drugstore, 251
New Oriental, 257
New York Times, 41
New Yorker, The, 17
Niger Delta, 120
Nigeria, 78, 120
Nigerian National Petroleum
  Corporation (NNPC), 80
NIIT, 256
Ningbo LNG project, 152
Nippon Koei, 233
Nippon Oil, 153
nitrogen injections, 101
nitrogen oxide (NOX), 144
nitrous oxide (NOX), 169, 184
Nixon, Richard M., 12, 23
Nobel Oil Group of Russia, 60
North Africa, security threats, 24
North Atlantic Treaty Organization
  (NATO), 11
North Sea
  decline of oil production, 102
  oil
    fields, 95
    production, 98
North West Shelf (NWS)
  development, 153
Norwegian Ministry of Petroleum
  and Energy, 97

Novartis, 247
Novo Nordisk, 248
nuclear energy, 90, 183-191
Nuclear Energy Law (Mongolia), 266
Nuclear Non-Proliferation Treaty
  (NPT), 188
Nutreco, 217
NWS Holdings Ltd., 228

O

official development assistance
  (ODA) program, 74, 233
offshore drilling, 114
offshore oil production
  Brazil, 115
  unconventional liquids, 121-126
  West Africa, 119-121
oil
  Asia, 132-133
  Brazil as a producer of, 115-117
  Cambodia, 273
  China, 18
  deepwater exploration, 111-115
  first commercial well, 83
  global production, 94
  Gulf of Mexico, 118-119
  Iran, 126, 129
  Iraq, 126, 129
  New Oil Age, 91-94
  peak, 95
  production. *See* production, of oil
  pumps, 97
  Russia, 126, 129
  sands, 121
  supply and demand, 130-132
  supply constraints, 94-98
  for transportation, 86-88
  unconventional liquids, 121, 124-126
  United States consumption of, 88, 91
  wells, types of, 97
  West Africa, 119-121
Oil & Natural Gas Corporation
  (ONGC), 125
Oil Age, 85-86, 91
oil country tubular goods (OCTGs), 132
Oil India Limited, 125
oil mining lease (OML), 75
Oil Search, 154
Oman, 49
onion dehydration businesses, 211
operations, offshore oil, 114
Orange, Texas, 111

order building, 21
Organization for Economic
   Cooperation and Development
   (OECD), 37, 137
Organization of Petroleum Exporting
   Countries (OPEC), 88
   oil production, 94
Orinoco Belt, 124
out-of-pocket health care
   expenditures, 240
overlapping claims areas (OCA), 273
Ovoot Tolgoi coal mine, 60
Oyu Tolgoi agreement, 265

P

Pacific Andes International
   Holdings, 216
Pakistan, 15
   nuclear capability of, 20
Paladin Resources, 191
Pan-Asia
   China, markets, 61-63
   sovereign wealth funds (SWFs), 47
      definition of, 55-61
      Kuwait Investment Board, 49-54
paper, 78
Papua, New Guinea, 154
Paribas Asset Management, 52
Parkway Holdings, 250
particulate matter, 169
Paulson, Henry, 54
Pazflor, 120
Peabody Energy, 176
peace and prosperity, 10-12
peak oil, 95
Peninsular & Oriental Steam
   Navigation Company, 30
pension plans, 37-38
Pentair, 213
People's Bank of China (PBoC), 56
People's Republic of China, 12. *See
   also* China
per square inch (PSI), 113
Persian Gulf, 40
personal computers (PCs), 138
Petrobras, 112, 117, 120, 130
PetroChina, 124, 129
Petrohawk Energy, 157, 158
Petroleo Brasileiro (Petrobras), 115
Petroleos de Venezuela SA
   (PDVSA), 115
Petroleos Mexicanos (Pemex), 99

Petronas, 129
Pfizer-Wyeth, 247
pharmaceutical companies, 243-248
Phnom Penh, 269, 272
photovoltaic (PV) solar cells, 195
Pike, Francis, 69
pipeline systems, 19
political reform, 14
political response to sovereign wealth
   funds (SWFs), 38-42
pollution
   coal, 169
   hydroelectric power, 184
polycentricism, 19, 21-22
polypill, 239
Port Arthur, Texas, 111
Port of Newcastle, New South
   Wales, 174
potable water, 206. *See also* water
Powder River Basin, 170
power plants, 68
   costs, 145
   scrubbers, 164
pre-salt finds, 116
prices of natural gas, 142
prioritizing diversification, 53
Private Equity Funds, 37
production
   of coal, 163
      *environmental issues, 169,
      172-173*
      steam, 164-168
      *supply and demand, 174,
      177-178*
   of hydrocarbon, 115
   of hydroelectric energy, 183-184,
      186, 188, 190-191
   in-situ, 122
   of natural gas, 136
      demand for, 140-149
      *electricity and industrial,
      136-140*
      *liquefied natural gas (LNG),
      150-154*
      Russia, 158-159
      shale boom, 154, 157-158
   of nuclear energy, 183-191
   of oil
      Asia, 132-133
      Cantarell oil field, 98-99, 102
      decline in, 102, 104, 107
      global, 94
      Gulf of Mexico, 118

Iran, 126, 129
Iraq, 126, 129
North Sea oil fields, 95
Russia, 126, 129
supply and demand, 130, 132
unconventional liquids, 121, 124-126
West Africa, 119-121
United States, 88
of solar energy, 191, 193, 195-196
of wind energy, 191, 193, 195-196
production tax credits (PTC), 194
profit
    fishing, 214-217
    for-profit education, 258-259
propane, 142
proppant, 155
Prudhoe Bay, 118
Public Bank, 273
public-pension plans, 38
public joint stock company (PJS), 51
pulp, 78
pulverized coal (PC) plants, 170
pumps, oil, 97
purposes of sovereign wealth funds (SWFs), 49
Putin, Vladimir, 13, 265

Q–R

Qatar, 49
    as producer of natural gas, 152
Qatar Investment Authority (QIA), 50
Qatar LNG (Qatargas), 152
Qatar Petroleum, 153
Qichen, Qian, 68

radical Islam, 16
railroads, 221-222
    China, 222-228
    Dedicated Rail Freight Corridor (DRFC), 231-234
    India, 228-230
Railway Board, 230
Range Resources, 157
Ras al-Khaimah, 49
Ras Laffan LNG Company (RasGas), 152
re-injecting natural gas, 97
recessions, Keynesianism, 2
Red Heart, 239
reduction of water demand, 207-211
refrigerators, 138
regulations, failure of, 3

reliability of natural gas, 142
removing sulfur, 169
renewables, 149. *See also* alternative energy
Renqing, Jin, 56
research and development (R&D), 130
reserves
    China, foreign currency, 55
    oil, 101. *See also* oil
reservoirs, oil, 96
respiratory illness, 149
reverse osmosis (RO), 205
Rio Tinto Plc, 264
risk, sovereign wealth funds (SWFs), 49
River Thames, 33
rock oil, 84. *See also* oil
role of UN (United Nations), 11
Rosneft, 127
Royal Dutch Shell, 80
    Iraq oil contracts, 129
Royal Group of Cambodia, 273
rupees, 230
Russia, 11
    capitalist states, 13
    democracy in, 69
    entrance into Venezuela, 125
    Georgian conflict, 23
    hydroelectric power production, 184
    natural gas production, 158-159
    polycentrism, 20
    relationship with Mongolia, 265
    Shanghai Cooperation Organization (SCO), 15
    state capitalism, 12
    The Great Game, 14
    trade with Africa, 79
    war in Afghanistan, 16

S

Sada division, 217
SAFE Investment Company, 56
safety of sovereign wealth funds (SWFs), 42
Sakhalin Island project, 127
Salamander Energy, 277
salt, pre-salt finds, 116
sand, 121, 155
sandstone, 96
Sanofi-Aventis, 247
Santiago Principles, 38, 41, 54
Santos Basin, 116
SARS epidemic (2003), 246

Saudi Arabia, 32, 49
  oil production in, 102
Savings Funds, 37
Schlumberger, 130
Schumer, Charles, 32
Schumpeter, Joseph A., 6
scrubbers, 164, 169
Securities and Exchange Commission
  (SEC), 57
security threats, 24
  Committee on Foreign Investment
    in the United States (CFIUS), 31
seed companies, 211
self-sufficiency in coal, China, 166
Senate Banking Committee, 31
Senegal, 72, 78
Sequenom, 250
sequestration, 172
shale boom, 154, 157-158
Shandong, 208, 249
Shanghai Cooperation Organization
  (SCO), 15-16
Shanghai Securities News, 60
Shaoqi, Liu, 12
Sharjah, 49
Shaw Groups, 190
Shek, Chiang Kai, 12
Shell, 153
Shenzhen Energy Group, 71
Sichuan, 208
Siemens, 222
Sierra Leone, 120
Simes, Dmitri, 23
Simmons, Matthew, 103
Singh, Manmohan, 77, 230
Sinopec, 120, 125
smog, 149
Social Security Fund (SSF), 224
Society of Petroleum Engineers
  (SPE), 103
SOCO International, 277
Soeya, Yoshihide, 21
solar energy, 182, 191-196
  in comparison to natural gas, 149
Sonangol, 119, 129
soot, 169
South Africa, 71. *See also* Africa
South America, Brazil as an oil
  producer, 115-117
South Korea, natural gas imports, 152
South Stream pipeline, 19

South-to-North Water Transfer
  Project, 202
SouthGobi Energy Resources, 60, 267
sovereign wealth funds (SWFs), 4,
  27-30
  China, markets, 61-63
  definition of, 55-61
  Kuwait Investment Board, 49-54
  Pan-Asia, 47
  political response to, 38-42
  United States, 30-38
*Sovereign Wealth Funds: A Critical
  Analysis*, 28
Soviet Union. *See also* communism;
  Russia
  capitalist states, 13
  dissolution of, 23
SOX, 169
SPDR Gold Trust, 58
sperm oil, 85
Spiegel Online, 53
Spindletop, 96, 111
sprinkler irrigation systems, 211
St. Malo oil field, 118
Standard Bank (South Africa), 71
State Administration of Foreign
  Exchange (SAFE), 56
state capitalism, 12, 14
State Council, 56, 225
State Energy Bureau (SEB), 187
State Palace of Mongolia, 264
state-owned enterprises (SOEs),
  28, 48
Statoil, 120, 173
  Iraq oil fields, 129
steam coal, 164-168
steam-assisted gravity drainage
  (SAGD), 122
Stevenson, Adlai, 68
Strait of Malacca, 18
strategies for sovereign wealth funds
  (SWFs), 28
strip mining, 122
Subsea 7, 131
Sudan, 68
sulfur dioxide (SOX), 148, 164, 184
sulfurs
  emissions, 149
  removing, 169
Sumatra, 18
Summers, Lawrence, 35
Suncor Energy, 124

SunPower, 195
supergiant oil fields in
    Saudi Arabia, 103
supply
    bottlenecks, 141
    coal, 174, 177-178
    oil, constraints of, 94-98
SURF (subsea umbilicals, risers, and
    flowlines), 131
Suzlon, 195
Syngenta AG, 211

T

Tahiti oil field, 113, 119
Tajikistan, 17
    Shanghai Cooperation Organization
        (SCO), 15
Talbot, Strobe, 14
Talisman Energy, 276
Tangguh project, 153
Tanzania, 78
Tanzania-Zambia Railway, 72
Tata Motors, 78
Tata Steel, 235
Tavan Tolgoi (TT), 266
teas, 246
Teck Resources, 58-60, 124
Telekom Malaysia, 274
Telekom Malaysia International
    Cambodia (TMIC), 274
television sets, 138
TeliaSonera, 274
Temasek Holdings, 4, 51, 267
Tenaris, 132
Texas
    Golden Triangle, 112
    Spindletop Gusher, 96
Thatcher, Margaret, 10
theories, Keynesianism, 2
Thermo Fisher Scientific, 250
thin-film solar market, 195
Three Gorges project, China, 184
Thunder Horse, 118
Thurrock, Essex, 33
ThyssenKrupp, 222
Tianjin Tasly Pharmaceutical, 246
Tiber, 112
Titusville, Pennsylvania, 83
Tomboco, 120
Total, 80, 119, 124, 153
traditional Chinese medicines
    (TCM), 246

trains, 221-222
    China, 222-228
    Dedicated Rail Freight Corridor
        (DRFC), 231-234
    India, 228-230
Trans-Sahara gas pipeline (TSGP), 80
Transmashholding (TMH), 227
Transneft, 126, 127
transportation, oil for, 86-88
trillion cubic feet (tcf), 143
Truman, Harry S., 11
Tullow Oil, 121, 130
Tupi, 116
Turkic Uighurs, 18
Twain, Mark, 88
twenty-foot equivalent units (TEU), 33
Twilight in the Desert, 103

U

Uganda, 78
ultimately recoverable reserves
    (URR), 99, 106
umbilicals, 131
Umm al-Quwain, 49
unconventional liquids, 121, 124-126
underground geologic pressures,
    control of, 96
United Arab Emirates (UAE), 32,
    35, 48
United Kingdom (UK)
    nuclear energy, 189
    oil production, 97
United Nations (UN), 11
United Nations Educational,
    Scientific and Cultural Organization
    (UNESCO), 252
United States
    consumption of oil, 88, 91
    Gulf of Mexico, 118-119
    hydroelectric power production, 184
    power plant costs, 145
    sovereign wealth funds (SWFs), 30-38
    The Great Game, 14
United States Liaison Office
    (USLO), 22
University of Auckland, 239
Uranium, 190. *See also* nuclear energy
urbanization, 261
US Africa Command (AFRICOM), 76
US Treasury Department, 34, 53
    definition of sovereign wealth funds
        (SWFs), 28
Uzbekistan, 15

V

vaccines, 247
Vale, 266
Vankor project, 127
vehicles, natural gas for, 145
Venezuela, 125
    as an oil producer, 115
Vestas Wind Systems, 194
Vietnam, 275-279
Vietnam Enterprise Investments
    Limited Fund, 278
Vietnam Growth Fund Limited, 278
Vietnam Infrastructure Ltd., 279
Vietnam National Minerals
    Corporation (VIMICO), 277
Vietnam Opportunity Fund, 278
Vietnam Property Fund, 278
Vietnam Steel Corporation (VSC), 276
Villain, Jean Paul, 51
VinaCapital Group, 278
VinaLand Ltd., 279
Vision 2030 strategy (Abu Dhabi), 51
volatility of sovereign wealth funds
    (SWFs), 36
von Richthofen, Ferdinand, 61

W

Wade, Abdoulaye, 72
warlord-ism, 12
wars, global war on terror, 20
Washington Consensus, 34
wastewater, 205, 208
water
    consumption of. *See* consumption,
        of water
    exploration, 203
    flooding, 97

wells (oil), types of, 97
West Africa, 112, 117
    global oil supply and, 119-121
West Cape Three Points, 121
Western Europe, 11
Westinghouse Electric Company, 190
wet gas, 142
whale oil, 85
wind energy, 182, 191-196
    in comparison to natural gas, 149
Wolfson Institute of Preventative
    Medicine, 240
Woodside Petroleum, 121, 153
World Bank, 74
World War II, 21
    acceleration of demand for
        oil after, 90
    effect of peace and prosperity, 10-12

X–Y–Z

Xiaoping, Deng, 12
Xinjiang province, 17
Xinjiang Uighur Autonomous Region
    (XUAR), 18
Xstrata, 177
XTO Energy, 154

Yadav, Lalu Prasad, 229
Yanzhou Coal Mining, 175
Young, James, 84
Yum! Brands, 274

Zambia, 78
Zedong, Mao, 12
Zhejiang, 208
Zhuzhou CSR Times Electric, 226
zinc, 58
Zoellick, Robert, 74